January, 2011

To my mother [barcode: D0926513], loving,
dependable, understanding, beautiful, silly, inspiring
mother. Heres to seventy years, to being
healthy, strong, bold and as pretty as ever.
Heres to all the adventures you've had and the
many more to come. What a life!
What a woman! An inspiration. Thank you
for giving me life, supporting me and
always loving me for who I am.

I love you so much,

Happy Birthday to you....

And many more.

Love Jenny

See page 22. (☺)

PRAISES FOR WE'MOON

The Power of Life
¤ Musawa 1999, WM'04

"The beauty of We'Moon is the beauty of oneness, putting all these nations under the same umbrella. I have absolute blessings for this Anthology. We can walk with this wisdom."
—Flordemayo, Mayan Grandmother, of the International Council of 13 Indigenous Grandmothers

"I have been using your calendar for years and years!!! Thank you for the incredible work We'Moon is doing. It is a blessing to be part of the We'Moon community."
—Alice Walker, novelist, poet, activist

"We'Moon is a beautiful collection of art, poetry and musings that have guided women's days and plans for decades now, providing us with a little hit of beauty and inspiration as we go about our lives. We'Moon is also an example of a long-lasting collective, women-run enterprise that remains successful after many years. I love We'Moon!"
—Starhawk, writer, global justice activist and organizer

"The We'Moon calendar is a gem! I adore the art in the pages, the layout, beauty and wisdom combined in We'Moon. Writing my autobiography, reading the past in my many books: I know we LOOOVED We'Moon."
—Zsuzsanna Budapest, psychic, Dianic Wiccan Priestess, author and teacher

"The We'Moon wisdom, sisterhood, and creative guidance in every calendar has kept my faith in a more just and peaceful world, grounded in the sacred feminine, alive and burning brightly in my soul. Flipping to any page, I may find goddess spirit, a deliciously insightful quote, a powerful illustration, a bright vision of creative protest or healing ceremony, balanced by spaces to plan my day. Instantly the week seems more manageable and exciting. Thank you, We'Moon, for weaving the red threads of succulent lifeforce together year after year, inspiring the new generations (that's me!) and honoring our elders. Blessings on the publication of this Anthology!"
—Rae Abileah, CODE PINK national roseroots coordinator

"We'Moon is a work of art! The circle of all these voices together is so profound. In some sense it feels to me that We'Moon is holding up the Women's Movement: we still have a Movement, we have We'Moon. It is so important for women's voices and stories to be heard. That's part of the healing of the world."
—Beth Beurkens, poet, shamanic teacher

"I like this calendar very much, and the teachings that are offered. Thank you for this good thinking you are doing here."
—Winona LaDuke, Native American activist, environmentalist, writer

"For years now We'Moon has been the sacred vessel that holds my daily life in beauty. It surrounds everything from dentist appointments to sessions with my clients to life-changing events with deep meaning, art, poetry and a reminder of the great cosmic dance. It's impossible to play it small using this 'calendar'—it reminds me who we are, who I am."
—Miriam Dyak, poet, teacher, counselor

"I remember my first glimpse of the original We'Moon calendar when it was still being produced in France! It was so radical—often featuring women's time-keeping, as was originally the case on this glorious planet. Lunar cycles and female-centered expressions of the passing seasons. Thirty years of marking female rhythms and sharing female art, writing and astrology."
—Vicki Noble, healer, artist, teacher, author

In the Spirit of We'Moon

Celebrating 30 Years

An Anthology of Art and Writing
Narrated by Musawa

🜊 Mother Tongue Ink 🜊

Front cover art: *Beauty* © Jeannine Chappell 2006
Front cover graphic design artist: Sequoia Watterson

Back cover artists: We'Moon cover artists from 30 years of We'Moon
Back cover graphic design artist: Sequoia Watterson

© Mother Tongue Ink 2010
www.wemoon.ws
wholesale: 503-288-3555
retail: 1-877-693-6666 or
541-479-4056
P.O. Box 1586, Estacada, OR 97023
mothertongue@wemoon.ws

We'Moon Founder/Crone Editor: Musawa
We'Moonagers: Sue Burns, Barb Dickinson
Special Editor: Bethroot Gwynn
Graphic Design: Sequoia Watterson
We'Moon Anthology Creatrix/Editorial Team: Bethroot Gwynn, Musawa,
Barb Dickinson, Sequoia Watterson, EagleHawk, Myshkin
Promotion: Lou Chain
Retail Sales/Order Fullfillment: Lou Chain, Myshkin
Production Coordinator: Barbara Dickinson
Production Assistant: Myshkin

Mother Tongue Ink publications feature creative work by women, celebrating earth-based spirituality and visions for a changing world. Since 1981, MT Ink has published We'Moon: Gaia Rhythms for Womyn—the well-known ecofeminist datebook, astrological moon calendar and daily guide to natural cycles—with art and writing from the growing edge of international women's culture.

Table of Contents

Amazing Grace
¤ *Cheryl Collins 2006, WM'09*

For 30 years, We'Moon has been created as a lunar calendar datebook dedicated to natural rhythms and filled with art and writing from women the world over. Rooted in womyn's community, We'Moon was originally planted as a seed in Europe where it sprouted on women's lands in the early 1980s. It was transplanted to the USA in the late '80s, where its roots took hold. We'Moon grew in abundance as a cottage industry on We'Moon Land in Oregon during the 1990s, and it continues to flourish into the 21st century in new communities of womyn, yielding colorful new flowers and fruits.

With this Anthology celebrating 30 years of We'Moon, we come full circle. The thirty moon phases on the cover represent the moon's journey around the earth in one month (in 29 ½ days, to be exact): one full round in the dance of earth, moon and sun in the universe. The front cover of the Anthology mirrors the ring of moons on the cover of the first We'Moon 30 years ago—and also reflects the thirty We'Moons on the Anthology's back cover, which have spiraled into creation in the meantime. Thirteen times the moon circles the earth, in all her phases, as the earth takes one full turn in her orbit around the sun each year. Thirty years (390 months of 13 "Moons" per lunar year) is a long dance!

Goddess of Laussel
© Lisa A. Tayerle 2000, WM'10

Anthology Origins—Interview with Musawa, We'Moon Founder and Crone Editor

Q: Putting together an Anthology of We'Moon over thirty years is a daunting task. What made you decide to do it? . . .why now?

A: 3 has always been my favorite number, so 3-0 makes sense to me as a watershed year (not to mention that it is the number of days in a lunar month, from one new moon to the next). And besides, I'm planning to retire from doing We'Moon after this year, so it is my last turn, coming full cycle. 30 years is long enough, don't you think?

Q: Yes, I can imagine it is. What kept you going with it all this time?

A: The main answer to that question is that We'Moon has a life of its own and has kept itself going. Like a child of your creating, you bring her into being and she takes off from there with her own life force, powered by the being she has become. We'Moon always had a lot of vitality, there is no stopping her!

Q: Did you ever try? To stop doing it, I mean.

A: Yes, several times. My partner Eagle (who is helping me pull together the Anthology now) had a big laugh when she was going back over the early ones and discovered that I was already trying to pass it on by the third We'Moon! (see the inside back cover of WM'84 on p. 35). But there were always womyn there to help with it all along—and to help carry it on when I couldn't. Now, after 30 years, there is a new generation of tried and true We'Mooners already carrying it as I pass it on for real this time—and I know it will continue in good hands!

What is We'Moon?

We'Moon: Gaia Rhythms for Womyn is more than an appointment book, it's a way of life! As a datebook that doubles as a handbook in natural rhythms, it allows readers to see events in their daily lives in relation to the larger cycles of the earth and heavens. Art and writing by wemoon from many lands give a glimpse of the great diversity and uniqueness of a world we create in our own image. We'Moon is about womyn's spirituality (spirit reality). We share how we live our truth, what inspires us, how we envision our reality in connection with the whole earth and all our relations.

Moon Dust
© Lena Bartula 1994, WM'99

Wemoon means "women." Instead of defining ourselves in relation to men (as in woman or female), we use the word wemoon to define ourselves by our primary relation to the natural sources of cosmic flow. Other terms wemoon use are womyn, wimmin, womb-one. We'Moon is a moon calendar for wemoon. As we'moon, we seek to be whole in ourselves, rather than dividing ourselves in half and hoping that some "other half" will complete the picture. We see the whole range of life's potential embodied and expressed by wemoon and do not divide the universe into sex-role stereotypes. We'Moon is sacred space in which to explore and celebrate the diversity of she-ness on Earth. We'Moon is created by, for and about womyn: in Her image.

Wemoon means "we of the moon." The Moon, whose cycles run in our blood, is the original womyn's calendar. Like the Moon, wemoon circle the Earth. We are drawn to one another. We come in different shapes, colors and sizes. We are continually transforming. With all our different hues and points of view, we are one.

Amaterasu
© *Hrana Janto 1991, WM'07*

Wemoon culture exists in the diversity and the oneness of our experience as wemoon. We honor both. We come from many different ways of life. At the same time, as wemoon, we share a common mother root. We are glad when wemoon from varied backgrounds contribute art and writing. When material is borrowed from cultures other than your own, we ask that it be acknowledged and something given in return. Being conscious of our sources keeps us from engaging in the divisiveness of either cultural appropriation (taking what belongs to others) or cultural fascism (controlling creative expression). We invite you to share how the "Mother Tongue" speaks to you, with respect for both cultural integrity and individual freedom.

Lunar Rhythms: Everything that flows moves in rhythm with the Moon. She rules the water element on Earth, pulls on the ocean's tides, the weather, female reproductive cycles and the life fluids in plants, animals and people. She influences the underground currents in earth energy, the mood swings of mind, body, behavior and emotion. The Moon's phases reflect her dance with Sun and Earth, her closest relatives in the sky. Together, these three heavenly bodies weave the web of light and dark into our lives.

Gaia Rhythms: We show the natural cycles of the Moon, Sun, planets and stars as they relate to Earth. By recording our own activities side by side with those of other heavenly bodies, we may notice what connection, if any, there is for us. The Earth revolves around her axis in one day; the Moon orbits around the Earth in one month (29 1/2 days); the Earth orbits around the Sun in one year. We experience each of these cycles in the alternating rhythms of day and night, waxing and waning, summer and winter. The Earth/Moon/Sun are our inner circle of kin in the universe. We know where we are in relation to them at all times by the dance of light and shadow as they circle around one another.

Cosmic Turtle
© *Christina Smith 1999, WM'10*

The Eyes of Heaven: As seen from Earth, the Moon and the Sun are equal in size: "the left and right eye of heaven," according to Hindu (Eastern) astrology. Unlike the solar-dominated calendars of Christian (Western) patriarchy, the We'Moon looks at our experience through both eyes at once. The lunar eye of heaven is seen each day in the phases of the Moon. The solar eye of heaven is apparent at the turning points in the Sun's cycle of seasons and balance points (solstices, equinoxes and the cross-quarter days in between). The third eye of heaven may be seen in the stars. Astrology measures the cycles by relating the Sun, Moon and all other planets in our universe through the backdrop of star signs (the zodiac), helping us to tell time in the larger cycles of the universe. *Musawa © Mother Tongue Ink 2008*

DEDICATION

We dedicate this Anthology to:

• The thousands of womyn who have answered the Call for Contributions to share their creative vision in the pages of We'Moon over the years—whether or not their work made it into print.

• The hundreds of community womyn who have participated in We'Moon Weaving Circles to help give feedback in our initial selection process for each edition.

• The hard-working Mother Tongue Ink staff members who, through countless Creatrix marathons and ongoing Matrix meetings have been part of the inbreath of We'Moon in creating and producing it, and the outbreath of getting it out into the world and into your hands.

• The hundreds of thousands of womyn who are part of the growing circle who have treasured and supported We'Moon year after year for three decades.

Thank you! May We'Moon continue to flourish and bear fruit to serve the upwelling of We'Moon Spirit, to be nourished and renewed from the source that keeps it flowing for the benefit of all beings in the interweave of Earth life.

Elemental Invocations on pages 10-13 have been adapted from Starhawk's work.

We invite you to enter a sacred space of
We'Moon heart-sharing,
invoking the Elements and Directions

In the Spirit of We'Moon

Saving Seeds © *Sequoia 2006, WM'10*

With these seeds of We'Moon spirit,
We cast a circle around Mother Earth
And join in Her embrace

(detail) **Passing Clouds** ¤ *Emelie Hebert / Deborah Wyatt 2005, WM'08*

By the Air that is Her Breath,
We call in the Spirits of the East

(detail) ***Beginning with the Light*** ¤ *Sheila Richards 2008, WM'11*

BY THE FIRE OF HER BRIGHT SPIRIT,
WE CALL IN THE SPIRITS OF THE SOUTH

(detail) **Dreaming: Eve of Heart's Delight** © *A. Kimberlin Blackburn 1992, WM'99*

BY THE WATERS OF HER LIVING WOMB,
WE CALL IN THE SPIRITS OF THE WEST

BY THE EARTH THAT IS HER BODY,
WE CALL IN THE SPIRITS OF THE NORTH

Coatlique © Hrano Yanto 1995, WM'04

GREAT MOTHER, ACCEPT OUR OFFERING.
WE INVOKE THE SPIRIT OF WE'MOON,
IN THE HEARTS OF ALL SHE TOUCHES

Flying Colors
© Schar Cbear Freeman 2003, WM'05

In the Spirit of We'Moon is An Anthology of We'Moon Art and Writing, celebrating 30 years of publication in "the Mother Tongue" (with Mother Tongue Ink as the publisher). The Mother Tongue speaks to each one in the native language of her own inner voice. It is unique to each individual and culture: the first language we learn from our mothers, in the dialect of our own individual life experience. And it is as universal as the language of Mother Nature. Who hasn't experienced the crack of thunder, the feel of warm earth, the light touch of a gentle breeze, the slap of rain? But what it means to you at any given moment, only you can know. In We'Moon, we let the Spirit of We'Moon speak for Herself, as it comes directly through the creative expression of womyn's own experience. What touches you on these pages? How are you moved by what you see?

It is a daunting task to sift through thirty We'Moons to distill the essence of the spirit of We'Moon into one book. Imagine putting together a scrapbook of the last thirty years of your life! Now magnify that by the thousands of womyn who have had a hand in creating We'Moon over the years! We couldn't possibly fit in everything we wanted to. It has been a huge project to contact the artists and writers, let alone to locate reproducible copies of their original work after all this time. So please accept our limitations and forgive our omissions.

The theme of this Anthology, as with every We'Moon I have ever worked on, worked on me as well. Naming the theme commits us to walk our talk. Like a mantra repeated over and over as we work with the material "in the spirit of We'Moon," it becomes a spiritual practice that holds us to Her Spirit in the process of creating this book. And, it is always gratifying to have a hand in channeling so much Beauty (the name of the owl in the circle of moons on the front cover) from the endless stream of We'Moon creativity!

Despite the immensity of this project, it was a joy to work with the talented, fine-tooled team that crafted this jewel of the Goddess in such a spirited way.

We ask for the Spirit of We'Moon to come through, as we offer it up, like a prayer, and let it go.

Great Mother, help us
carry out this divine work
with a touch as light
playful and profound
as the work in process
that is your ever-unfolding
spiral dance of creation.
© Musawa 2010

Muse Musawa
© Annie Ocean 1989, WM'90

15

Labyrinth ¤ *Witchhazel Wildwood 2001, WM'03*

All over the lands
of the earth
I see the
labyrinth's way
returning and
you my daughters
following silver
threads.
Praise be.
excerpt © Cora Greenhill 2001, WM'03

16

Walking as Before

Look to each other across chasms of ancient time.
We are moving round a single unchanging point.
Move to the very edge
where the old world ends
and something else begins.

And we have always been walking through this land.
And we have always worn its vision like a skin.
The track is strongly felt, walking as before.
And our footsteps fit, walking as before.
Move to the very edge, where the old world ends
And something else begins, something else begins.

excerpt © Carolyn Hillyer 1997, WM'00

© Marcia Patrick, WM'91

bone-singers

When near the sea,
the water within us sings
like the pure stone tone of
a bell carved from
bone. We are flutes
in the wind's mouth,
unearthed from the cave
of our ancestors' memories,
bone-singers
learning a forgotten
song.

© Jill Stephanie Morgyn 2006, WM'08

Spirit Dancer *© Yasmin E. Brown 2001, WM'08*

The Path of the Little Sisters

There is something happening on Earth right now that has never happened before. We are not going to be able to think our way out of it. But there is a way to live through this, and it has to do with allowing ourselves to be guided. To be a little one again, to become like little children, allowing each step to be guided.

excerpt © Zelima Xochiquetzal from
Walking the Sacred Path, *Sor Juana Press* 2005, *WM'09*

Matriarchy *© Shoshona Rothaizer, WM'91*

Because

Because the world is being broken
into allotments of dollars and loss
we will plant our fruit trees and lilies
in the cracks between paving stones.

Because the world is rinsed scarlet with blood
we will take our own reds of passion and heart
and place them in hearths and love's look
knowing their potential for healing fire.
Because the world's spirit is being torn
we will mend our own webs of connection,
that fine lace, stretching between us
connecting us into life, in every direction.

Because the sky is being clouded over
with smoke and dirt and armored stars
we will stand in the dark of mountains
in the backstreet alleyways and in the deserts

to call out old names of the starry ones,
the sky dancers: Astarte, Arianhod, Venus, Aditi,
our eyes shining, our eyes shining with hope.

© Rose Flint 2005, WM'07

Baba Yaga *© Hrana Janto 1995, WM'11*

Prayer

Mother of All
thank you

You Who calls my name
and I come running

◻ *Shemeya Mountain Laurel, WM'93*

Salutation *© Nancy B. Holley 1997, WM'07*

Magical Medicine Pouch © *Cathy McClelland 2006, WM'09*

The Promise

We are pieces of
ancient earth,
bits of sacred story
soaked in intellect and dirt
excerpt ¤ Oak Chezar 2008, WM'11

Meditation © *Cathy McClelland 2000, WM'09*

Listen deeply for what
your soul already knows, weave
your overflowing
love for the earth
into your daily life.
excerpt © Patricia Dines 2007, WM'09

Each Woman
carries within
her the medicine
for her healing.
Sometimes
it is hard to
see and feel
the one who holds
the medicine bag.
She is there.
We must
never
stop listening
for her arrivals.
Shhh...
Silently she comes
bringing what is
now needed.
Believe...
© *Shiloh Sophia McCloud 2007, WM'09*

Remembering Joy © *Nancy Watterson 2005, WM'11*

Pachamama © *Hrana Janto 1991, WM'03*

Sow New Seeds!
Seedlings rise, radical,
Blueprints for the future,
Vision pulls us
into a new world.
        excerpt © Silvie Jensen 2009, WM'11

The Trance Dance © *Calley O'Neill 1988, WM'11*

Women carry the ancient knowledge of the Divine Feminine deep within the very cells of their being, the Grandmothers say.... We must be strong and walk in our innate knowledge and power under the protection of the four directions. With the world on the brink of destruction, women must wake up this great force they possess and bring the world back to peace and harmony. When women and men set in motion this enormously transformative feminine force of unconditional love they carry within, great healing and change will come about.

Carol Schaefer, excerpt from
Grandmothers Counsel the World,
Shambala Publications Inc.,
© 2006 Carol Schaefer, WM'09

Remember the Future
¤ *Katya (Nina Sabaroff) Taylor 1974, WM'05*

Festival Parade © *Cedar Kindy 2009, WM'11*

When the Drummers Were Women

When the drummers were women
people moved to the sound
of the heartbeat of Gaia
slow, steady rhythm
energy flowing
in all hearts and mind.

When the drummers were women
people danced to the sound
going barefoot on Gaia
in meadows, on mountains
earth energy healing
in all bodies and souls.

Grandmother Drum
¤ *White Eagle Medicine Woman, photo
by Barbara Shugg 2001, WM'04*

When the drummers were women
people slept to the sound
lying down on the earth
Gaia supports us completely
warm mother nurturing
to all who are around.

And she is still waiting
patient and receptive
to hear women drumming
in honor of her presence
the feminine aspect
in all that abounds.

¤ *Annalisa Cunningham 2001, WM'05*

21

Redtail Mandala ◻ *Jennifer G. Metz 2008, WM'10*

Mandala I: Spirals & Tulips © *Karen Russo 2004, WM'06*

Re-Invent the Wheel
© *Sandra Lory 2008, WM'10*

Center: **Transformaiton Mandala**
© *S. Grace Mantle 2002, WM'10*

Sunflower
© *Annie Ocean 2006, WM'08*

Grandmother Flordemayo says the Mayans are among those whose prophecy reveals that a new consciousness is preparing humanity for the spirit of the feminine and the spirit of the Grandmothers, when humanity will walk from the four directions into the light at the center.

excerpt from Grandmothers Counsel the World, *Shambala Publications Inc.* © *Carol Schaefer 2006, WM'09*

Three Decades: Broad Strokes

Creating this Anthology has been like an archeological dig, uncovering layer upon layer of women's culture and consciousness through the creative outpouring of We'Moon art and writing. In a period of great change, it is surprising to see the consistency of themes—voices just beginning to be heard 30 years ago, that are so urgently relevant today. This Herstory section presents a chronological overview of We'Moon's 30 years, decade by decade.

The 1980s were the formative years of We'Moon, the origins: Roots. In the beginning it was more like an '80s version of a 'zine, a collective "labor of love" with a multi-cultural country lesbian edge. The first five editions were pocket-sized, home made, and continually evolving in format, design and technology, changing languages and focus every year. With roots in women's land communities, it was created by a growing network of friends and carried by traveling women from one land to another and on into the cities, transplanted to different countries from one year to the next. We saw ourselves as "Amazons" seeking sanctuary from patriarchy, trying to find a way to make a life for ourselves living close to the earth in community with women. We'Moon was a vehicle for sharing creatively what we were learning.

The 1990s were years of steady growth, sustainability: Shoots. We'Moon settled down in one place (a women's land community founded originally by myself, my sister and friends in the early '70s). The calendar pages settled into a consistent format from 1990 on. Mother Tongue Ink incorporated as a cottage industry/home business with paid employees. During this period, we learned how to do the business of publishing and distributing, as well as reaching out to a larger network of artists, writers and readers. The technology changed from type-written to type-set and word processor, and eventually took us into the computer age with email and a website. The gay nineties were busy and abundant, and as our numbers swelled, so did the workload, supporting a year-around paid staff of We'Moon Land community members who lived and worked together.

The early 2000s were the years of We'Moon expansion, producing seeds of change: Fruits. Our own Y2K crisis was a fire that razed our community home and business and led eventually to the dispersal and fracturing of both. But the phoenix rose from the ashes and led to our re-building from the ground up at We'Moon Land, and re-locating the We'Moon home business to different parts of Oregon, initiated by a new generation of We'Moon co-managers. And through it all, We'Moon was growing by leaps and bounds. Having to learn everything by the seat of our pants, we became more skilled with experience. Our network of contributors, our staff and our products were expanding, as the technological expertise, visual beauty and quality of We'Moon continued improving year after year.

1980s: We'Moon Roots!

Herstory Section: Overview

There are pages in this section from each of the 30 We'Moons. At the beginning of each decade, there are additional pages of narrative, weaving in various We'Moon voices: those involved in creating We'Moon, contributing artists and writers, and readers sharing their pieces of the story of We'Moon. Personal narrative voices are separated from the original content of the We'Moon calendar pages, and from our editorial commentary, with a line: —————— Unless other speakers are named, the narrator's voice, either in personal story or as an editorial guide, belongs to Musawa. In the 2000s, many of the Introductions to the Theme were co-authored by Bethroot Gwynn. The section on the 1980s includes substantial narratives about the origins of We'Moon, when there was no set format or specific guiding theme for the datebook. After the initial year (1981-82), each We'Moon has a four page display. Editions in the 1990s and 2000s have specific themes, based on Tarot imagery. The second page of each year's display draws on material from any We'Moon to deepen understanding of that Tarot card's wisdom. The calendar pages were printed in black and white for We'Moon's first 22 years. In our display for the early We'Moons, we have sometimes reprinted in the original handwritten form. We have used full-color versions of the original art when they are available

We'Moon Origins

We'Moon was inspired by the rising tide of women's liberation in the emerging people's movements of the 1960s and 1970s and came to fruition in the 1980s as a vehicle for the creative expression of women's empowerment and earth-based spirituality. The collective counter culture impulse of the '70s energized small bands of women in many countries to venture away from the confines of patriarchy and improvise new life options, by settling in independent communities of women living together on the land. The original "women's lands" (including Women's Peace Camps) were as far-flung as Australia, Denmark, France, Hawaii, Italy, New Zealand, Spain, Germany, the UK, Wales, and ranging from the Ozarks to Oregon in North America. The idea of We'Moon originated at Kvindelandet, an international women's land in Denmark where 50 to 60 lesbians from different countries lived together in the late 1970s. It was inspired by our learnings about living together as womyn in a creative and magical way, in harmony with the Earth and her cycles. Our astrological charts, hanging on the living room wall, gave us better understanding of each other despite language barriers. In 1980, we were literally "undermined" by a multinational corporation that expropriated our land. Faced with loss of our home base, we turned to the Moon, Sun and stars to keep us in touch with ourselves, each other and the Earth's cycles.

We'Moon was conceived as a handbook in natural rhythms, letting us know when to celebrate the New Moon or Solstice: we could continue circling together even if not in the same place! We wanted to stay in touch through the "Mother Tongue" across time and space and man-made borders. Since 1981, when the first We'Moon was self-published in France under the name of Mother Tongue Ink—as a pocket-size astrological moon calendar diary, hand-written in five languages—this little handbook in natural rhythm has steadily expanded in artistic quality, scope and readership. It has remained a unique vehicle for the expression of women's creativity during an extraordinary period of our herstory, with the (re-)emergence of eco-feminism, goddess spirituality, and global women's culture.

Shoshana Rothaizer: One of the most dynamic aspects of lesbian life in the 1970s was "women's land." Many lesbians left the cities and created environments where we learned from experience we had all the skills we needed to create our own lives. On women's land we had multiple lovers, wrote songs, danced around campfires, repaired cars and tractors, did gardening in the nude, and made decisions with the help of Tarot cards and astrology.

The World © Shoshana Rothaizer 1979

Ten of Cups © *Shoshana Rothaizer*

Kvindelandet Memories of our Wild Anarchistic Women's Land Times (1979-1982)

Puma Lichtblau: I arrived at Kvindelandet for the first time in August, 1979, and it was as if the dream that I and many others had long dreamed of had now materialized. It was harvest time, and vegetables and flowers were spread out in the courtyard—and hay was being brought in—and many inspiring women were in the courtyard and on both breast-like hills and a tipi stood on one of them, and I laid down on the ground and tears flowed and I knew I was home.

To lie above in Seventh Heaven and to hear the women below in the yard talking, laughing and singing was for me paradise. "Seventh Heaven" was the name of the one room upstairs in the house in which one could sometimes sleep but that no one could reserve for themselves. The only rule was that alcohol and men were forbidden—this last part I had already decided for myself.

Instead each one could do or be whatever she wanted. Love and sex and creativity, and once a day a common warm meal; we might look after the kitchen, cut wood, work in the fields, create and share songs, consult oracles, astrology and healing ceremonies, take a bath under the stars, tell relationship stories of love and pain, find a crystal ball and a red stone all in one place together somewhere on the land, have an escape place. And the opportunity was always there, if feelings threatened to become overpowering, to get high and not take the practical things of life so seriously. Everything belonged to everyone and some things were also private. There was a great openness for all that moved us deep inside and for how different and the same we also were, that each one could for the first time be the way she was.

Shoshana Rothaizer: I lived at Kvindelandet from 1979-80. Looking at early We'Moon almanacs brings back memories of spirituality, love and friendship.

Astrology and the Tarot were inseparable from our daily routines on the land. We planted and harvested by the phases of the moon and planets. Quite a few women knew a lot about astrology, and there was always an ephemeris available. One wall of the living room was full of individual women's charts, and another large chart showed all of the women's signs together. Tarot was also important

in our lives. We had a casual morning ritual where a Tarot deck was fanned out face down on the windowsill where we ate breakfast. Women would pick a card and place it on the frosty windowsill as her significator for the day.

Women were always playing music, writing, drawing, painting, knitting, sewing, and creating. We had a succession of common journals full of beautiful art and writing, mostly in English, which was our common language. The earliest editions of We'Moon sprang from this pool of creativity.

Musawa: We'Moon was inspired by my fresh new look at what women's culture and spirituality could be, as experienced in the first blush of womyn's land on the other side of the ocean—where the grass was greener as it was all still so new. I loved the different nuances of phrase, gesture and culture among us, as we sang our songs, grew our food, cooked our meals together and learned to know and love each other in our different languages.

There was a community closet of clothes contributed by whoever wished to share: a sweater hand-knit by a Danish woman's grandmother, French work pants and billowing peasant shirts, Spanish hats and boots, the latest in accessories from lesbians in Berlin. We could pick out what costume to put on, what role we wanted to play, what name we might take on today. For a while, I took on a different name every day while I was learning the days of the month in Hawaiian (the 30 moon phases in a Moon month that the days were named after). Although I was not very successful in getting anyone to call me that (or even in remembering my own name from day to day), I was learning the chant of days in Hawaiian and celebrated being Hina at New Moon or Mahealani on Full Moon, as I went through all the changes in between.

It was a rarified world of our own creating that didn't last long although it had a lasting effect. When we had to move on, We'Moon was a way to continue sharing what we were learning and staying in touch when the ground got pulled out from under us.

Nada, WM'85

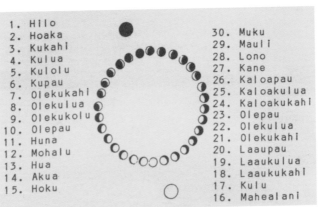

1. Hilo		30. Muku
2. Hoaka		29. Mauli
3. Kukahi		28. Lono
4. Kulua		27. Kane
5. Kulolu		26. Kaloapau
6. Kupau		25. Kaloakulua
7. Olekukahi		24. Kaloakukahi
8. Olekulua		23. Olepau
9. Olekukolu		22. Olekulua
10. Olepau		21. Olekukahi
11. Huna		20. Laaupau
12. Mohalu		19. Laaukulua
13. Hua		18. Laaukukahi
14. Akua		17. Kulu
15. Hoku		16. Mahealani

Looking Back: Kvindelandet Gathering 25+ Years Later: June 29, 2006

Dear Sisters,

Last weekend we had our wonderful meeting in the middle of the forest with a lot of place to be outside, put up tents, make a big fire and meet in a big circle or in little groups.

We were 35 wemoon from 6 countries and I was especially glad that some of the founders of our land also had come: Verdende, Arnika and Alraune/Jette. From Norway Idun/Babos were there, from Holland Antje and Mayana, from France Moutsie, Fea/Chantal and Nada, from Santa Fe Marion—and a lot of German wimmin I cannot all mention here. We were so happy to see each other again and it happened very quickly, that the atmosphere turned into the atmosphere of the old times, it was incredible! Sitting each evening at the fireplace and playing the old songs, making musik like if we have done it thousand times before, doing a healing circle for wemoon remembering the wemoon who have left us and this earth already—and telling stories from Kvindelandet and also reflecting, how we had been in these young years and how we see our experiences from where we are now. It was very moving to hear that for each woman this experience was so important for her life!! There was laughter and tears and a kind of being connected, which I wouldn't have expected, being still so strong.   —Saheta Susanne Weik

spes dolphin, WM'81

26

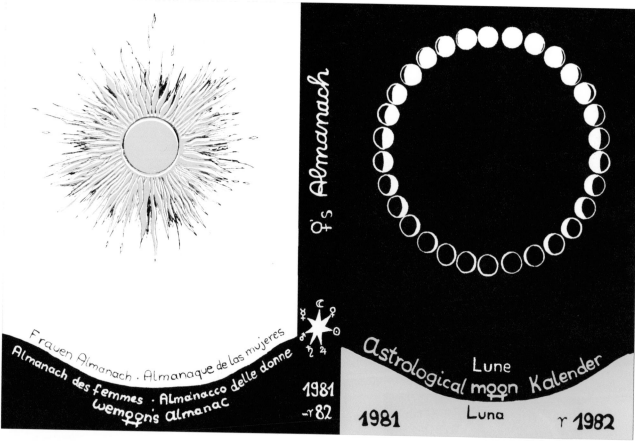

Nada, Cover Art, WM'81

The image shows cover art with text:

♀'s Almanach

Frauen Almanach · Almanaque de las mujeres
Almanach des femmes · Almanacco delle donne
wemoon's Almanac

1981
~r82

Astrological moon Kalender
Lune
Luna
1981   ♈ 1982

Nada: The time we had spent together in Kvindelandet had been wonderful. Rich, free, wild, creative, crazy. But after one year of nearly total commitment to the group, I (or we?) felt the need for some space for privacy, intimacy, for couple-life and some quietness. And then Musawa came up with this idea of creating a women's calendar, her way to extract some of the spirit of Kvindelandet and incarnate it in this vision of wemoons moving through time differently.

Einführung

Wir haben diesen Kalender mit viel Liebe gemacht, hoffentlich könnt ihr sie finden.

INTRODUCCION

Hemos hecho esto calendario con mucho amor, esperamos que tú lo sentirás.

Introduzione

Noi abbiamo fatto queste calendario con molto amore, spariamo che tu lo sentirai.

En commençant

Nous avons fait ce calendrier avec beaucoup d'amour, nous espérons que tu le sentiras.

INTRODUCTION

WE MAKE THIS CALENDAR WITH A LOT OF LOVE THAT WE HOPE YOU CAN FIND.

Musawa: The first We'Moon was put together by Nada and me on the kitchen table huddled in front of a big fireplace in an old farm house in Southern France, where Nada's sister and her lover had taken us in that first Winter after leaving Kvindelandet. It was late October, 1980, when we started and by the time we finished, Winter Solstice was already upon us, so we hastily added three more months, ending on Spring Equinox, 1982. We had no idea how much work it would be when we began it—especially when friends came by and translated it into five languages and everything had to be written five times over. This first We'Moon consisted mostly of charts and writings about natural cycles gleaned from our collective studies at Kvindelandet— with some drawings by Nada, who wrote most of it by hand. There was only one anonymous piece of original art in it—one we found in a portfolio behind the door.

When the moon changes sign
Wann die Mond das Zeichen wechselt
Quando la luna cambia nel segno
Quand la lune changel la signe

Middle Europe Time (for moon-changes only)

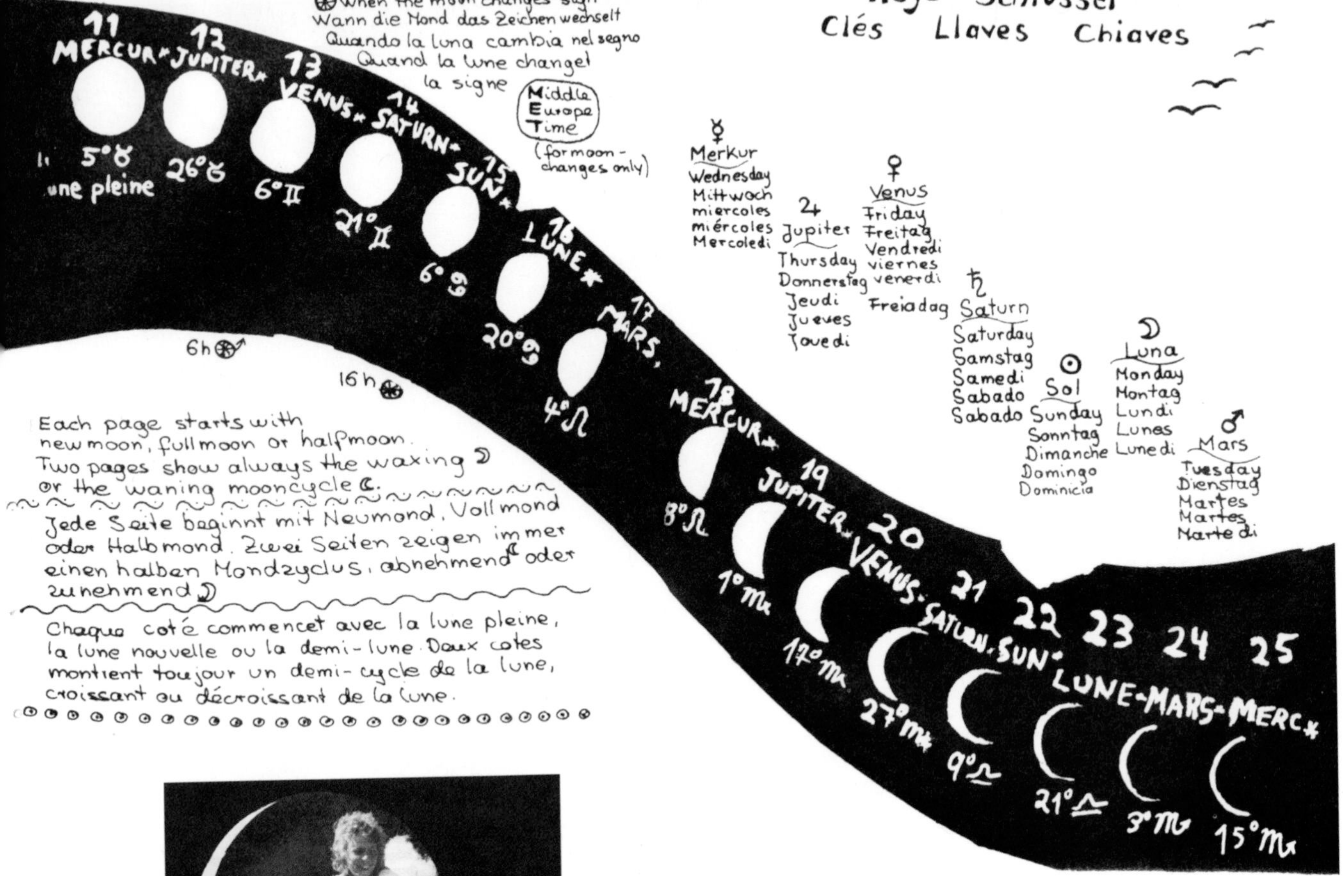

11 MERCUR
12 JUPITER
13 VENUS
14 SATURN
15 SUN
16 LUNE
17 MARS
18 MERCUR
19 JUPITER
20 VENUS
21 SATURN
22 SUN
23 LUNE
24 MARS
25 MERC
5° ♉
lune pleine
26° ♉
6° ♊
21° ♊
6° ♋
20° ♋
4° ♌
8° ♌
1° ♍
17° ♍
27° ♍
9° ♎
21° ♎
3° ♏
15° ♏
6h
16h

Keys Schlussel
Clés Llaves Chiaves

☿ Merkur
Wednesday
Mittwoch
miercoles
miércoles
Mercoledi

♃ Jupiter
Thursday
Donnerstag
Jeudi
Jueves
Jovedi

♀ Venus
Friday
Freitag
Vendredi
viernes
venerdi
Freiadag

♄ Saturn
Saturday
Samstag
Samedi
Sabado
Sabado

☉ Sol
Sunday
Sonntag
Dimanche
Domingo
Dominicia

☽ Luna
Monday
Montag
Lundi
Lunes
Lunedi

♂ Mars
Tuesday
Dienstag
Martes
Martes
Martedi

Each page starts with newmoon, fullmoon or halfmoon. Two pages show always the waxing ☽ or the waning mooncycle ☾.

Jede Seite beginnt mit Neumond, Vollmond oder Halbmond. Zwei Seiten zeigen immer einen halben Mondzyclus, abnehmend ☾ oder zunehmend ☽

Chaque coté commencet avec la lune pleine, la lune nouvelle ou la demi-lune. Deux cotes montrent toujour un demi-cycle de la lune, croissant ou décroissant de la lune.

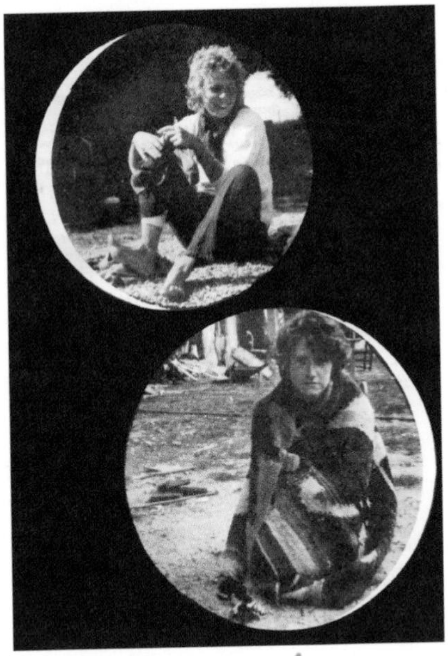

Beginning

We make this calender with a lot of love that we hope you can find. We are 2 ♀♀ who lived (together with wimmin of many different cultures) the last year's growing cycle on wemoon's land — Kvindeland in Danamark (one Nozamamerican, one deutsche, currently in South-Francia). Living on the land with wimmin and with the elements in a culture of our own nature. We want this calender to help us stay in touch with the natural rhythms in our lives, wherever we are. Made for our sisters of many lands and languages to strengthen our connection through all separating borders. Let the mother-tongue speak, hear her in the silence in the music of the spheres, in her touching.

To translate all this in words on two-dimensional paper is not easy. This is why we leave so many pages blank for you to fill in with the other dimensions of your daily lives. Signs, symbols and images of heavenly being's mark the time. But still we need to use words — have patience with our limitations and irregularities. It comes from where we are now.

Our approach to time comes from the far edges. Nada (♎) wants to dissolve it and Musawa (♉) wants to learn to live with it (the opposite is also true).

This almanac is based on natural time: the dance of the earth, moon, sun, stars and us each moves from her own center in relation to all others. Natural time comes in waves, is cyclical and is never the same. When we let her flow through us we come in touch with the spirit that moves us. Time is, how you experience the flow, not how you measure it — inside and out.

Life without fear comes from knowing that all is one.

Inclusif:

★ Einführung · En Commencment
   Beginning · Introducione ★

✳ Astrologie · **Astrologia** · Astrology
   ⊙☉☽☿♀♂♃♄♅♆♇ ♈♉♊♋♍....♓ ★

▲ Ephemeriden · Ephemerist · Efemeridi ▲

★ astrologische Aspects ★

✳ ♀ Keys · Schlüssel · Llaves · Clés · Chiaves

○ ☀ – ● – ✳ – Calender – Diary
   toutes faccias de la Luna   Diario

☽ MOON

● Luna negra – Schwarze Mond ●

⊙ SUN – seasons · Goddesses · Elements
   Quatre saisons

🌼 One day – Saluda au soleil

🌿 Invocazione da Diana – Anrufung von Diane

✿ Assoziationen zu d. **Sternzeichen** – Signs

★ Inner and outer – interieur et exterieur · espace

✳✳ Signs + Constellations · ✳ – bilder + Zeichen

C Planting by the moon – Pflanzen n.d. Mond

〰 Biorhythms · Biorhytmes

★★★ ✋ 🤚 🌐 Cartas : mano, pie, mundo

➜ Adresses · Adressen · Indirizzas
   direccionas

as the moon circles the earth, she always shows the same face to the earth – only the light changes according to where she is in relation to the sun

1 mes
mese
mois
monat
month

outer circle: moon as seen from the sun

inner circle: moon as seen from earth

Musawa: The first We'Moon was written in the different languages of the women who came along to help put it together. Originally, We'Moon was a sharing among friends, a love song arising from the interstices of our lives in a world we were creating together. Everyone who helped create the first We'Moon (Frauen Almanach, Almanaque de las Mujeres, Almanach de Femmes, Almanacco delle Donne, Wemoon's Almanac) was a guest in our home, a personal friend, part of a growing extended family of women living together on land, here or there, in this country and that, a circle that eventually spiraled out to include women from all over the world. We were creating our lives anew, exploring relationships among women, in intimate relationships and in community, on a journey of self-discovery within ourselves and each other—in close relation with the Earth—growing our food, living simply, mostly outside, in rhythm with the cycles of nature and our own hearts.

Nada: My first and strongest memory of the wemoon-calendar is jealousy. I didn't like it because it took so so so much time and energy for and from Musawa, who was my partner and lover at the time. It was her vision, her baby and her lover and I felt there was not much left for ME and US. Not that she was exclusive, not at all, it was just such an absorbing undertaking that there was not much space left for anything else (it seemed to me!). Although I was quite involved in it, I didn't really get the depth and the power of this approach (which kept living for so many years afterwards!)

Looking back at it now, I feel that Musawa was a visionary for wemoon's culture, and I was much more into the down-to-earth approach of here and now. It's been 25 years since I went "back" to the world where men and women live, love and work together. But this experience of wemoon's culture is in my basic psychic and spiritual structure— is, in a way always a reference point for me with its values and beauty.

Astrological Wemoon's Kalender: 13 moons, 1983

WEMOON ALMANAC
19   83
MONDFRAUEN KALENDER
AGENDA DES FEMMES DE LA LUNE

Nada, Cover Art, WM'81

Musawa: When Nada decided not to continue co-creating We'Moon after the first one ended on Spring Equinox, 1982, we let it go for the rest of the year. In the meantime, we had moved to a place of our own: an old abandoned farmhouse built out of huge hand-hewn stones by the family that was now our neighbors in the foot hills of the Pyrenees in Southern France. There was electricity but no running water. It was heated only by the fire in a large open fireplace in the kitchen. We cut and hauled wood with horses, who also helped us plow the fields. We grew vegetables and herbs that we also wild-crafted and sold at the nearby village market once a week. We slept upstairs in the attic under a slate roof that was hot in the summer, cold in the winter, but just right for us.

Then friends began coming to visit and brought new energy and enthusiasm for starting another We'Moon. . .

Puma: I remember a hot summer of 1982 in South France at a wemoonsland „La Serre Darre". Nada and Musawa lived there and some wemoon from Kvindelandet and elsewhere in Denmark visited.

Musawa brought us together to write and draw by hand one of the first We'Moon calenders. She was so motivated and convinced about this project, that we all did our very best to bring it to the materialisation. From our life at Kvindelandet we had collected many experiences while improvising with few materials and technical comfort. And we had so many possibilities to study the changing moonsigns on the changing mood of the wemoon and atmosphere on the land, what could happen and what not, living there with 30 to 60 wemoon.

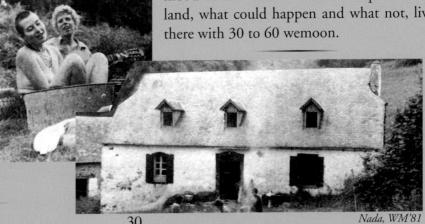

30

Nada, WM'81

Like all heavenly bodies, we are each influenced by the movements of all others. Unlike the ones in the sky who follow their courses naturally, we choose our own life paths and yet are moved at the same time by forces we hardly even know are there.

In our not knowing, we are easily thrown off balance. Becoming conscious of the larger whole we are a part of helps us to find our way to move freely within it, each from her own center. Especially now, in the world war of 'Man Against Nature'... we need to turn to the natural sources and strengthen our connection with the inner resources of our own nature. Viva la Resistance! Wemoon rising...

You can use this calender on whatever level fits your experience:

> a calendar-journal through all the phases of the thirteen moons and the twelve sun signs of the year... given in half moon cycles.

> an astrological guide with a complete ephemeris of planetary positions and aspects for every waxing and waning moon... including monthly astronomical star maps.

> an almanac of cosmic energies in daily life with articles on astrology, healing, planting, and various charts of inner and outer spaces...
· with a cross-cultural, earth-loving, woman-centered view.

It is written in the languages of the wemoon who contributed to it: English, French and German. The world of nature speaks to all in her own tongue — we can only translate in the ones we know and hope that this reaches across the borders to wemoon of other cultures with whom we would also like to share.

All views expressed here are not meant to be seen as the ultimate truth. Each article represents one (fairly simplified) approach among many. Take what fits your own experience and use it with care, knowing that we are all different, no matter what sign!

This is dedicated to the goddess in us all. May we create lands and cultures that support her growing in our lives, as we learn to move with natural rhythm.

---

13 moon months
Mond monate
mois lunaire

Winter l'hiver / Spring Frühling printemps

1. moon INANNA
Dez	Mo (Dez)	20	27	3	10
1982	Tu	21	28	4	11
♑	W	15	22	29	5	12
1983	Th	16	23	030	6	13
Jan	F	17	24	31	7
	Sa	18	25	1 Jan	8
	So	13	26	2	9

4. moon PERSEPHONE
Mar	Mo	14	21	028	4	11
♈	Di	15	22	29	5	12
	Mi	16	23	30	6
	Do	17	24	31	7
April	Fr	18	25	1 April	8
	Sa	19	26	2	9
	So	20	27	3	10

2. moon FEBRUA
Jan	Mo	17	24	31	7
	Tu	18	25	1 Feb	8
♒	W	26	2	9
	Th (Jan)	20	27	3	10
Feb	F	14	21	028	4	11
	Sa	15	22	29	5	12
	So	16	23	30	6

5. moon MAIA
April	Mo	18	25	2	9
	Di (April)	19	26	3	10
♉	Mi	13	20	027	4	11
	Do	14	21	28	5
Mai	Fr	15	22	29	6
	Sa	16	23	30	7
	So	17	24	1 May	8

3. moon ISIS
Feb	Mo	14	21	28	7
	Tu	15	22	1 mar	8
♓	W	16	23	2	9
	Th	17	24	3	10
	F	18	25	4	11
Mar	Sa (Feb)	19	26	5	12
	So	13	20	027	6	13

6. moon SAPPHO
	Mo	16	23	30	6
Mai	Di	17	24	31	7
	Mi (May)	18	25	1 June	8
♊	Do	12	19	026	2	9
	Fr	13	20	27	3	10
Jun	Sa	14	21	28	4
	So	15	22	29	5

summer Sommer été

7. moon HERA
Jun	Lu	13	20	27	4
	Ma	14	21	28	5
♋	Me	15	22	29	6
	Je	16	23	30	7
Jul	Ve (June)	17	24	1 July	8
	Sa	11	18	025	2	9
	Di	12	19	26	3

Automne, Herbst

10. moon ARTEMIS
Sep	Mo	12	19	26	3
	Tu (Sept)	13	20	27	4
♍	We	7	14	21	28	5
Okt	Th	8	15	022	29
	Fr	9	16	23	30
	Sa	10	17	24	1 October
	So	11	18	25	2

8. moon SELENE
Jul	Lu	11	18	25	1 Aug
	Ma	12	19	26	2
♌	Me	13	20	27	3
	Je	14	21	28	4
Aug	V	15	22	29	5
	S (July)	16	23	30	6
	D	10	17	024	31	7

11. moon HEKATE
Okt	Mo	10	17	24	31
	Tu (Okt)	11	18	25	1 Nov
♏	We	12	19	26	2
	Th	6	13	20	27	3
Nov	Fr	7	14	021	28
	Sa	8	15	22	29
	So	9	16	23	30

9. moon DEMETER
Aug	Lu	8	15	22	29	5
	Ma	9	16	023	30
♍	Me	10	17	24	31
	J	11	18	25	1 Septem.
Sep	Ve	12	19	26	2
	Sa	13	20	27	3
	D	14	21	28	4

12. moon MINERVA
Nov	Mo	7	14	21	28
	Tu	8	15	22	29
♐	We (Nov)	9	16	23	30
	Th (Nov)	10	17	24	1 Dec
Dez	Fr	4	11	18	25	2
	Sa (Dec)	5	12	19	26	3
	So	6	13	020	27

13. moon LILLITH
	L	5	12	19	26	2
	Ma	6	13	020	27
	Me	7	14	21	28
♑	J	8	15	22	29
	V	9	16	23	30
	Sa (Dec)	10	17	24	31
	So	4	11	18	25	1 Jan 84

Explaination
● 13 = Newmoon the 13th
○ 27 = Fullmoon the 27th

1983

The Phases of the MOON ~ DANCE

☉♂☽
new moon • neue monden • nouvelle lune

☉□☽
half moon. Waxing ☽ halbe mondin: zunehmend ☽ demi lune — decroissante

As the moon circles the earth she always shows the same face to us ~ but her relation to the sun change: casting a different light across the face she shows to us

☉□☽ half moon ☽ waning ☽ abnehmende mondin ☽ halbe la lune demi decroissante

☉♂☽
full moon volle mondin la lune pleine

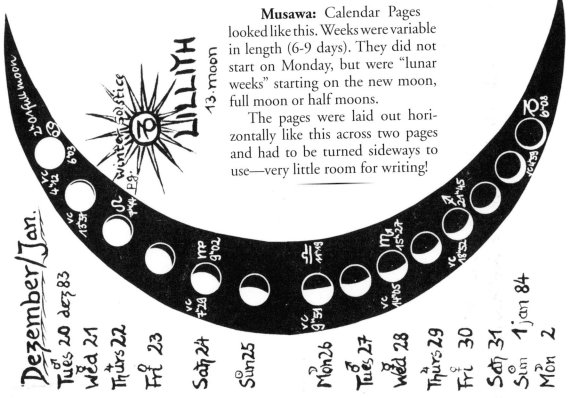

Musawa: Calendar Pages looked like this. Weeks were variable in length (6-9 days). They did not start on Monday, but were "lunar weeks" starting on the new moon, full moon or half moons.

The pages were laid out horizontally like this across two pages and had to be turned sideways to use—very little room for writing!

13. moon

Winter Solstice pg.

Dezember/Jan.
Tues 20 dez 83
Wed 21
Thurs 22
Fri 23
Sat 24
Sun 25
Mon 26
Tues 27
Wed 28
Thurs 29
Fri 30
Sat 31
Sun 1 jan 84
Mon 2

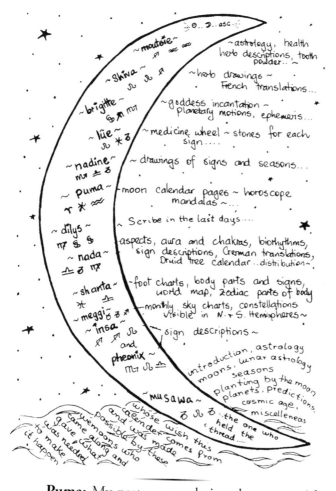

~astrology, health herb descriptions, tooth powder..~

~herb drawings ~ French translations...

~goddess incantation ~ planetary motions, ephemeris...

~medicine wheel ~ stones for each sign....

~ drawings of signs and seasons...

~moon calendar pages ~ horoscope mandalas ~...

~ Scribe in the last days....

aspects, aura and chakras, biorhythms, sign descriptions, German translations, Druid tree calendar...distribution~

~foot charts, body parts and signs, world map, zodiac parts of body

~monthly sky charts, constellations visible in N. + S. Hemispheres~

~ sign descriptions ~

introduction, astrology moons, lunar astrology seasons planting by the moon planets, predictions cosmic age, miscelleneas

~moutoie~ ~Shiva~ ~brigitte~ ~lüe~ ~nadine~ ~puma~ ~dilys~ ~nada~ ~shanta~ ~meggi~ ~insa~ and pheonix~ ~musawa~ ~the one who held the thread~ whose wish this calender comes from and was made possible by these wemoons who came along and gave what was needed to make it happen

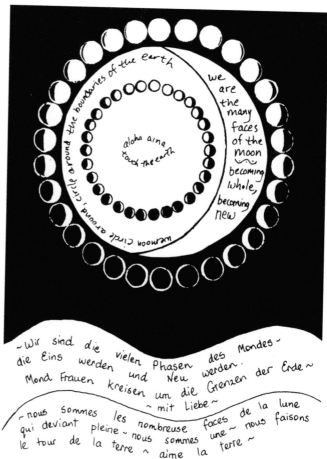

we are the many faces of the moon ~ becoming whole, becoming new

circle around the boundaries of the earth

wemoon circle around

aloha aina touch the earth

~ Wir sind die vielen Phasen des Mondes ~ die Eins werden und Neu werden. Mond Frauen kreisen um die Grenzen der Erde ~ ~ mit Liebe ~

~ nous sommes les nombreuse faces de la lune qui deviant pleine ~ nous sommes une ~ nous faisons le tour de la terre ~ aime la terre ~

Puma: My part was to design the pages with the moonphases and other drawings. Sometimes we got tired but Musawa wouldn't let us out. For otherwise the calender wouldn't be ready in time. Every prophesy and healing method we knew, we wrote down and translated into 4 languages. What a big project on a place without any technical comfort. But nice to include so many wemoon with the translation and writing and later reading and understanding. I looked after it during the printing (where we had complications to make corrections). But then we hold a beautiful pocket calendar in our hands. Thank you, Musawa, for your love and perseverance in 30 years wemoontime.

Musawa: This second We'Moon was reduced to three languages; there were still no straight lines marking off the days in We'Moon '83, and the sideways swath of Moons left hardly any space to write in. As with the first one, the main focus was on charting the natural cycles.

Nada: I have one example of the We'Moon almanac here from 1983, with Lue playing the flute on the beach on the cover and all writings are written by hand, all drawings quite simple, and in three or four languages, I recognize my handwriting on some of the pages. Strange . . . so long ago. I also have some unpleasant memories struggling with the printing place, where communication was extremely difficult since we both barely spoke French. For the ordinary French men working there we were totally strange creatures and there was no mutual understanding whatsoever.

33

Nadine Zenobi, Cover Art, WM'84

Musawa: "1984" was a much publicized watershed year at the time (like the Harmonic Convergence in 1987, Y2K in 2000, or 2012 now), when Orwellian fears that "Big Brother is watching you" were looming large in the collective consciousness. I took my first trip back to the U.S. since 1978, during the time it took to produce We'Moon '84. I met up with old friends in New Mexico who had been part of our earlier attempt to start a "matriarchal village" on Mama Mountain in Northern California in the mid-1970s. They had since settled on women's lands in New Mexico and Oregon—that are my home lands to this day. I knew Nadine Skyrivers from mutual migrations that led us both to Kvindelandet, and now to New Mexico. She did a lot of the art for We'Moon '84, including the beautiful cover, the season drawings, and some of the photos of Kvindelandet days (along with Shoshana who was now living in New York City working as a photographer). I wrote most of the text for it in a small one room adobe house on the edge of the desert in Chimayo. I had the honor of participating in my first Native American peyote healing ceremony

◻ *Musawa*

nearby, which as it turns out, was called in honor of Grandmother Margaret Behan, who was a young mother at the time and subsequently became one of the founding members of the International Council of 13 Indigenous Grandmothers.

Suisun, WM'84

34

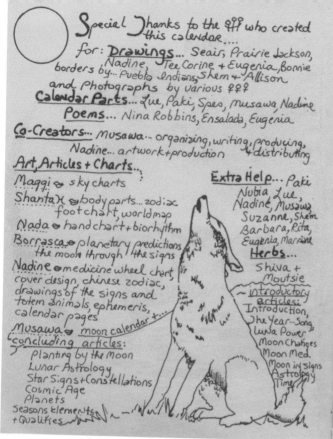

Special Thanks to the ♀♀♀ who created this calendar....
for: **Drawings**... Seair, Prairie Jackson, Nadine, Tee Corine + Eugenia, Bonnie
borders by... Pueblo Indians, Shem + Allison
and Photographs by various ♀♀♀
Calendar Parts... Lue, Paki, Speo, Musawa, Nadine
Poems... Nina Robbins, Ensalada, Eugenia
Co-Creators... Musawa... organizing, writing, producing, + distributing
Nadine... artwork + production

Art, Articles + Charts..

Maggi ☉ sky charts
Shanta ☿ body parts... zodiac
foot chart, worldmap
Nada ☉ hand chart + biorhythm
Borrasca ☉ planetary predictions
the moon through the signs
Nadine ☉ medicine wheel chart,
cover design, chinese zodiac,
drawings of the signs and
totem animals, ephemeris,
calendar pages +...
Musawa ☉ moon calendar +
concluding articles:
  Planting by the Moon
  Lunar Astrology
  Star Signs + Constellations
  Cosmic Age
  Planets
  Seasons, Elements
  + Qualities

Extra Help... Paki
Nubia, Lue,
Nadine, Musawa,
Suzanne, Shem,
Barbara, Rita,
Eugenia, Marrine

Herbs...
Shiva +
Moutsie
~ introductory
articles:
Introduction,
The Year... Song,
Luna Power,
Moon Changes,
Moon Med.,
Moon in signs,
Astrology,
Time

Moon in Aquarius © *Mari Jackson 1979, WM'84*

This is a lunar calendar, with days given by the phases of the moon, and months given by the thirteen revolutions of the moon around the earth, from the new moon before Winter Solstice to the new moon of the following Winter Solstice, when the sun cycle renews. It also includes a guide to planetary energies with a complete ephemeris and aspects each day, articles and charts on cosmic energy sources for use in everyday life, such as planting by the moon, healing and seasonal celebrations; with introductory explanations of astrology that anyone can use—from a cross-cultural, earth-loving, wemoon-centered point of view

This book is recyclable!

The moon returns to the same phases, on the same days and dates, in the same sign and degree of the zodiac, every nineteen years (her metatonic cycle). If you save this We'Moon Almanac 1984 until the year 2003, you can use it again—if the earth, and we who wish to live in peace with her, can survive that long to make it possible. One cycle at a time, here's hoping we make it to the next metatonic return of the moon! If we learn to keep in touch with her and other heavenly beings in this time—along with ourselves and each other here on earth—we will be living in natural harmony, in tune and ready for the next round, in whatever form that comes to us. All one family, we of the moon, matakaisi, aloha aina: love the earth, mother, we are all one.

excerpt Introduction

Every year, so far, the Wemoon Almanac has been printed in a different country... France (1981-82) Germany (1983), N. America (1984).
Where, when + by whom it continues is an open question. It is time now to pass it on, or change the process. If you wish to be part of this... write: "Wemoon Almanac" % Musawa at the contact address given in front (Woman Spirit - U.S.A; or France) by springtime. Aloha aina

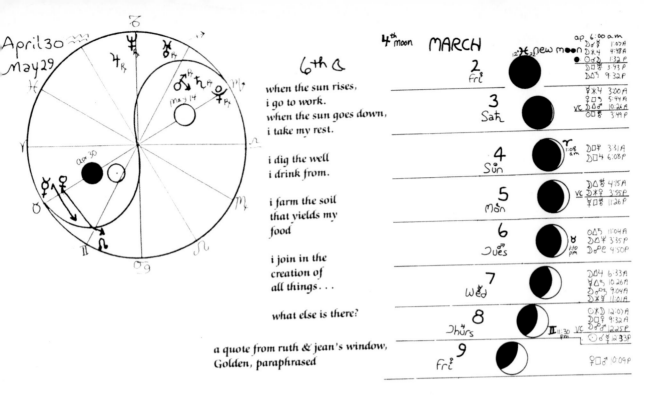

April 30 ♒
May 29

4th moon **MARCH**

6th ☽

when the sun rises,
i go to work.
when the sun goes down,
i take my rest.

i dig the well
i drink from.

i farm the soil
that yields my
food

i join in the
creation of
all things . . .

what else is there?

a quote from ruth & jean's window,
Golden, paraphrased

2
Fri

3
Sat

4
Sun

5
Mon

6
Tues

7
Wed

8
Thurs

9
Fri

Nadine Zenobi: My connection to We'Moon comes from early on. Musawa communicated her vision to me as we sat around a table in New Mexico, as dear old friends, and she asked me to design the visuals for the 1984 edition. I remember assembling it and as I look at it now it makes me smile at its simplicity. During the years, women volunteered in a grassroots endeavor to make it a continual reality. It was a beautiful, affirming, creative, unified, flowing experience for me with fond connections and memories. Women's lands were in prime time and we traveled and organically the input became stronger and more solid as the years went on. I cannot even believe it has been 30 years since then. It is so wonderful to open awareness of how one woman with a vision, can find unison with the flow of other women to put this vision into manifestation. May we all find inspiration and awareness to live our lives in such a way.

© Nadine Zenobi, WM'84

© Shoshana Rothaizer, WM'84

36

The Tractor Race © *Shoshana Rothaizer, WM'84*

© *Shoshana Rothaizer, WM'84*

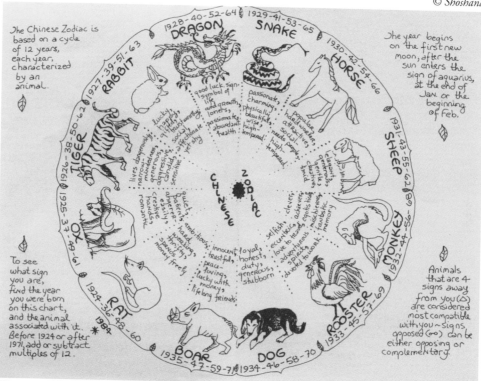

The Chinese Zodiac is based on a cycle of 12 years, each year, characterized by an animal.

The year begins on the first new moon, after the sun enters the sign of aquarius, at the end of Jan. or the beginning of Feb.

To see what sign you are, find the year you were born on this chart, and the animal associated with it. Before 1924 or after 1971, add or subtract multiples of 12.

Animals that are 4 signs away from you (△) are considered most compatible with you — signs opposed (◯◯) can be either opposing or complementary.

1928-40-52-64 **DRAGON**
1929-41-53-65 **SNAKE**
1927-39-51-63 **RABBIT**
1930-42-54-66 **HORSE**
1926-38-50-62 **TIGER**
1931-43-55-62-89 **SHEEP**
1925-37-49-61 **OX**
1932-44-56- **MONKEY**
1924-36-48-60 1984 **RAT**
1933-45-57-69 **ROOSTER**
1935-47-59-71 **BOAR**
1934-46-58-70 **DOG**

CHINESE ZODIAC

Chinese Zodiac © *Nadine Zenobi, WM'84*

WM'84

Nuage and Nada ▫ *Musawa, WM'84*

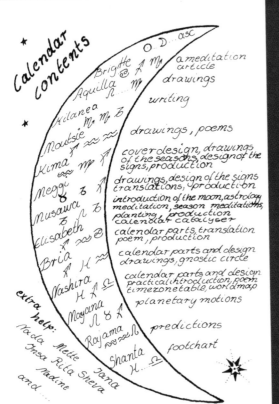

Musawa: Having just returned to Europe, I was in no shape to turn around and produce the next We'Moon immediately, and women from a nearby women's land (Kvindelandet women who then settled in Rouvenac in the Mediterranean region of Southern France) stepped in to carry the day. As you can see from the Table of Contents to the left, they created it collectively (see the story of the Great Mother and the gifts she gave to her twelve daughters in the Astrology section (p. 197) and the group photos illustrating each sign. They also did a lot of the artwork, drew charts, made photos and wrote poems—which were mostly not credited individually. Thank you Rouvenac Womyn for your creative collective process and for carrying the torch when it was needed for We'Moon to continue for another year! "Step by Step the longest march, will be won, singly none, singly none…"

Elisabeth, Igelin/Eagelin: What to say about making these photos in Rouvenac. It was great fun and actually I remembered just a couple of weeks ago. This Scorpio photo (p. 207) was for me a pure expression of my sexuality, the first time in my life then, I felt my Mars in Scorpio. That was a great opening!

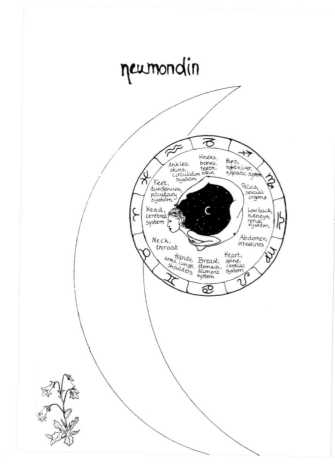

neumondin

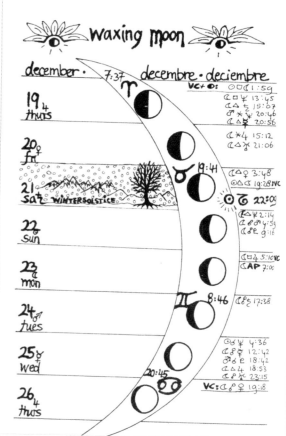

Waxing Moon

december · 7:37 · decembre · deciembre

		VC+☉:	☉☌☽ 1:59
19 thurs	♈	☽△♆ 13:45	
		☽△♄ 15:07	
		♂⚹♆ 20:46	
		☽△♄ 20:56	
20 fri	♀	☽⚹♃ 15:12	
		☽△⚷ 21:06	
21 sat	♉ 19:41 WINTERSOLSTICE	☽△♃ 3:48	
		☉☌☽ 19:28 IVC	
		☉☌♀ 22:09	
22 sun	♊	☽△♀ 2:14	
		☽♂♂ 4:59	
		☽♂♄ 9:16	
23 mon	♋	☽△♃ 5:10 IVC	
		☽△♇ 7:00	
24 tues	♊ 8:46	☽⚹♄ 17:38	
25 wed	♉	☉☌♆ 4:36	
		☽♂♀ 12:42	
		☽♂♃ 18:42	
		☽△♃ 18:53	
	20:45	☽♂⚷ 23:15	
26 thurs	♋	VC: ☽♂♀ 19:18	

GUIDED MEDITATION

Meditation gives a way to experience cosmic energy by letting it flow through us and consciously working with what that opens in us.

It is a path we'moon are beginning to explore more and more as we seek to live our meditation.

The meditations given in this calendar come from ten years of we'moon spirit wanderings in different countries--in the early days of our rediscovery of spirituality and healing and trying to live it on land. I have put together some of the basic teachings we'moon have passed around to each other in learning how to meditate.✳

As we go through the seasons with these meditations, we tune into the special powers generated by the turning of the wheel of the year...

Winter Solstice we reach down into the earth for grounding; Spring Equinox we reach up through our individuality point to the cosmos; Summer Solstice we surround ourselves in a cone of white light; Fall Equinox we work with the polarity of our breathing to find balance, inside and out. In the mid-season celebrations we practice visualization (Candlemas), shining up the chakras (May Day), energy circles (Mid-Summer Day), and ritual (Halloween).

Moon Priestess © Mari Jackson 1985, WM'85

39

☾meditation:

The Spiral Dance: A Rebirth of
   the Ancient Religion of the
   Great Goddess, by Starhawk
   (H & R, New York, 1979)

Mother Wit: A Feminist Guide to
   Psychic Development, by
   Mariechild (The Crossing Press,
   N.Y. , 1981)

Creative Visualization, by Shakti
   Gawain (Whatever Publishing,
   Mill Valley, Cal., 1978)

Psychic Healing by Amy Wallace
   and Henkin (Wingbow Press,
   Berkely, Ca. 1978)

wimmin's tarot: ★

Motherpeace Tarot
P.O. Box 1511
Cave Creek,
Arizona 85331
          USA

The Amazon Tarot
Hecuba's Daughters
P.O. Box 488
Bearsville. N.Y.
12409   USA

the Aquazon Deck
Morgan Maxwell
4748 Edgeware Rd.
San Diego, Cal.
92116   USA

Goddesses of
   the Tarot
susun Weed
P.O. Box 64
Woodstock, N.Y.
12498   U.S.A.

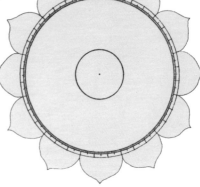

☾ ♀♀♀'s peace camps:

photo by Shoshona

Greenham
Women's Peace Camp
Outside Main Gate
RAF Greenham Common
Newbury, Berkshire
England

Italian Women's
   Peace Camp
La Ragnatela
Comiso, Italy

Seneca Women's
   Peace Camp
Seneca, New York,
        USA

Women for Survival
(Pine Gap)
Alice Springs,
Australia

lune croissante

This book is recycleable...
the moon returns to the same phase, on the
same days and dates, in the same sign and degree
of the zodiac, every 19 years (her metatonic cycle). In the year 2004
you can use the We'moon Almanach again. Bon courage

see two butterflies--as you gaze at them, you give yourself wings,
the ability to travel between dimensions

La Ragnatela, Comiso
Italian Women's Peace Camp

Women's Peace Song

We are womyn
We are crying
We are singing
for the earth.

Wind keeps blowing
rivers flowing
trees are growing
on the earth.

don't give up now
times are changing
keep on loving
for the earth.

no more soldiers
no more slaughter
no more missles
on the earth.

break the silence
speak your own words
keep on trying
for the earth.

Closing the gap at Pine Gap,   Alice Springs, Australia

Colette Gardiner: Receiving my first We'Moon was one of those watershed events that changed the course of my life. It was the early eighties and a friend handed me a copy of the almanac. As I leafed through the pages it felt as though all the separate threads of who I was, all the little rivulets of ideals, magic, earth awareness, and feminism came together to create a great river of possibilities, a river that could guide me into the future I envisioned. And so I started my journey, using the We'Moon as a wellspring of inspiration, incorporating the knowledge of seasonal and moon cycles into my magic and my work as an herbalist. [Colette became the We'Moon herbalist in the '90s].

As I submitted writings to the almanac, it was reassuring to realize that there were women ahead of me, making it easier for all of us to move forward. Many years later I'm amazed at how far we've come. I look back and see how the work of those women has expanded who we all are. Now when students ask me how I started my work, the story of picking up my first We'Moon is always part of the telling. As I watch my students opening their own herb schools, offering magical counseling or creating Tarot decks, I can't help but wonder how many other We'Moon inspired streams of change are out there. All rushing along, gathering strength and speed, changing the course of reality, a bit at a time.

Queen of Wands, Amazon Tarot
Billie Potts, WM'85

© Karin Orleander, Cover Art, WM'86

The We'Moon Almanac '86 was begun in Denmark and completed in England, with help from Danish, Norweigan, Swedish, English, Scottish, Irish, Welsh, Spanish, French, German, Japanese and American wemoon (mostly one of each!). Wemoon have no country, the whole earth is our land . . . but still, we come from different parts of it. Karin, who designed the calendar pages (and the cover), made a big effort this year not to fill them up with all our creations, to keep them clear for you. The other wemoon in the original calendar/healing circle in Denmark—Tove, Rayama, Verdende, Dani, Shanta, and Margrete, with inspiration from Jytte—were a great help in getting it started and leaving me on my own to journey to where the moon goddess seemed to be calling. In England, Cornwall wemoon (especially Grete, Liz and Sarah Goatwoman), and Greenham wemoon (especially Io, Mari and Jo) were a strong support and inspiration in making it happen, as was Monica Sjöö.

Creating this year's almanac was a serpentine journey to living goddess sources on a strong flowing current through we'moon culture. The places and experiences, as well as the wemoon I met along the way, gave a substance to what it is about: the wemoons' peace camps in Denmark and at Greenham; healing circles and spirals of wemoon needing and giving healing energy everywhere; the walk to reclaim the sacred land across Salisbury Plain from Silbury Hill Avebury, on Beltane — to Stonehedge, Scorpio full moon and lunar eclipse—30 miles in 3 days with 150 wemoon and children of all ages through a military artillery range on an ancient mother pathway; journeying along great goddess ley lines from Avebury—Glastonbury to Wales and up to Cornwall, a gathering of Women for Life on Earth at Malvern and a squat in Rotherhithe where the final labor took place. All along, wemoon were meeting in special ways and places for the new and full moons, Equinox, Solstice, and Fire Festivals, contacting deep sources of goddess energy which we take in, share, and generate out in the touching. Singing and dancing as we go: Aloha Aina, in the presence of the spirit of love, heal ourselves, heal the earth.

"We walk upon sacred ground, with every step we take..." And it is so. Aloha Aina: heal the earth. *excerpt, Introduction*

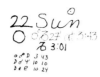
22 Sun
○ 0°♏27' ♑ 3:43
♑ 3:01
♂□☽ 3.43
☽□♃ 10.10
☽♂♇ 10.24

FULL MOON
in
CAPRICORN

23 Mon
○
☽♂♂ 11.36
☽✶♃ 14.22
☽□♀ 22.36 vc

JUNE

24 Tues
○ ♒ 2:51
☽✶♄ 10.12
☽□♇ 10.28
☽♂♀ 20.16

SCT. HANS

25 Wed
○ ☽ ☿
☽✶♅ 11.44 vc

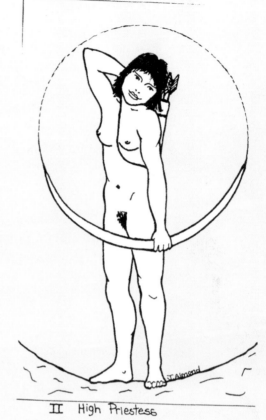

II High Priestess

III MATRIARCH

"Matriarch" Amazon Tarot

Praire Jackson Amazon Tarot

Every culture has its own version of the **Cosmic Weaver**. It is always a woman—she who spins, weaves and cuts the thread of life as we live it: The three Fates, the three Norns, the three Muses, the three Marias, the Triple Goddess, Changing Woman, Spider Woman. Not so well known is the fourth aspect—the all/one who exists in the dark space between the worlds from whose depths all form emerges. She is usually either forgotten, denied, or violently suppressed out of the fear of the unknown; the greatest female power is a mystery, despised by the patriarchy which cannot take over what it cannot name. It is she who holds the key to becoming the weavers of our own fate. When we can accept her as part of ourselves, she becomes an ally to guide us instead of an enemy to fear . . . in the underworld journey where all boundaries are dissolved as we meet the fragments of our divided selves, where we find power to heal and change. When we experience our wholeness (holiness), we pass by her in some ways every time we step out into the unknown at the end of one growing cycle and the beginning of another.

excerpt, Introduction

43

Invocation to the Goddess

© Monica Sjöö, WM'86

Naertus
Ancient Mother (Urmuder),
You, our first goddess,
born of the field of Dana,
the virgin forest, the song of Spring,
fertile power who bears the fruit
of the earth,
Mother we call you. Be with us.
As we wandered
in the past times with peace.
we wander now.
Listen to us. Be with us.
where ever you appear, Naertus,
all weapons disappear, Naertus.
all weapons disappear,
peace fills your path.
Naertus, we will fill your earth
with seeds of peace.
where you travel,
happiness flowers.
Naertus, we call you,
we awaken you
be with us now.

© Dani, WM'86

Nerthus
a ninefoot high cloven oak branch

© Monica Sjöö, WM'86

♀ for survival - Cockburn Sound ♀'s Peace Camp
December 84 - Western Australia

Earth Mother ▫ Jenny Croxford, WM'86

44

Musawa: I went to England in the middle of producing We'Moon '86 to do a We'Moon workshop in Cornwall that never happened and instead, met up with a group of Greenham women involved in the "Walk across Salisbury Plain" and joined in on my first spiritual political action. It was deeply reminiscent of ancient mass migrations, as we moved together by day and set up camp by night, magically eluding police lines in an unstoppable stream of women moving with sacred purpose to liberate an ancient goddess site from U.S. military occupation. That's where I met Monica Sjöö (and followed her home to Wales afterwards), whose art and writing on the ancient Goddess sacred sites was a major inspiration for We'Moon '86—and also Starhawk, who, as another goddess-inspired political activist, took a leadership role on that walk in bridging the gap between these two traditionally separate camps (women's spirituality and political activism) in the famous "Bog Roll ritual" our first night at Stonehenge. Her "Poem for Women who Live in the Open" (p. 56) was inspired by that walk.

Another friend from that walk ended up joining us in France at an auspicious time. This is her story of how she helped move We'Moon to its next destination:

Many many moons ago, two wimmin, new friends, sat in a café in France musing about the plight of funding for the fast approaching We'Moon publishing commitment in London. The funding (proceeds from the sale of the previous We'Moon) was stuck in francs in a French bank, unable to leave the country, victim of a sudden embargo on the franc. So a daring plan of trust and courage was hatched and grew to fruition. One of the women went to the bank, obtaining the francs, giving them trustingly to the other, who tucked this precious cargo safely in her knickers for its trip across the water and border. Arriving safely, she then helped birth that year's We'Moon.

© Shoshana Rothaizer 1982, WM'84

Seed Meditation:
For Renewal/Self-Healing

Imagine you are a seed full of life. Plant this seed of your Self in the warm earth and water it gently until it begins to open. Feel your little roots reach down between the particles of earth, drinking in nutrients. Feel the sprout unfold from the seed into the air. Your leaflets begin to raise up towards the sun, soaking in her rays. You become green-growing-green. All that you need is given . . . for growing, for well being—you give all that is needed. You are in radiant health.

Individuality Point:
a point a metre above your head where your individual soul meets cosmic consciousness . . . the crown point of your astral aura through which pure cosmic energy is streaming into your physical being all the time.

Egypt: 6000 years ago

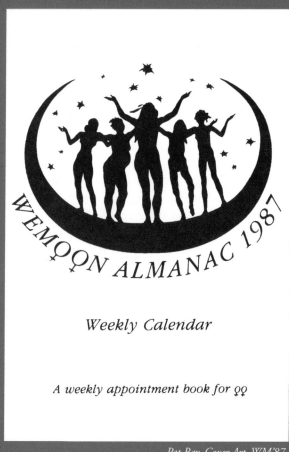

WEMOON ALMANAC 1987

Weekly Calendar

A weekly appointment book for ♀♀

Pat Ray, Cover Art, WM'87

Yemaya: The Moon D.O.M. Tarot © Ffiona Morgan 1986, WM'87

For the past five years, We'Moon Almanac has been created by wemoon from different countries, primarily in Europe—lesbians living on land, re-creating wemoon culture from our common natural roots in the Mother Earth. The network of women dispersing out over many lands, like seeds in the wind, was the source of its creation for the next five years.

The We'Moon Almanac was raised in an extended community of wemoon on land from all over. Wherever I was when the time came to put it out, there were wemoon who wanted to see it happen enough to be the midwives and comadres. Drawings, photos, research, poems, ideas and inspiration for the contents came floating in almost effortlessly each time. The free-floating fund of wemoon creativity out there just waiting to be appreciated is truly inspiring; the hardest part was always pulling it together and putting it out in print.

Being the one consistent thread holding it together all this time through all the changes was becoming wearing. Particularly as I was in a different country each time, mostly on the road or on women's lands where we had to walk at least a mile each way to the telephone or post box, without even a typewriter (until the third year), operating on a shoestring, distributing We'Moon in vans and backpacks over borders, always racing across boundaries of time and space and nationalities.

By the time I returned to America, where I had come to concentrate on other work (healing), the thread had worn to the breaking point and I was ready to let go. Whenever I had reached this point before, there were so many wemoon who wanted it to go on so much, that someone or other would come forward in the end to help do it. This time it was Women in Constant Creative Action.

We'Moon started out with wemoon living on the land; it has now broadened out to include wemoon of varying life styles and experiences. It is part of the ebb and flow, of who is here now for it, that makes it possible to go on at all.

from We'Moon Herstory, WM'87

The asteroid belt between Mars and Jupiter is the celestial pathway for the cycling of thousands of fragments of a planet that either exploded millenia ago, or of a planet that never was able to form herself into a whole because of the gravitational pull of Mars on one side and Jupiter on the other. This is symbolic of the nature of power embodied in the asteroids, since they represent an aspect of the feminine principle which has never been allowed to come to wholeness within us. As daughters of patriarchy, we are conditioned into a split consciousness, the Goddess repressed and fragmented by the patriarchal authority of Jupiter and the agressive Mars.

© Yana Breeze 1986, WM'87

— drawing down the moon —
Prairie Jackson

The Mandala of the Asteroid Goddess

The silver Light of the Moon reflects
the Ground of Lunar Energy—
The Undifferentiated Feminine Prior to Manifestation
with Her Powers of Fertilization.
and Transformation.

Arising from the Center is Venus Aphrodite,
Core Essence of the Feminine Nature in Her Manifest Form,
Through Her Powers of Divine Beauty
and Magnetic Desirability as Love
She awakens the Impulse to Life.

In Her Emanation to the North,
the feminine appears as Ceres
Representing Her Procreative Aspect as Mother
in Her Propagation and Nurturing of the Species.

In Her Emanation to the South,
the Feminine appears as Pallas Athene
Representing Her Creative Aspect as Daughter,
Giving Rise to Mental and Artistic Progeny.

In Her Emanation to the East,
the feminine appears as Vesta Representing
the Self Containment of Feminine Nature as Virgin
and Sister, Complete-in-One-Self, Belonging to No Man.

In Her Emanation to the West, the Feminine appears
as Juno Representing the Union of the Feminine Nature
with the Masculine as Consort and Wife through
the Sacred Marriage, Conjunction.

© Demetra George, WM'87

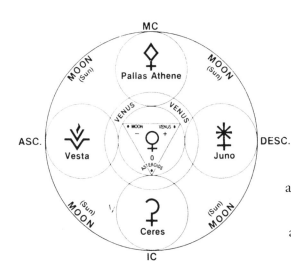

I am the cup of the moon
the crystal crescent
silver, silver
My open arm
receive pure pouring light
pouring through
I am sweet surrender
the open heart
    of the moon

*Wahaba (Nuit Cat,
Cottage Grove, OR),
WM'87*

© *Jenna Weston, WM'87*

The Pythia © *Max Dashu, WM'87*

Sunday Feb. ☽ 18° ♐ 4'   22
☐ ☿
♂ ♄

Monday ☽ 2° ♑ 26   23
⚹ ☉
△ ♂
☐ ♃
♂ ♅
♂ ♆

Tuesday ☽ 1°♑ 2   24
♂ ♀

48

Kali: The Awakener D.O.M. Tarot © Ffiona Morgan 1986, WM'87

Mother Tongue Ink landed this year at the We'Moon Healing Ground—a women's land I helped start 13 years ago. This almanac grew out of a journey that began from this place and led to many different women's lands in other countries. Returning to the starting point, I see the land herself in transition. We would like to start with creating a healing environment in which to live and work. Since the theme of the next We'Moon Almanac is on Healing Ourselves, Healing the Mother, we would like to encourage wemoon living close to the earth in a healing way to contribute your experiences. Musawa can be contacted at We'Moon Healing Ground.

Footnote to We'Moon Herstory, WM'87

Musawa: When We'Moon moved from Europe to North America, We'Moon '87 provided the transition—and it was a rough landing. The process of transplanting our little We'Moon seedling from one continent to another proved to be quite a shock on its fragile root system that had been tended consistently by women living on land, even if on many different lands. The only way We'Moon had survived so far was as a labor of love—we worked on it for free and put all the proceeds from one year into producing the next year's edition. It grew organically, like strawberries on runner roots that stretched from one to the next. But somehow, it was not able to bridge the oceanic gap between cultures. We ended up losing our shirts, financially, on this first edition produced here, and we had nothing to go on with—until the Oregon Women's Land community picked up the thread and offered to carry it on. Jemma Crae loaned the money to produce We'Moon '88, and two other friends (NíAódagaín and Kaseja) offered to co-produce it at OWL Farm (Oregon Women's Land) in Southern Oregon.

As the footnote to the We'Moon Herstory (above) indicates, the idea of soliciting art and writing on particular themes for each edition of We'Moon was beginning to emerge, although the theme for '88 transformed in the meantime from "Healing Ourselves, Healing the Mother" to "Wimmin's Lands."

we heal ourselves
As we heal the earth
almanaque de las
mujeres • frauen
almanach • almanacco
delle donne • almanach
des femmes • wimmin's
almanac •
we heal the earth
As we heal ourselves

We'Moon
Almanac
1988

a moon calendar
for wimmin

Daucus-Blossom, Cover Art, WM'88

The Earth—turning, rotating, orbiting; holding us to her, carrying us with her. We stand upon her —living, breathing, loving, wimmin. Healing ourselves as we atune to her, co-creating with her as we redirect our energies toward living with her in balance. As we grow food from her body; as we stomp our feet to the drum and feel her vibrate; as we sit and feel the heat of the open fire; as we sing the songs of praise to her, we heal ourselves.

This project began with a letter to wimmin's lands in the U.S., Canada and England. We asked wimmin to tell us of their experience in healing as they live close to the Earth. From their responses, we have created the 1988 We'Moon Almanac. We hope that during this year, the We'Moon will assist you in understanding and learning ways wimmin on land, together and alone, in communities as diverse as the Earth's plants and animals, join with the Mother's energy to bring about a healing way of life.

We felt too, that the theme of Healing the Earth, Healing ourselves would not be complete without the presentation of two lands where wimmin are working in direct struggle against the United States government, in an effort to stop the destructive policy this nation continues to perpetuate throughout this world. Thus, we have included poetry, narrative and photographs of Greenham Common, the Wimmin's Peace Encampment of England, and the story of the Dineh nation whose wimmin are playing a major role in resisting relocation of their people from their ancestral homelands. Furthermore, in a statement of solidarity with the wimmin of Big Mountain, 10% of all profits from this almanac will be given to the Big Mountain (J.U.A.) Legal Defense/Offense Committee.

Over the course of eight months, the wimmin who have worked on the formation of the Almanac also learned much about healing. Differences of class backgrounds, ideology, time constraints, financial restraints and the process of collective decision making produced struggles which needed to be recognized and resolved before we felt we could be truthful in presenting an Almanac with the theme: Healing the Earth, Healing ourselves.

The need for integrity pushed us to confront these issues, within ourselves and with our co-workers. Through honest sharing of feelings and needs, we were able to produce what we feel is a beautiful exposé of wimmin in struggle to heal themselves, and their Mother Earth.

Blessings to you,   *excerpt, Introduction*
by honora peace ní aódagaín, kaseja odanata

50

O.W.L. Farm Main House
□ Sharon Gillars, WM'88

April~Avril~Abril

Full Moon in Libra ♎ 1:22am PST
9:22am GMT

Billie Miracle, WM'88

2 ♄
Sat

3 ⊙
Sun
☽→ ♍ 10:27am PST
☽→ ♍ 6:27pm GMT

4 ☽
Mon

5 ♂
Tue
☽→ ♏ 6:30pm PST

6 ☿
Wed
☽→ 2:30am GMT

7 ♃
Thur

RELOCATION IS GENOCIDE

HONOR
MOTHER
EARTH

REPEAL P.L. 93-531

Emma Joy, WM'88

Christine Venghaus, WM'88

51

Fly Away Home Ritual

I

Silence

The women are silent.
All day. Both of them.
Most every day.
Until supper, when they sing a song
　　　and eat a meal
　　　and rave about the food they grow
　　　report on dreams,
　　　dog and cat events of the day,
　　　the newest aching joint
　　　the latest flower-bed scheme.

Keeper of the quiet forest temple.
Keeper of quiet:
a magic trick of tongue and will
　　　to make Solitude
　　　in the company of another.
Each one free to hear plants grow and die
to follow the deep sound of private mind.

We edge the sacred mountain with silence.

Keepers of the temple: and women come
only women come
to be still
to sing out their hearts
to wear the spirits
in between one world
and another.

© Bethroot 1986, WM'88

Spring Equinox © *Shoshana Rothaizer, WM'88*

Rosh Chodesh
A Jewish Ritual of the New Moon

Rosh Chodesh has always been female-oriented, born of the natural connection between the lunar and menstrual cycles. Here are some ideas from traditional and radical sources, for honoring the new moon:

hold an outdoor, evening ritual (for an authentic touch, include dancing)

say "shalom alcheim" (peace to you) to three people who respond with "alcheim shalom" (to you, peace)

eat round foods (pizza?) and new fruits of the month

give tzedakah (to charity: support causes and projects you believe in)

light candles

begin a new project; wear a new piece of clothing, learn a new song

What quality or skill would you like increased, what need or wish filled, as the moon "grows" this month? Claim this moment of womanly power, when darkness offers all possibilities.

© Laura Philips, WM'88

© Emma Joy, WM'88

52

Reclaiming the Earth

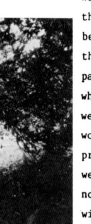

```
We are two wimmin walking arm in arm
the earth is staked with razor wire
bearing damp bedding
through midnight mist
passing shadowed soldiers
who mark our movements
we circle the base
woodsmoked nomads
property of no man
we travel camp to camp
no compromising
with each step feet massage the earth
and know sorrow in her smooth stones
```

art and writing:
**Two Sides
of Greeham Common**
© Oak Chezar, WM'88

Tribes

You say to us: if this is a tribe, why do you never stay still? Why do you meet only long enough to exchange stones, shells, feathers, amulets? Why can you pass though the center only alone and in absolute darkness? You say, if this is a tribe, what is the given language? What is its name, who belongs? You challenge our assumptions. You say, what kind of people is always on the road, alone, only speaking to each other in crisis, at connecting points, in crowded intersections on dying cities, in drug stores in small towns where no one knows your name, and then dispersal?

This is our answer: our language is poetry. Do you understand? Our language is signs, symbols, sacred objects; we are a sacred people. We have magical properties. There are many things to be done, people to be healed, houses to be built. It is not a time to be together, It is a time to be separate, to learn what it means to be alone.

We tell you this: we are doing the impossible. We are teaching ourselves to be human. When we are finished, the strands which connect us will be unbreakable; already we are stronger than we have ever been.

Thus we move: silently, separately; our name is buried in various sacred spots all over the land, We are waiting until it is safe to claim it. Though we move silently, separate, can you hear our joint voices singing, singing our women's songs in ever widening circles?

Listen: we are making ready. Hear our music across the dying land . . .

© Martha Courtot, WM'88

*▢ Zana, WM'88
an outdoor shampoo*

Musawa: What a relief to find our tribe again on this side of the ocean, after 10 years away. The stitch that got dropped the previous year was picked up the next and woven back in seamlessly. We'Moon was nurtured by the co-creators of We'Moon '88 at OWL Farm who worked diligently to produce the datebook—and so richly portray the diversity of wimmin's lands that responded to tell of "their experiences in healing as they live close to the Earth."

WE'MOON '89

A DAILY GUIDE
TO NATURAL RHYTHMS

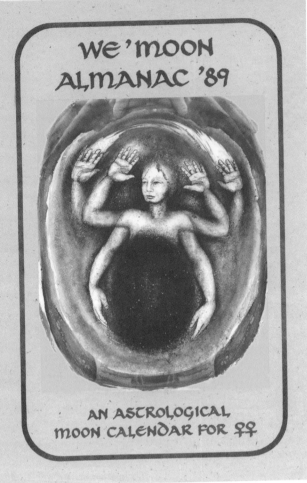

WE'MOON
ALMANAC '89

AN ASTROLOGICAL
MOON CALENDAR FOR ♀♀

© Deborah Koff-Chapin, Cover Art, WM'89

Musawa: "Spirit Healers" was the theme for We'Moon '89, even though themes were not announced on the covers until the '90s. This was the first time since We'Moon began that the calendar had a regular 7 day week starting on Mondays, rather than whenever the new, full and half moons happened to fall (every 6-9 days). With this edition, we began to number the 13 Moons throughout the pages of the lunar cycle (Moon I–XIII). It was also the first edition to be printed on 100% recycled paper, including the covers, with the founder of *Sage Woman Magazine,* Anne Newkirk Niven of Arena Press, a small, independent, (almost) local press as the printer.

This time, another friend stepped in—Rashani (pictured on the facing page), whose many "Spirit Healer" friends graced the pages through photos and writings of their healing work. Rashani came to We'Moon Healing Ground, (as We'Moon Land was called in those days) and helped me put it together, with her beautifully clear hand-written calligraphy. And once again, reminiscent of the earliest We'Moons, not a straight line was to be seen in delineating the flow of nights and days. With the close of the 1980s, We'Moon had settled on women's land in Oregon, where it took root and flourished for the next decade and a half, with the help of many old and new We'Moon friends.

© Shoshana Rothaizer 1982, WM'84

Rashani © Ellen Claire, WM'89

Saving the Redwoods

From Santaya Galana*: My people are fire survivors. This is because we are silky people, a soft people. We are also a people that let go, that peel, that slough off old layers of bark. We open the the fire that other trees try to block. The fire enters our hearts and lays them bare. When this happens to other trees, they die. But we live, and grow. Our hearts are hollow; creatures take shelter there. In this strength and our joy: the joy of the hollow heart, opened by the fire of spirit, providing shelter to all who come near.

© Frodo Okulam, WM'89
* Santaya Galana is a Redwood at Camp Gualala in northern California. She has been hollowed by fire. You can stand in her hollow heart, yet she is green and growing.

there is only awakening! Awakening to who we are......

There comes an indescribable moment when we realize that what we've spent years searching for is within ourself...... and that everything that has ever happened to us was intended for bringing us closer to Self understanding.

When we arrive at true Self acceptance (which is a step - or leap! further than Self-understanding) we have the power to alter our life forever and to transform opposition into opportunity. And, eventually, see that everything is an opportunity to evolve...... All of the energy that was previously used to be someone other than we were is suddenly available for other things!

My "vocation", according to my astrologer, is 'bartering magic for magic'. I do this in many ways, every day of my life. Every morning, my son and I find at least three miracles. This sets the tone for the rest of the day......

Whether performing, creating rituals, taking 8 year olds on shamanic journeys, waiting at a bus stop or walking alone in a forest, I enter into relationship with whomever I'm with... including myself and nature. I create a context: a sacred, safe space in which to touch & explore what is... A space in which "the shadow self" is no more, no less ugly or beautiful than our radiant goddess self. We experience our magnificence and a new level of power when we embrace and integrate our shadow and our "beauty". It empowers us to be effective instead of being at the effect of others.

Let us love the forces that oppose us
and understand them
well
let us suppose, the shadows
in ourselves
were elves in need of shade'

Rashani, Visionary poet, songwoman,
carpenter, craftswoman, spiritual midwife

© Rashani Réa, WM'89

© Sudie Rakusin, WM'89

A Poem for Women Who Live in the Open

A woman carved of rock
solid
A woman rain can beat against
who will not wear away
A plain woman
      whose dance bear breasted
      in the great freed stones
is a slow upcurving grace
a swan's neck rising from the river
a swan's head turning to listen to watch
      as the light grows

as an imp child beats the drum
that passes from woman to woman

barbed wire razor wire
cannot keep back this river
      women bring water to the imprisoned stones

this is our time of power in the moon's eclipse
and we will walk where we will to walk
over the chronically shelled Plain
that is sacred land
(all land is sacred land)
step by step we go forward on it

© Sudie Rakusin, WM'89

police soldiers
cannot dam this river
women surge through the stones   a cleansing
      and the light grows . . .

here we are free
      and the light grows
a crescent between stone thighs
it has been a long long time   since we were free
since we sang the moon here
      and the light grows
and we will not be free for long
      a moment eclipsed out of time
      a hole clipped in barbed wire

tomorrow they will jail us
tomorrow they will repair the fence that surrounds us
      but never completely

for tonight we touch freedom
      and the light grows
a crescent wedded to our own shadow
pulling a rising invincible river

the moon is full and the dark is holy
and we are women who live in the open

© Billie Miracle, WM'89

excerpt © Starhawk, written on the Salisbury Plain, May 1985, WM'89

56

Through my work with birthing women, I have experienced first hand the beauty and the power of the female body in its most raw and sacred aspect. My studies of the earth-based religions of Africa, North America and Europe have taught me that woman's body was humankind's earliest symbol for the mysteries of life, birth, death, the universe and creation. In my work with dance I seek to have us re-member the body - to create a space where women experience the sense of sacredness and joy in the body that is the spiritual heritage of our physical being! I do this through dance because dance, like sound, is our body's spiritual language. It is how we speak spirit, or more importantly, how spirit speaks us.

Arisika Razak, Midwife and Spiritual Dancer

© *Arisika Razak and Rashani Réa, WM'89*

© *Rashani Rae, WM'89*

© *Greta Boann Perry, WM'89*

Throughout the '80s, no art or writing was copyrighted and credits were sporadically given. . .until this last year of the decade:

Giving Credit Where Credit is Due:
The main return that contributors to the We'Moon Almanac receive is to have their work known. In past issues, credit has not always been given in a good clear way. For all the oversights of the past, please accept a deepfelt We'Moon apology. This year, we are making sure to credit each one for her work where it appears, as well as with the descriptions of each one in the Contributor By-lines. Thank you for sharing your beauty.

preface to Contributor By-lines, WM'89

Sudie Rakusin: We'Moon has been very important in my life as an artist. We'Moon was one of the first publications, along with *Sinister Wisdom* and *Woman of Power*, that accepted my artwork. I have always appreciated being given a theme for each year that would go into such depth. It would challenge me and spark my imagination. I have felt honored to be part of We'Moon through the years.

© *Sudie Rakusin 1985, WM'89*

57

1990s: We'Moon Shoots!

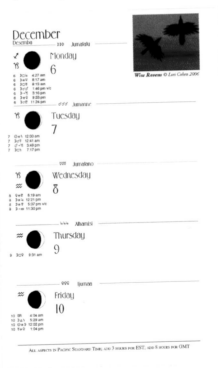

Judgement © *Motherpeace: a pseudonym for Karen Vogel and Vicki Noble 1981*

Judgement

As specific themes began emerging for each year at the end of the 1980s, we called on sources of spiritual guidance to consciously evoke the focus we wished to energize for the future. We found we were already using Tarot as our oracle to divine the themes for upcoming editions (which we now do 2-3 years in advance), and so we began specifically naming themes based on particular Tarot cards—to help us tap into underlying currents of spiritual evolution for reading the pulse of the times to come.

The Herstory section for the next two decades continues to be organized chronologically with a 4 page format of art and writing for each We'Moon year. With the 1990's, we add into the mix a thematic focus on the first 2 pages. The front cover heads up the first page, usually with an excerpt from the Introduction to the Theme, plus art and writing from that edition. The facing page focuses on the meaning and imagery of the corresponding Tarot card—drawn from all We'Moon editions. When we are choosing the theme, we play We'Moon Tarot: using Tarot imagery in a mystical, magical, playful process of conjuring themes unique to We'Moon. Using a combination of We'Moon numerology (the last two digits of the year) and the cosmic themes depicted in the Major Arcana of the Tarot (with Roman numerals for each Tarot card), we divine

our own interpretations of the Tarot symbology for the next year's We'Moon. We then send out our Call for Contributions of art and writing on that theme, and after a labor-intensive community selection process, we fill thirteen Moons of calendar pages with art and writing. Beginning in 1992, each of the Moon chapters has a named subject-theme beginning on a double-page spread with featured art and writing.

In 1990, We'Moon calendar pages began to take the shape that you see now in contemporary editions: the week begins on the left-hand page with Monday. Saturday and Sunday are usually on the facing page, depending on Holy Day features. The days of the week are named in four different rotating languages. The international roots of We'Moon continue to manifest, as we arranged for a German language edition from the '90s on. Gisela Ottmer, Rosemarie Merkel and Beate Metz were the faithful translators/distributors who made the German edition possible. Christel Göttert carries it on with help from Alice Holzer, Kerstin Weber and Gisela, who continues to help with translation.

In the 1990s, We'Moon settled down in one place and became a sustainable community business. At last, we were selling enough We'Moons to have some money left over to begin paying ourselves. This self-publishing venture was incorporated in 1995 as a home business with a part-time staff of paid employees made up of community residents. We'Moon remained a cottage industry for We'Moon Land for over ten years, in a mutually supportive partnership where We'Moon provided livelihood for womyn living on the land and the community did the work of We'Moon, with each helping stabilize, inspire and energize the other.

Wise Ravens © *Lori Cohen 2006*

We'Moon Community Members: Past, Present, Future

(back to front, left to right) Lori Katz, Amy Schutzer, Pandora, Carruch, Musawa, Linda Meagaen, Beth Freewomon, Marna Hauk

□ Linda Meagaen 1995, WM'97

We'Moon: Calendar / Land / Community

We'Moon is not just an appointment book, it is a way of life!

It is not just something we do on paper, it is something we create as a small intentional community of wemoon living on land in Oregyn. We have the special task of interweaving our life on the land with our work on the calendar throughout the year. Publishing We'Moon is the main cottage industry supporting we'moon living in our community.

We'Moon Gaia Gals got Gaia Rhythm! We dance to the Directions, end our weekly meetings with a Schoom! We celebrate the cycles, grow our food, drink water from the ground, live with fire, breathe! We have check-ins, feelings meetings, work in the garden, do yoga and body work, eat together, take breaks. Each one holds a piece of the truth, we honor the sacred in our work, make altars in the office, name computers after goddesses, bring the theme home, birth We'Moon with magic.

Like the moon, we go through our changes and have our differences. While the old cultural divides of class, race, age, culture, nationality, spirituality and sexual identity continue to challenge and teach us—they can also raise our consciousness. Consensus training has helped us to value and work through our differences. As a group, we are learning to survive conflict with love and humor.

We are all beginners at this thing called community—whether we have been doing it for 20 years, or are just passing through—it is a drop in the bucket of patriarchal time. We are re-membering community and creating culture as wemoon loving wemoon. We still have much to learn, but we're committed to keeping on keeping on.

□ *Musawa 1996, WM'97*

© *Sonja Shahan 1994, WM'96*

Beth Freewomon: I felt a calling to go to wimmin's land in 1990. Something in me was longing for land-based community and for balance with Nature.

My travels took me to OWL Farm the summer of 1990. There I learned about an opportunity to help out with the production of the 1991 We'Moon almanac. I had come to love We'Moon recently and this felt like an exciting opportunity. I worked in a variety of capacities for the production marathon and when that was over, Musawa invited me to continue to work with her to help finish up production. I said "Yes!" I felt so enthusiastic about the future potential of being part of Mother Tongue Ink that I desired to make myself indispensable. This was a powerful invocation and indeed became answered prayer!

On October 8th, 1991, I moved to the land. I helped out with some administrative tasks and looked for a "real" job. In the first years I learned the ins and outs of Mother Tongue Ink. Eventually I said "Yes" to the We'Moonager job. It felt like a coming of age, rite of passage when I stepped up as We'Moonager. For eight years I held the reins of We'Moon, guiding her towards her destiny to become a full-color edition. Her press circulation had increased from 13,000 to 39,000 over the 11 years I was a part of We'Moon.

Beth was the first full-fledged "We'Moonager"—a "plenty-time" business manager who also functioned as an editor, book-keeper, production coordinator, page lay-out and graphic designer, sales and accounts/promo and distribution manager, Matrix and Creatrix team leader—an all around Wonder wemoon! who was ably supported by a part-time staff of amazingly talented community members through the years. My first We'Moon pay check went into buying a car and taking a "Crone's Year Off"—at age 50!

Gretchen Lawlor joined our annual team effort as our beloved "Year-at-a-Glance" We'Moon astrologer, as did Susan Levitt, Chinese New Year writer. Sandra Pastorius, AKA Laughing Giraffe, continued to offer her poet/astrologer wisdom. Heather Roan Robbins joined this team of brilliant astrologers in 2003. In 1996, Bethroot Gwynn became our "special guest editor"—for ever after! That title does not even begin to describe what all invaluable work she does for We'Moon. She is also co-author with me of many of the Introductions to the Theme from then on. The quality of our work in all areas continued to improve with the skill and experience of our spirited and gifted staff and contributors—our friends, land mates and close circle of We'Moon steadies!

Osha, WM '93

Bethroot Gwynn: Musawa and I first met at the first National Women's Liberation Conference in 1968. Parallel paths carried us deep into the feminist movement and the women's land community, where innovative forms of spiritual practice and lesbian culture were thriving. I landed in Southern Oregon, Musawa at We'Moon Land to the north. She brought her magnificent "child," the We'Moon datebook, and it became a sacred text in country dyke culture: women living close to the earth, creating ritual and song, buildings and poetry, sisterhood for the long haul.

I joined We'Moon staff when the 1998 Datebook—with the theme Wise Womyn Ways—was being prepared. The staff crew called on me because they felt the need for an older, more crone-ish voice among them, given the ancient wisdom roots for this theme. I did not feel especially ancient, but at 55, I was an available elder to work with these women in their 20s and 30s. I plunged in, had a wonderful time working with the staff, and the art and writing. I have stayed on as Special Editor through several more evolutions of staff turnover, stabilized now with a wonderfully experienced and creative staff team. The intergenerational mix of us—our differences in taste and culture, assumptions and life experiences—make for a spicy and enriching work environment.

Editing seems a natural bent for me (my Critic gets free rein: I'm supposed to find mistakes!) Imagine how much fun I have, drenched in the ocean of We'Moon submissions! Musawa and I have fierce intellectual battles about word choices. Each of us has met her match for verbal stamina. Sisterhood for the long haul.

As our roots grew deeper down into the earth for sustainable growth, our branches reached far and wide. The network of wemoon artists and writers from around the world grew in this time, as well as our readership. As a budding young teenager, We'Moon was becoming popular!

We'Moon continued to be created as a community effort by a growing network of wemoon. Thousands of wemoon were receiving the Call for Contributions for art and writing each year. Wemoon throughout Oregon were coming to our "Weaving Circles" to review the hundreds of pieces of submitted art and writing, and to participate in our preliminary selection process.

Hawk Madrone, 1997:

We'Moon Weaving at Fly Away Home

we of the moon,
with our canine companions,
women together
for two sun cycles, weaving
"Wise Women Ways": We'Moon 1998

we are in our 30's, 40's, 50's
some old friends,
some newly met
all sisters
in the making of this fabric.
boxes of poems and prose,
paintings, drawings, photographs:
our warp and woof.
round and round go
countless folders of writing

women's words
spun from
   joy despair insight simplicity
thick folders of graphics
handed out
   as succulent visionary reward
for giving each written voice
quiet attention.
the knowing
the questioning
the imagining
of the weavers
spin the threads
sent by women far and wide
into a growing web.

Katya Sabaroff Taylor: How has the spirit of We'Moon moved through my life? Like the moon itself, steadily, glowing, sometimes delicately hiding in mist, other times accompanied by bright stars, yet other times dim and dark and then, suddenly comes the crescent piercing the night sky. As women are linked to the moon, so are we linked to one another, and We'Moon has been an encyclopedic compilation of our thoughts, words, hopes, art, always unfolding with new insight and ancient wisdom.

◻ *Guida Veronda 1994, WM'97*

WE'MOON '90

BIRTH·DEATH·LIFE·TRANSITIONS
an·astrological·moon·calendar·appointment·book·for·wemoon

© Sudie Rakusin, Front Cover Art, WM'09

Traditionally wemoon are the ones who stand at the gates between the worlds and bring people though. This is true coming and going (as mothers and midwives, nurses and hospice workers). It is true through all the stages of life, growth and transitions in between. Wemoon are the caretakers (ie. the caregivers), the ones who nurture, guide and raise the generations of humanity—and "all our relations" who share life on the planet. This is true not only in ordinary everyday states of being and doing, where spirit reality is matter-realized. It is true of the transformations in extraordinary states of consciousness and forms of being. Wemoon are the original oracles, shamans, psychics, healers, priestesses, witches ("wise ones"), teachers, lovers and spiritual leaders. We are the daughters of Mother Earth, who inherit and pass on her life.

excerpt, Introduction to the Theme

© Billie Miracle 1989, WM'90

Menarch Ritual

My daughter had her first bloods in December, 1987. We did ritual, singing her song. All her gifts were red. We ate red apples and red cake. She was given a medicine bag, with blood stone. She was offered, in love, to the goddess. She was received in love to the circle.

▫ Therin Jensen 1989, WM'90

Mid-Winter Waiting, Sun-Standing-Still
© Cathy Dagg 1989, WM'90

Open Hayfield

While the night is still young in diamonds
wind howls like a cat past my chilled ears.

As the sky shapes itself, stars stream over the earth.

Standing deep in an open hay field,
tears stream down my face.

In my somber flesh and skin I am
what I am and I fear not what's in me.

While the night is still young in diamonds,
listen to me:

Living is not for the other side of life
because one don't know how they will end

I ask for respect as you turn the other way;
my body quivers to be held.

Wild. . .the night is still young in diamonds.

I'm not ready to die yet.

© Jeanette Spencer 1987, WM'90

Goddess of the Tarot
□ *Susun S. Weed 1982, WM'85*

Black Pearl

I had believed old age
to be the rumpled smell
of Nan stuttering to her commode
on Grancha's arm,
the staleness of her handbag
sticky with burst fruit sweets
and melted chocolate,
perpetually wiping my fingers
to salvage her love-letters
but this octogenarian woman
who dances everyday,
who has remet her first love
after 50 years and tells me
of her passion, now,
is an open oyster offering me
her black pearl.
□ *Llinora Milner 1994, WM'98*

***Out of Winter Come Spring,
Hail Persephone's Return***
□ *Oriol Dancer, WM'90*

Nature Lovin' Granny © *Sara Glass 2007, WM'09*

My Grandma's Hands

Helping hands, so powerful. so strong
plowed, planted,
sung her sweet song
veins, wrinkles,
like roads she walked
tough, hard,
roving, she stalked
the road to freedom,
so long, so near
the exit from slavery,
so deadly clear
fist full of memories,
the sturdiness of dreams
molded, flooded;
overflowed my streams
a hint of beauty,
a gleam of knowledge in my eye
my grandmother's hands,
the reason why
© *Laura Irene Wayne 1992, WM'98*

Latin America:
Tree of Life-Nunca Mas-Never More
(a homage to mothers of the disappeared)
etching © Betty LaDuke 1986, WM'90

Some thoughts
while visiting you in jail. . .

Some prisoners count the days
and long for the future;
others are mourning for the past.
The wise ones take refuge
in each moment,
knowing that the inner world is vast
and that being imprisoned
is a state of mind
occupied by many
who think they're free.

Our world is filled with prisoners:
look closely and you will see
the slavery called freedom
in our own society!

Written for Diane Poole, who was arrested
for blockading ammunition trains at the Concord Naval
Weapons' Station excerpt © Rashani Réa 1989, WM'90

Fruit of the Tree...

It used to bother me—still does sometimes—
that if I do not have a child from my own body
this lifetime,
then I am breaking a long chain of life passed on
from mother to daughter from the beginning of time
until now.
Who am I to break that chain?
Can I honestly stand here,
look back at my entire lineage of foremothers, and say:
This is it! I am the fruit of your life-giving labor—
the final fruit?!

But when I look at the whole tree
each life line leaves, I see how she branches,
and how she bears far more fruit
than she needs for seeds
to reproduce herself, generation after generation...
It is part of her design!
Fruits are meant to be eaten—and enjoyed,
to feed the living goddess.
Her leftovers go to seed
future generations.
Now I see. . .when the fruit becomes the tree,
the gift of life is free.
I AM A FRUIT, GREAT GODDESS, EAT ME!
I AM A TREE, COME, GROW IN ME!

© Musawa 1989, WM'90

© Eaglehawk 1989, WM'90

5:55 I was born,,,5:55 I will be reborn...Ritually...
into the last half of my life...I feel///time enough to
perfect myself...in LOVE...So...this could be my last
incarnation...my last carnation...and I wanna smell
good! like luscious!

© Moon at 55, 1989, WM'90

"Die Rufende" am Hexenturm von Gelnhausen enthüllt am Tag von Tschernobyl. Stellvertretend für alle, die als Hexen gefoltert und getötet wurden, ruft sie, heute wach zu sein für das Leben."

On the day of the Chernobyl event (August 26, 1986), this statue "The Summoner"' was unveiled at the Witches Tower in Gelnhausen, Hessen, West Germany. She is a reminder of all those worldwide who were tortured and killed as witches. On behalf of all these she summons us today to be awake for life.

Die Rufende/The Summoner *sculpture and writing © Eva-Gesine Wagner 1989, WM'90*

Life and Death *© Anne Berg 1987, WM'90*

Moving On

Death is a fool,
inside of me
Something I have learned to live with.
© Jeanette Spencer 1983, WM'90

Self Portrait with Guide *Oriol Dancer, Back Cover Art, WM'90*

We'moon '91

Gaia: an astrological moon calendar & appointment book for we'moon

Missa Gaia: This is my body
© *Judith Anderson 1988, Front Cover Art, WM'91*

The theme of this year's We'Moon is Earth. Her living Spirit is embodied in the myriad forms of being that compose the web of life, this planet. Originally, the theme was defined as "Stones, Power Places, Earth Magic": the bare bones of her teachings, passed on in the power of place, written in stone. By the time the Call for Contributions for We'Moon '91 went out, it had evolved to "the Living-Dying Earth and All our Relations," including the more generally acknowledged "animate" forms of Earth Being—the plants and animals and human forms of life now—as well as the stone people from ages past. The artwork and writings in this calendar are contributed by wemoon who responded to the call for materials—only a few were specifically solicited, when they fell in my immediate path while gathering material on this theme. They all came together quite naturally as aspects of the living body of Gaia: the final evolution of the theme.

What wemoon sent in was then grouped into the headings for each of the 13 Moons, creating a serpentine path through the year of ways wemoon are touched and inspired by Her.

excerpt, Introduction to the Theme

She is the affirmation of natural power that does not wear away over the ages but only changes form. Here, the body of Earth is alive in Spirit, and experienced in those special places where the mystery within is revealed. © *Musawa 1990, WM'91*

Opening © *Annie Ocean, WM'91*

Full Moon Eve, Callanish. 1987

A moment in time I share—
the moment—just a moment—
when rocks still moved
when the stones still flowed—
fluid no more—
frozen movement
for mortal eternity—
not so long for stone.

The frozen moment stands till the wind takes it to dust.

Kalpas and kalpas.
What's a kalpa?
the time it takes
for a butterfly's wings
to wear away a mountain

I share the moment
the last moment
before the movement
froze.

excerpt © *Jill Smith 1989, WM'91*

Gaia is the Greek name for the Goddess of Earth. There is currently a growing body of scientific findings named after her: the Gaia Hypothesis. It has grown out of the irrefutable evidence of the "New Biology" that the Earth is a living, growing, self-healing organism just like we are—only on a much grander scale, like a goddess! They acknowledge that Earth's incredibly complex adaptations on every level of being seem to be guided by a kind of wisdom that can only be the function of a living being. Now people are starting to believe what we have always known: The Earth is alive!

The sources we draw on pre-date modern science. We go back before the times when women were burned as witches for believing the Earth was alive and for passing on Her teachings. Our sources are much older than books. They go back to the times when all people knew the Earth as Mother, and worshipped Her as the creator, through whose body all life forms return in death. These teachings were written in stone, some as long ago as 30,000 years ago, and survive today to inspire wemoon who are now open to receiving them.

excerpt, Introduction to the Theme

Wisdom ◻ *Luz-Maria Lopez 2004, WM'11*

Mother Gaia

We cannot blame her
For crying great torrents of rain
So great is her sorrow
For sobbing sometimes uncontrollably
and shaking her great shoulders
So intense is her pain.

excerpt ◻ Lesley Weldon 2002, WM'08

Engraved bone discs drawn from an exhibit of Ice Age art in San Francisco. 1979. From Petersfels. Germany and Badergouce, France, 17,000-11,000 B.C., WM'91

Birthing Danger, Mt. St. Helens
© *ScharCbear Freeman 1998, WM'08*

Cytherea

...Cytherea is angry
that we have poisoned her oceans
at night she climbs the waves
straddles the white foam
and calls to her whales
"are you catfood yet?"

She is unforgiving
and methodical
when a dolphin gets tangled
in a tuna net
she grieves
when a single cell of green algae dies
she knows it...

the rusting barrels of nuclear waste
drive Cytherea to distraction
she plots revenge
with the cunning of a shark—she
who was so peaceful...

Now she sits in a dark cave
consorting with morays
sipping poison drinks
concocted from the venom
of Australian stone fish
counting the tankers
that rumble overhead
breathing the oil-fouled water
assimilating the toxins
through her seaweed softy skin
she is not pleased
she is not amused

Cytherea is planning something
down there
something she tells only
to the spiny batfish
and the sea dragons
perhaps she has decided
to call back the oxygen
and leave us gasping
perhaps she has decided
to melt her ice caps
rise and take back all the cities
that ever emptied sewage
down her throat
perhaps she has decided to show us
a mercy we don't deserve—
but don't count on it

Cytherea
the flowers we throw to you
come back oil-soaked
and dying
We stand on your beaches
calling you up
but you no longer appear
at our feet you scatter
pieces of styrofoam cups
tin cans, beer bottles, hunks of insulation,
stinking fish and dead birds
and sometimes a jellyfish
pulsing and dying
like a punctuated soap bubble
like a human heart
gone bad.

excerpt © Mary Mackey 1989, WM'91

© Sudie Rakusin 1989, WM'91

Mandorla of the Spinning Goddess

... The almond form is the Yoni, the sacred gate of the vagina, a place of mystery and birth. And so the intersecting circles may be thought of in many ways: inner and outer, self and other, the unconscious and the conscious, life and death, the Alpha and the Omega, controlling and letting go, and so on. This conjunction of opposites will show strange paradoxes in balance, rather like the Yin and Yang circle.

So we are looking at the birth of the Goddess, she who spins the web of life and death, whose womb of earth bears, sustains, and receives in death all creatures and growing things. All of these women's hands, young and old—some of which are my own—are spinning and moving the threads. I am intrigued by hands not just because hands are the very instruments of creating, of working, of loving touch. Women's hands do much of the work of the world: hard labor and menial work, the work of transmuting elements in cooking and sewing and breast feeding, the nurturing of children, the sick and the aged. Our hands help create the fabric of life; in many sacred acts, our hands weave the will of the Goddess.

*etching and writing © Judith Anderson
1982 (photo by J. Colando), WM'91*

from Grandmother Earth, What You Give Away

(iv.)
Grandmother Earth, what you give me
is the awareness of being in love
with you, this is a love epic to the one
who holds up my feet, who gives me
a beautiful place to stand and walk, rooted
by the belly, to you, old sexual crone.

(v.)
Living in the presence of
White Buffalo Woman
in her brilliance and beauty
our hopes open involuntarily to trust and love

You are our deepening of spirit, Grandmother Earth
Among our circles, you are the solitude in the garden
you are the tending, the cultivating, the new
growth (I used to call it change), the reflection
by the creek, the kestrel fledglings' flight

Your work is all these women's hands at work
tanning   painting   beading
hands peeling poles to pitch a tipi
to make a home there in the weather
fire-ring   firewood   campsite
for the coming snow

excerpts from A Basket of Light © *Melane Lohmann 1989, WM'91*

Rebirth © *Patty Levey, WM'91*

Eagle's Home
© *Eaglehawk 1984, WM'91*

Cromlech Goddess
© *Monica Sjöö 1982, Back Cover Art, WM'91*

WE'MOON '92

GAIA RHYTHMS FOR WOMYN

Goddess © *Durga Yael Bernhard 1989,*
Front Cover Art, WM'92

In ancient times, people lived in close kinship with the animals. They provided our food, shelter, clothes, tools, our source of livelihood. They were also our greatest teachers in the mysteries of life. Together, we shared in the bounty of Earth's great give-away. People who live close to the Earth Mother still honor animals as allies in the exchange of everyday life energy, as well as in the spirit realms. This is reflected today in the art, poems and stories on the pages of this We'Moon, where the animals are our guides, friends and familiars.

As wemoon, we can listen to the voices of the ones who have come before and be guided by our animal nature. Animals are the ancient spirit guides of the people. By their example, may human animals learn again how to walk gently on the Earth.

excerpt, Introduction to the Theme

Tiger-Crane-Moon
© *Catherine Firpo, WM'92*

Salmon at Callanish

...I am Salmon
I swim free
I leap in the sunlight
I leap in the moonlight
I leap in Loch Roag
on the island of Lewis

I leap and see
the ancient stones
standing silent
standing strong
echoing the colors of my body
echoing the patterns of my spirit
echoing the cycles of my life...

...I am Salmon
wise Salmon
let the flash of my body
catch your eye
silver in the sunlight
let me dance for you
let me leap for you
for I know the freedom
of the oceans of the earth

I am Salmon
I swim free
I leap

but for how long...
excerpt © Jill Smith 1989, WM'92

La Panthére Noire

Black Magik is
Night's mistress.
The raven-robed shamaness
Melts into darkness,
One with the Power.
She prowls softly,
A were-pantheress
Of shadows shaped.
© *Ilona Garrett 1991, WM'92*

Animal Wisdom—like Body Wisdom, the Inner Child, or the Higher Self—is a part of us, whether we are in touch with it or not. But, like the cultures we live in, we tend to deny and devalue our essence. We often organize our fragmented lives in such a way as to not experience that part of us that is in touch with our wholeness.

The Wild One teaches us that the worlds are not separate from each other, *I am the free part of you, do you hear? Do you see? . . .*

Animal spirits are always close by as guides on this journey to the source. Lets listen now to the teachings of the ones who have come before us on Earth, the ones who are leaving now. Who are they? What is their special gift? What can we learn from their passage on Earth that might help show us the way to heal what is hurting. Animal Wisdom: Spirit Teachings of Earth's earliest inhabitants.

excerpt, Introduction to the Theme

Strength
© Chesca Potter 1999, WM'01

Samovila: Guardian of the Animals

Samovila is an Eastern European goddess who protects the animals of the forest. She brings harm to anyone who harms them.

art and writing © Sandra Stanton 1989, WM'92

Elephants in My Soul
detail © Christina Alice Siracusa 2003, WM'09

Bestiary

Short-tailed albatross, whooping crane, gray wolf, peregrine falcon, hawksbill turtle, jaguar, rhinoceros. In Geneva, the international tally of endangered species, kept up to date in looseleaf volumes, is becoming too heavy to lift. Where do we now record the passing of life? What funerals or farewells are appropriate?

Reed warbler, swallow-tail butterfly, Manx shearwater, Indian python, howler monkey, sperm whale, blue whale. Dive me deep, mother whale, in this time we have left. Deep in our mother ocean where once I swam, gilled and finned. The salt from those early seas still runs in my tears. Tears are too meager now. Give me a song. . .a song for sadness too vast for my heart, for a rage too wild for my throat.

Anteater, antelope, grizzly bear, brown bear, Bactrian camel, Nile crocodile, American alligator. Ooze me, alligator, in the mud whence I came. Belly me slow in the rich primordial soup, cradle of our molecules. Let me wallow again, before we drain your swamp, before we pave it over and blast it to ash.

Gray bat, ocelot, marsh mouse, blue pike, red kangaroo, Aleutian Goose, Audouin's seagull. Quick, lift off. Sweep me high over the coast and out, farther out. Don't land here. Oil spills coat the beach, rocks, sea. I cannot spread my wings glued with tar. Fly me from what we have done, fly me far.

Golden parakeet, African ostrich, Florida panther, Galapagos penguin, Imperial Pheasant, leopard, Utah prairie dog. Hide me in a hedgerow, badger. Can't you find one? Dig me a tunnel through leaf mold and roots, under the trees that once defined our fields. My heart is bulldozed and plowed over. Burrow me a labyrinth deeper than longing.

Thick-billed parrot, zone-tailed pigeon, desert bandicoot, Southern bald

□ *Hawk Madrone 1985, WM'92*

eagle, California condor, lotus blue butterfly. Crawl me out of here, caterpillar. Spin me a cocoon. Wind me to sleep in a shroud of silk, where in patience my bones will dissolve. I'll wait as long as all creation if only it will come again—and I take wing.

Atlantic Ridley turtle, pearly mussel, helmeted hornbill, sea otter, humpback whale, monk seal, harp seal. Swim me out beyond the ice floes, mama. Where are you? Boots squeeze my ribs, clubs drum my fur, the white world goes black with the taste of my blood.

Orcas © *Angela Von Lintel Lobitz 1990, WM'92*

72

Gorilla, gibbon, sand gazelle, swamp deer, musk deer, cheetah, chinchilla, Asian elephant, African elephant. Sway slowly through the jungle. There still must be jungle somewhere, my heart drips with green secrets. Hose me down by the waterhole, there is buckshot in my hide. Tell me old stories while you can remember.

Fan-tailed flycatcher, flapshell tortoise, crested ibis, hook billed kite, bob cat, frigate bird. In the time when his world, like ours, was ending, Noah had a list of the animals too. We picture him standing by the gangplank, calling their names, checking them off his scroll. Now we also are checking them off.

Ivory-billed woodpecker, brown pelican, Florida manatee, Canada Goose. We reenact Noah's ancient drama, but in reverse, like a film running backwards, the animals exiting.

Ferret, curlew, cougar, wolf. Your tracks are growing fainter. Wait. Wait. This is a hard time. Don't leave us alone in a world we have wrecked.

© Joanna Macy 1988, from
Thinking Like a Mountain: Towards A Council of All Beings,
New Society Publishers, WM'92

© Sudie Rakusin 1990, WM'92

Nuage and Musawa
© Nada 1983, WM'92

Deer Totem
© Durga Bernhard 1986, Back Cover Art, WM'92

We'Moon '93

GAIA RHYTHMS FOR WOMYN:
INVOKING SPIRIT

Nile River Goddess
© *Nancy Blair, Front Cover Art, WM'93*

This We'Moon is about calling the power of Spirit into our lives. Spirit is always present; we are not. Becoming present, turning inward, allowing awareness, being inspired, getting the spirit...whatever the words used, it comes through experience in the present moment in relation to the wholeness of being. How do you invoke Presence? What is your magic? How do you go between the worlds? Each of the 13 Moons explores a different pathway to Spirit, as offered by We'Moon contributors on this theme.

excerpt, Introduction to the Theme

© *Onyx Owens 1991, WM'93*

For a Cleansing Ceremony On Winter Solstice

Spirits of the East we invoke you, we call we call.
Oh Inanna. bring your windbreath of clarity.
Come back come back
from your journey to the Great Below
and with your sweet fresh breeze
gently blow our confusion away.
**Watchers and ancestors and animals of the East
be welcome to our sacred Circle.**

Spirits of the South we invoke you, we call we call.
Oh Kali, Queen of fire and rages,
bring us your courage to destroy
that which needs to be destroyed.
Illumine illumine the truth in us.
**Watchers and ancestors and animals of the South
be welcome to our sacred circle.**

Spirits of the West, we invoke you, we call we call.
Oh Maria, with your waters wash away from us
our grief and shame and fear.
Bathe us in our own innocence.
**Watchers and ancestors and animals of the West
be welcome to our sacred Circle.**

Spirits of the North, we invoke you, we call we call.
Hecate, Mother of the Longest Night,
give us your grounding, your deep winter dreaming.
Guardian of the Crossroads,
bring us your green child of hope.
**Watchers and ancestors and animals of the North
be welcome to our sacred Circle.**

¤ *Susa Silvermarie, WM'93*

XII. The Hanged One

Endarkening

Conjuring up the shadows
Watching them spiral in and out of our lives
Putting a new dark on things

Invoking inward energy
Going inside the dark
Inviting insight, intuition
Making invisible that which needs protection
Endarkening

Valuing the cave, the womb, the night
Gestating, germinating, releasing, resting
Being that which lives instead of
That which watches
Endarkening

Experiencing ecstasy
Eroticism in the dark
Experiencing pure sensation
Sensing with the heart, the hands, the belly...

Feeling depth in the dark
Following dark wisdom which does not
         need to know
Flowing with the dark
Claiming the freedom to move as we chose
         in the dark
Finding that it nurtures
         as it endarkens

Opening to the dark
Reveling in mystery that
Reveals dark truth
Revering our female truth
Letting no man talk us out of it
Returning joyfully to the dark inside
Endarkening

□ Antiga, WM'93

© Deborah Koff-Chapin, WM'93

Mask for Samhain
© Sheila Broun 1992, WM'93

© Patti Levey 1991, WM'93

Rosemary (Rosmarinus offincinalis)

In the small rituals of everyday life, one of our greatest needs is protection and the clearing of negative energies. In the European tradition rosemary is one of the oldest incenses used for this purpose. Rosemary wands, by themselves or dipped in saltwater, can be used to define sacred space, provide protection, or cleanse a house. It is also frequently burned to clear the air of harmful energy. Sacred to Isis and Mary.

© Colette Gardiner 1992, WM'93

© Melissa Harris 1992, WM'93

Winter Solstice *© Sudie Rakusin 1991, WM'93*

Bay (Laurus nobilis)

Bay's powers are protection, psychic awareness, purification, healing and strength. Priestesses at Delphi chewed fresh bay leaves to induce visions. A few leaves brewed into a tea also increases psychic awareness and helps to impart wisdom. Bay leaves can also be added to dream pillows for prophetic dreaming. It is associated with the Goddess Ceres and to a lesser degree with Althena.

© Colette Gardiner 1992, WM'93

Chanting Up the Moon

Between Grandmother Moon and our
    song, breath rises in sheets
    of mist
We move sensuously, we open our robes,
We are not afraid.

Yes! Now we can, O Women, now we can
    be awake and dance to tell
    about it.

The chant rises—ancient and sacred
    it rises and rises, the moon
    herself rises
And rises until no heart could hang hard
    and heavy in any breast.

We rise to join you, Grandmother Moon,
    lifting our arms, drawing down the
    light, bringing our burdens, our
Joy, our treasure as offering; it dissolves
    in the mist of our songs, making a
    veil for you, a halo.

We bring our silver breath to you,
    our strong bodies,
    our creative hands raised,
    lifting up our lives
    in praise.

© Jane (Saya) Wolf 1992, WM'93

© Boudyke, WM'93

Homeself, Sacredself

I would counsel you to be still
To move away from everything for a time
To wait quietly until you come home to yourself

There will be signs

Songs will be sung from your lips
Your body will dance with you
Your eyes will see magic
Where you keep the fresh flower
Where you burn the candle
Also where you cry and where you bleed

There will be signs

The magic of your homeself, your sacredself
Will take you to the sky
Luna will welcome your flight
With silver embraces
Comets will be your lovers

Trails of stars will carry you inward
Until, at your core, a cataclysm will burst
In celebration of homecoming
To the magic of your soul

◻ *Ila Suzanne Gray 1986, WM'93*

"Kakaken" also called by name of "Dance of Hiten," is an old Chinese way of meditation through movement, In the deep breathing, together with a silent movement, the energy of the universe is sucked into the body, and it is aimed to activate the inner energy in order to regulate the nerves and internal organs and the inner secretions.

photo and writing © Cathy Cade 1990, WM'93

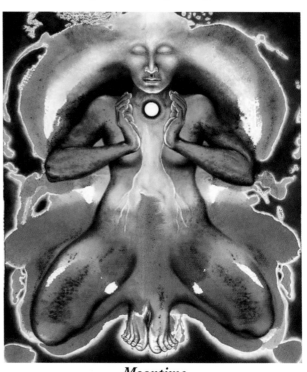

Moontime
© *Deborah Koff-Chapin, Back Cover Art, WM'93*

WE'MOON '94

GAIA RHYTHMS FOR WOMYN
CYCLES

Africa: Rite of Passage
© Betty LaDuke 1993, Front Cover Art, WM'94

In the '94 We'Moon, we have taken what is always in the background of We'Moon and brought it into the foreground with this year's theme: Cycles!

Ancient matriarchal cultures supported life on this planet for ages by honoring the wisdom of cycles and the essential oneness of the living Goddess in all Her diversity. Patriarchy lost sight of this in developing technologies that imitate natural forces without integrating the underlying cyclical view which sustains them in connection with the whole web of life.

A linear world view has taken over curvilinear reality. Life has become fragmented and the Earth flattened, sending us off the planet on a tangent from which we may never return.

By marking the passage of time in our lives with universal cycles, we enter into conscious relationship with the greater movement of growth and change. Having a sense of the whole and the different parts that go into it allows us to move with the changes instead of resist them at each new step.

Becoming conscious of cycles shows us the known steps as well as the unknown, and teaches us that the darkness, like the light, is to be welcomed, not feared. It is a natural part of every change, the gateway to renewal.

excerpt, Introduction to the Theme

First Blessing—First Bath
© Gloria Tinker 1992, WM'94

Woman in the Hourglass
© Ruth Zachary 1993, WM'94

I Am Bone Tired

I am bone-tired from traveling that hard last mile with you.
The blasted holes and smoking stumps along the way
have drained the sun from me.
So heavy, so heavy—this weight of tears,
this burden of love.
Yet were you to ask, my heart would leap
and drop all trophies to walk with you again.
How flimsy is weariness when balanced against
One more glimpse, one sound, one touch of you?

Come back! There are still more words to find,
more heart to open.
My conceit decrees that it is not Your Time
Listen—I will say when—and it is not now!
And who am I to decide your date? I will tell you.
I am the one who washed your feet,
wiped your sweat, smelled your fear,
And still held on. I am the one who loved beyond pain,
through exhaustion,
past stench, beyond doubt.

Yet if the sands of time in both worlds
were poured out for me
Could I stop your coach from its homeward journey
or ease the wrenching of your death?
When the sun is gone I look inside for illumination
At the dark of moon a question forms slowly—
For whom do I mourn?
You—now whole and free,
dancing in the light;
Or me—wandering my hard last mile
without your frail arm to guide me?

¤ Lyrion Ap Tower, HPS 1998, WM'09

Celtic Mysteries © Angela Werneke 1989, WM'98

Fit for a Queen

crone living with cancer making friends with death
lesbian clan singing
as i enter the third trimester of my life
a celtic warrior queen walking with ancestors
time now to prepare my beloved daughters
my precious sisters
my devoted family my special friends
for my journey towards a complete and peaceful death
warrior queen reigning over life
wounds healed in heart mind and spirit
wisdom and life stories shared and stored
wrapped in a magnificent croning cloak
decorated with thoughtfulness by my female clan
patches stitched beaded and drawn
celebrating each woman's connection to me
inspiring creative colourful moving delightful
patches continue to arrive as cloak is destined for shroud
when living is done   safe nurtured and cloaked in love
when journeying to the land of the dead
no queen will travel as gloriously robed as i
in the colours and handcraft of my precious
friends family and beloved lesbian clan
scottish lass to celtic warrior queen
i delight in the depths and joys of this time of my life

excerpt ¤ Anah Holland-Moore 2007, WM'09

Between Two Worlds © Rachill 1999, WM'09

Aging Amazons

Aging amazons wander the city
      looking for lost causes
issues turned into windmills
      when the decade changed

warhorses are restless in the pastures
they look for the battles
      they know they never finished

grey heads bend over a new generation
      looking for sparks in young eyes
the only hope is time
      ¤ Ila Suzanne Gray 1988, WM'94

Extinction © *Amy R. Hanford 1992, WM'94*

To My Love

And you stepped over me
filling my breath with the scent of you
filling my face, nose, lips, mouth
with the nectar of you
opening my passion with the warmth of you
entwined so close together—
we bloom as one
excerpt © Catherine Firpo 1989, WM'94

© *Tee A. Corinne 1992, WM'94*

The Dress You've Been Waiting For . . .
The Perception Shift
© *Oriol Dancer 1993, WM'94*

(detail) **Sunflier** © Ruth Zachary 1991,

creek   rushing   singing
rock   knowing   deepening
trees   reaching   deepening
soil   crouching   spreading
wind   circling   swinging

moon   glows
rain   falls
sun   warms
cloud   floats

And so

© Laura Irene Wayne 1993, WM'94

Run   Shine   Play   Taste
Hear   See   Wonder
Grin
Fly   Spin   Sit
Climb
Touch
Honor
Celebrate
Love
¤ *Pandora Cate Judge*
1992, WM'94

Girls Got Muscles Too
© Laura Irene Wayne 1991, WM'94

© A. Kimberlin Blackburn, Back Cover Art, WM'94

81

We'Moon '95

GAIA RHYTHMS FOR WOMYN

SURVIVORS: THE HEALER WITHIN

Healing Hands/Healing Heart
© *Julie Higgins 1992, Front Cover Art, WM'95*

'95 Theme: Survivors/ The Healer Within

We are using a broad definition of survivors to mean anyone who has survived deep loss, dis-ease or abuse in any form—mind or body, heart or soul. Abuse is whatever violates the Spirit of any being on any level: by overpowering, doing violence to, inflicting one being's will onto another, or dishonoring the integrity of value of any being.

As survivors, we develop strategies for protecting ourselves and living in the world in a safe way. These survival strategies are resourceful and creative means to stay alive and be as present as possible. As we grow and the world we live in changes, these strategies may begin to limit our experiences in ways that no longer serve us. Arising from the underworld with new wisdom, survivors become healers, and often can serve as guides to others who have lost their way.

Deep Blessings to all Survivors! May we all continue to transform our hurts, put them in the compost bin, and tend them with sun and self love. May we rage and cry, create and change. Blessed Be.

excerpt, Introduction to the Theme

Chiron: The Wounded Healer

In November of 1977 a small planetary body was discovered between Saturn and Uranus. It was subsequently named Chiron, after a mythological centaur who was half-horse and half-human.

Chiron was teacher, prophet, physician, and musician. He was a healer who taught the medicinal use of plants, surgery, and the laying on of hands. When Chiron was accidentally wounded in the knee by a poisoned arrow, for all his healing knowledge, he was unable to cure himself.

Archetypally, Chiron represents the quintessential shamanic healer. What distinguishes a shaman from any other kind of healer is that the shaman is always wounded first; it is the wound, in its sacred aspect, that serves as the initiating journey.

When Chiron is an active archetype in our lives, we experience a physical, psychological, or spiritual crisis which engenders great suffering. We descend into the underworld of the unconscious where we meet the shadow demons, face death, and develop a communication with the world of unseen spirits and guides. As we begin to learn the secret ways of nature, or psychic channels are opened; we discover our special talents in our role of helping others. This experience of personal crisis, followed by a deepening of self-mastery and healing ability, is the critical act through which we can access our divine nature and heed the call for service to the community and to the planet.

© *Demetra George 1994 WM'95*

Cradle of Love
© *Nancy Bright 1988, WM'95*

XIV: Temperance

Lightning Tree

Look, look at my scars,
see how it has healed,
leaving a sign of what I have survived.
Your scars will heal in this way
leaving their reminder of past trauma.
Grow strong, deeply rooted,
you will be stronger for surviving.
Show your scars, do not hide them,
they are part of you,
a sign for all time.

© Shulamit Tziporah 1988, WM'91

Illumination *© Marion Cloaninger 2005, WM'08*

Medicine Woman *© Ruth Zachery, WM'93*

Libations

when there are no answers,
I go to the water;
she offers me her wisdom

when I am hurt, in pain
I go to the water;
she heals me with her power

when there are no feelings,
I go to the water;
she opens me to my heart

when I am stuck, in mud
I go to the water;
she moves me with her passion

□ Jacqueline Elizabeth Letalien 1999, WM'01

© Tee A. Corinne 1992, WM'95

Amazon Angel
© Megaera 1991, WM'95

Declaration of Self

I am a woman flanked by lionstrength, and
angels circle hawklike above my head.
I am a woman
holding my ground against
a hurricane of patriarchal opposition, but I am
only one of many sisters:
We will reclaim our Earth, our Selves. our Goddess.
I am independent, but accept help when it is needed
without guilt, without shame,
without a feeling of indebtedness.
I am loved.

excerpt © Diana Rose Hartmann 1993, WM'95

Survivors

Seven women from the north
Two from the south
and two from Fly Away Home
sat in circle
under Their Great Shelter
and began to weave for We'Moon

We all took piles
in our cross-legged
leaning back
rocking chair laps
and began to read,
at first with much spontaneous chatter,
then, in the silence of our bodies.

We read for hours in that ten-sided house,
expanding and contracting
with the theme of our task:
surviving

The south-faced windows
stretched bigger than life.
The wind whittled down to nothing.
Not even the trees spoke.

From time to time
one of a few would get up,
go over to the table in the best of daylight,
lean or sway over the artwork
so painfully, plainly presented.

"I don't know if I don't like it
or if it just hurts me to see it,"

one woman said into the space.
Heat rising when I saw the drawing myself,
I wanted to recoil, not wanting
it to be true that
the demons we draw
are the demons
we've experienced.

Hardwood floor. Wings
rushing around the woman
in the rocking chair.
I feel her crying in the extra breath
she draws from the room.
Pencils drop.
Later she lays in front of the fire
her head and naked torso
covered by a pink, tattered blanket.

I want to cup her feet,
I want to lay my body over hers
protecting her from the light.
This whole time
I have been wanting
to curl my hand in a "c"
and run my thumb and fingers
down every woman's back;
the trembling fibers are singing,
the trembling fibers
are trembling,
and even as they're snapping
the stringed instruments of our bodies
are playing a healing song.

¤ Caroline Brumleve 1993, WM'95

Bitter Sweet Resonance

I have been honed by pain
as the fine resonate cello
is honed by time—
and grief has kissed my face
leaving its mark upon my brow
changing forever my vision
sweetly, ever so bitter sweetly opening
my heart a little more

© Catherine Firpo 1989, WM'95

It was for this
       I incubated in the mud,
slowly basting
       in generations of pain,
until the frozen heart
       agreed to beat again.

¤ Sherri Rose-Walker 1991, WM'95

**Broken Hearted Butch Madonna
Mends Her Own Heart**
© Sierra Lonepine Briano 1991, WM'95

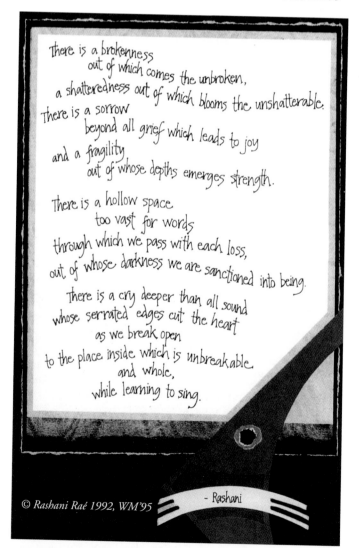

There is a brokenness
    out of which comes the unbroken,
a shatteredness out of which blooms the unshatterable.
There is a sorrow
    beyond all grief which leads to joy
and a fragility
    out of whose depths emerges strength.

There is a hollow space
    too vast for words
through which we pass with each loss,
out of whose darkness we are sanctioned into being.

    There is a cry deeper than all sound
whose serrated edges cut the heart
    as we break open
to the place inside which is unbreakable
    and whole,
    while learning to sing.

© Rashani Raé 1992, WM'95

– Rashani

The Healing © Nancy Bright 1986, Back Cover Art, WM'95

GAIA RHYTHMS FOR WOMYN:
EARTH MATTERS

Tahoma—Spirit of the Cascades
© *Michelle Waters 1993, Front Cover Art, WM'96*

Earth Matter. Earth Mater. Earth Mother. Like a mother who gives birth, the earth has the power to bring spirit into form—to *mater-realize*. The material level is not separate from the spiritual level. Matter is spirit embodied. Earth and spirit matters are intertwined. Earth is a living, self-regulating, self-healing organism, a sentient being.

Every being, every particle on and in and around this planet is intricately connected. We are all literally flesh of the same flesh. We breathe air that moves in our blood, eat food from the earth that then becomes soil. Rocks turn into pebbles to sand and to soil that grows plants that drink the sun, purify the air, and feed us. The water goes from sky to land to ocean, through deer and birds and fish. We are one being, eating our ancestors from our gardens. Earth-based spiritualities recognize this interconnection, valuing *all* entities as holy, equal, and intrinsic. What happens to her, happens to us.

How incredible that we walk, pulled down by gravity, to the center of the earth! Every entity we come in contact with is an aspect of the living goddess, a wild mystery, unique unto itself. We can re-infuse all we do with spirit and all we witness with wonder. May we tend our visions with care, enjoy and share the fruits of our labor, replenish and be replenished by the sustainable garden of earth.

excerpt, Introduction to the Theme

Rock Recycling

IGNEOUS
(formed by fire; a molten
mix from other rocks)

METAMORPHIC
(formed through heat and
pressure on preexisting rocks)

SEDIMENTARY
(pressed from particles of
preexisting rocks)

Mother Earth includes everything in her spiral of change. Biological biodegrading and human remelting or remaking are not the only forms of recycling. Rocks recycle and recombine constantly. Molton material makes its way up through the crust to either erupt in fiery splendor as lava from a volcano (*extrusive ingenous*) or cool slowly underground to form rocks with crystals of various sizes (*intrusive ingenous*). Particles of gravel or sand from all kinds of rocks weathering at the surface are deposited and buried, and under high heat and pressure become *sedimentary* rocks. Any of these basic rock types under high heat and pressure become *metaphoric* rocks. Each of these types may be reworked into any of the others in a continuous dance that recombines the elements!

◻ *Guida Veronda 1995, WM'96*

Spiral *(compressed peat moss bricks)*

Spiral

The organic materials and processes I use create a living artwork which has a life cycle of its own. The piece generally recycles/returns back into the Earth, part of the cycle of creation, death, and regeneration.

photo and writing © Lycia Trouton 1995, WM'96

Historically, in Western worldviews, womyn, earth and people of color are considered "low" and "dark"; bodies, sensuality and physical existence are inherently "evil." Heaven is "up above," far away from earth, not of this life; and all good is seen as coming from "the light."

Countless essential movements are striving to recover the balance, such as the struggles for indigenous peoples' lands and cultural rights, for the environment, as well as the work to attain peace, justice and equality for all beings. It is *all* the same struggle.

Wemoon are gathering in circles and/or working alone to heal the patriarchal splits through a vision of wholeness, providing inspiration, support, and creative forms for magic and spiritual activism.

excerpt, Introduction to the Theme

Oh Earth,

scorned, stripped
of your jewels
and secret voluptuous dells
by humanity's unending numbers,
crowded, paved, beloved Earth,
do not be angry,
renew yourself, be strong,
be well.

© *Janine Canan 2006, WM'08*

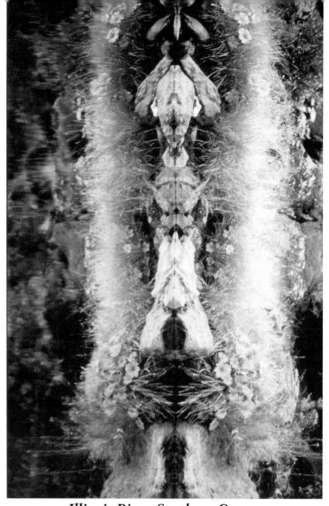

Illinois River, Southern Oregon
© *Annie Ocean 1987, WM'96*

**Great Mothers
Birthing the Future**
© *Selina Maria di Girolamo
2001, WM'03*

Otter's Painting ¤ *S.J. Hugdahl 1994, WM'96*

What She Grew and What She Saved

Over her head clouds sprouted cabbage leaves,
coarse and broad, cupped against a sky
colored like weak tea.
She pruned rose bushes to the shapes of stars.
When the rains came
she misunderstood and placed umbrellas
over the rhubarb. She followed the moon.
Planted in circles a garden that grew
more like a tide as the summer waxed,
cresting at the edge of lawn.
In her fingers the muscles and bones crooked
into dense twigs until it was impossible
for her to know what she held in her hands:
dirt, dandelions, or honeybees?
When the sun came and stayed
sharp and hot for a month
she remembered all the secrets
she kept closed in her heart
and lay down in her garden
to become as quiet as the earth.

¤ *Amy Shutzer 1994, WM'96*

open the window to
the blessed night air.

Rainbringer
begins her
thigh-slapping dance

with small waterbell
movements

she comes
(and comes and comes).

¤ *marna 1992, WM'96*

© *Billie Miracle 1994, WM'96*

Ceres © *Nancy Ann Jones 1994, WM'96*

© *Marcia A. Gómez 1988, WM'96*

Madre del Mundo

Save the Mother
Save the Land
Honor Treaty Rights
Stop Nuclear Testing on Our Sacred Earth

This sculpture was originally installed in U.S.-occupied Shoshone Land across form the Missile Test Site in Mercury, Nevada. She was part of a Mother's Day Peace Action opposing the bombing and desecration of our Sacred Mother Earth.

© *Marsha A. Gomez 1988, WM'96*

In the beginning, according to the Wise Woman traditions, everything began, as everything does, at birth. The Great Mother of All gave birth and the earth appeared out of the void. Then the Great Mother of All gave birth again, and again, and again, and people, and animals, and plants appeared on the earth. They were all very hungry. "What shall we eat?" they asked the Great Mother. "Now you eat me," she said, smiling. Soon there were a very great many lives, but the Great Mother of All was enjoying creating and giving birth so much that she didn't want to stop. "Ah," she said smiling, "now I eat you." and so she still does.

excerpt from Healing Wise ¤ *Susun S. Weed 1989, WM'96*

The Beginning World © *Durga Yael Bernhard 1993, Back Cover Art, WM'96*

WE'MOON '97

GAIA RHYTHMS FOR WOMYN
WOMYN IN COMMUNITY

No Limits © *Christine Eagon, Front Cover Art, WM'97*

'97 Theme: Womyn in Community

Community is not a new idea. It is human nature, Gaia nature. Community is the natural tendency of all beings to group together organically into patterns that form a larger whole—whether mineral, plant, animal, or human, in inner or outer space. Ions do it. Molecules do it. Cells and organisms do it. Societies and solar systems do it. Wemoon do it.

Traditionally, "women's role" has been to relate, to take care of others, and to create family and community. In most cultures, womyn's community persists in some form or other (the moon lodge, quilting bee, womyn's support groups, etc.). Over the last three decades, womyn's communities have emerged from (and encouraged the growth of) various liberation and civil rights struggles, especially the womyn's liberation movement and the creation of lesbian culture. In this We'Moon, we explore womyn's experience of community in our lives today.

We need to find the center of the circle again—in ourselves, the earth, in our communities—and reconnect with the source of wholeness. When we learn how to create ways of being that nurture and sustain us in a balanced relation to one another, seeds of community sprout and leaf and blossom and fruit again. Womyn, the givers of life, the nurtures and sustainers, creators and transformers of cultures are leading the way. This is the revolutionary potential of womyn in community.

excerpt, Introduction to the Theme

Greenham Women's Peace Encampment
¤ *Tracy Litterick 1985, WM'97*

Africa: Women On the Move
© *Betty LaDuke 1993, photo by R. Jaffee, WM'97*

XVI: Tower

The Tower is the Tarot card we associate numerologically with We'Moon '97 (9+7=16=the Tower in the Major Arcana). Community is a power greater than the individual ego, capable of toppling the tower of patriarchy and its power-over politics that permeate all our relationships. Ideally, in community, the whole is greater than the sum of the parts, differences are a source of strength, not divisiveness, and everyone stands to gain by the empowerment of all its members. Community is based on common bonds—the same land, neighborhood, culture; a common purpose, vision, task; an affinity to one another, a sense of belonging, shared values and commitments, a heart connection. *Community is the extension of relationship from the personal to the collective. People give to the community and the community gives back.*

excerpt, Introduction to the Theme

House of Cards ¤ *Dorothy Rossi 2001, WM'97*

Full Circle Temple:
Sanctuary, Universe-ity, and Place of Worship for Womyn of All Ages

Calling forth: all womyn pregnant with faith, that our combined resources can create holy Temple.
Calling forth: midwives whose skills are vast and are ready to catch this Temple.
Calling forth: tenders of the fire.
Calling forth: priestesses from all walks of life, teachers and students of the healing crafts, facilitators of sacred time and space.
Calling forth: scribes, to maintain our archives.
Calling forth: web weavers, the ones who bring the circle tight and intricate.
Calling forth: womyn who know how to receive, and can teach others.
Calling forth: prayer, residents, visitors, offerings in all forms.

It is time to light the sacred flame once again.

¤ *Tia Ma for the Full Circle Temple 1995, WM'97*

MudGirls Natural Building Collective
Sam Barlow ¤ MudGirls Collective 2008, WM'10

In our oral teachings, we were told that at this particular time it will be the women who lead the nations. I bow to the spirit of the women from the beginning of time, the spirit of woman that is within us all...

Flordemayo, excerpt from Grandmothers Counsel the World © *2006 Carol Schaefer, WM'09*

The Power of Womyn
¤ *Shelley Stefan 1997, WM'99*

School of Women
© *Megaera 1992, WM'97*

An Open Letter to My Sisters on the Land

Yes, meetings are difficult. Yes, coming together as wimmin outside the dominant male ruled culture is difficult. Why?

I believe it is because we carry into our meetings a lot more than agenda items. We carry our family-of-origin material. Who do you remind me of? What buttons do I push for you?

We carry our conditioning, including definitions learned in a male-dominated society: definitions for words such as *power*. What is power? What is power over, what is powerlessness, who's got the power, how do we take it away from who's got it? Is there enough to go around? If I am powerful, then who is not? What is empowerment?

We also carry into our meetings class issues, cultural issues, ablebodiedism, internalized homophobia, racism, just to name a few. So, it isn't surprising that meetings are difficult. In fact, what is surprising is that we think they shouldn't be.

I hear my sisters talk of the revolution, of creating new paradigms, of bringing down the patriarchy. How do we do that if we can't figure out how to sit in a "meeting" together without huge pain?

Traditionally, our wimmin's way has been oral, sitting around a task such as weaving, quilting, cooking, shelling peas, or cleaning herbs, talking about ourselves, our families, our work. Historically, we wimmin have been silenced. I ask you to search with me for a way to return to what is truly a wimmin's world—gentle communication; honest communication; loving communication; loud, boisterous, exhilarating communication; but, in all, communication.

Communicate, commune, common, commonality, community.

◻ *NíAódagaín 1990, WM'97*

To my Land Sisters

First, we want to thank all of you who entered this year's Annual Refrigerator-Cleanout-and-Guess-What-Food-This-Used-To-Be Contest. Carruch, our soul judge this year, said that the entries were fascinating and varied, providing a number of stunning visual, as well as olfactory surprises!! Well done, leftover artists! However, we're sad to report that, since so few of you (in fact, none of you) signed or dated your entries, we're unable to identify the creator of the winning selection: Vegetable? Medley with Sauce?? So this year's grand prize will go unclaimed.

Call For Contributions:

Next year's contest begins with today's food, so rush your entry now to Hazel House refrigerator. Because the number of entries was so large this year, we'll be strictly enforcing our documentation rules, meaning that only **signed** and **dated** entries will be considered. If you neglect to sign and date your entry, it will be discarded at the first sign of decay as if it were ordinary decomposing food, regardless of your artistic sensitivities. Please check bottom shelf of the refrigerator to see if any of this food is a possible entry for next year's contest. The judge especially enjoyed the entry Four and Two-halves Egg Cartons with Less Than Three Eggs Each. While food inside was still recognizable, she felt this entry had great promise given a few months. Please mark your entries **immediately** so that we can credit you next year. **Thanks again to all the artists!!**

◻ *Carruch 1995, WM'97*

Mirror of My Future, Reflection of My Past
© *Mara Berendt Friedman 1995, WM'97*

well no,
so far the neighbors haven't been
what you call friendly
◻ *zana 1993, WM'97*

root wy'mn

the root wy'mn theatre company is an ensemble of Afrikan American wy'mn formed to present a herstory of Afrikan-American wy'mn's stories through performances, workshops, and presentations.

root wy'mn's primary objectives are to present a portion of the lives of various coloured wy'mn and to chronicle the herstory of Afrikan-American wy'mn, honoring the Indigenous People of Turtle Island, acknowledging the mixing of the Souls/the surviving-Spirits/the diverse and brave wy'mn of dark blood/those still to come.

root wy'mn uses words/performance/visual art/dance/music to reach the Ancient/the universal in us, to awaken Spirits, to connect and inspire.

Women in Ritual Dance
© *Nancy Blair 1995, WM'97*

it is our hope that the power of
combining art forms will incite
healing/bridging/reclaiming/movement
towards
self-love and unification
and that the result of
like-vision lacing
will be a tribute to
COLOURED WY'MNS
of all times
and places.
© *the root wy'mn theatre company 1996, WM'97*

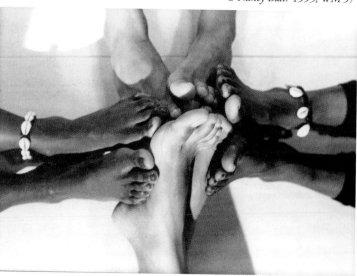

Root Feet
© *Rita DeBellis,*
Back Cover Art, WM'97

WE'MOON '98

GAIA RHYTHMS FOR WOMYN
WISE WOMYN WAYS

Bone Hill Hag, Brown Birds Turning,
Songi Night Hidden, Grandmother Turtle
© *Carolyn Hillyer, Front Cover Art, WM'98*

Who are the wise womyn? Where do they come from? Maybe your great-great grandmother was one...

The We'Moon '98 "Call for Contributions" for art and writing started with this adaptation of an old circle song (substituting *wise womyn* for *witches*). Wise women were persecuted as "witches," a word which comes from "wicca," which means *to bend or shape* and is the root of the word "wisdom." If nine million womyn in Europe and North America were burned at the stake for practicing *wise womyn ways* just a few centuries ago, the threat to patriarchy was obviously great. Is this a clue to the patriarchy's undoing? The power of womyn's wisdom may be forced underground, but it never dies; it bends and shapes ever new pathways as needed to survive. We'Moon '98 calls for womyn's wisdom ways to reemerge in us all. As the unsung last line of the above verse states:

...There's a wise womyn in every woman today!

excerpt,
Introduction to the Theme

The Offering
© *Karen Russo 1996, WM'98*

The Wise Woman Tradition

The Wise Woman tradition is invisible. Without healers and diseases, without cures, certificates and guarantees, it exists. It has no rules, no right answers, no promise of life eternal. The Wise Woman tradition is a spiral of uniqueness, everchanging, like a woman, steeped in a rising out of the blood mysteries, the wisdom of womb-ones, the knowledge of those who hold their blood inside.

The Wise Woman tradition honors the ordinary and avoids the exotic, works simply and steers clear of complication, accepts failure, chaos, and the eternal void with humor instead of fear and dread. The Wise woman tradition is compassionate and heart -centered. It honors the Earth. It is local and ecological and urges us to use our dooryard weeds instead of the latest miracle herb from far away.

The Wise Woman tradition maintains that health is best defined as flexibility and that deviations from normal offer us an opportunity to reintegrate parts of our selves that we have cast out. Illness is understood as an integral part of life and self-growth, with healer, patient and nature as co-participants in the healing process...The Wise Woman Tradition reminds us that wellness and illness are not polarities. They are part of the continuum of life. We are constantly renewing ourselves, cell by cell, every second of our lives. Problems, by their very nature, can facilitate deep spiritual and symbolic renewal, leading us naturally into expanding, more complete ways of thinking about and experiencing ourselves.

The Wise Woman Tradition encourages us to work towards good health from the inside out. And to remember that our healing choices influence not only ourselves but the entire planet.

◻ *Susun S. Weed 1997, WM'98*

The Star. Each year we select the theme using our own magical blend of We'Moon numerology, Tarot, Gaia Rhythms and we'moon wisdom: We'Moon '98 adds up to 17 (XVII), the Star card in Tarot. The Star is the radiant one through whom the wisdom of the ages shines, inside and out. Tara, whose name means "Star" (Astarte, Ishtar and Isis) is a Tibetan Goddess of wisdom, compassion and liberation. In Tara meditation, her light streams through our hearts "like the simultaneous rising of a thousand moons," inviting us to awaken our true nature, to become the stars we are. With this We'Moon, we invoke the Star, who is both Goddess and the wise womyn within, to be with us now as we reclaim our ancient wisdom ways and learn what the Goddess is teaching us now.

excerpt, Introduction to the Theme

The Goddess Re-Turns
¤ *Selina Maria Di Girolamo 2008, WM'10*

The Star

Gently truth will touch you, when she comes
No loud fanfare blares her forth
But in the deepest space of silence
Angel's silver calls embrace the earth. . .
excerpt from a song written for the Star card in the Tarot through
© *Shekhinah Mountainwater, WM'90*

women bootleggers

we have been

collecting
sorting
memorizing

Brewing

Distilling
and running

our issues
underground
since prohibition

moonshine

of potent

portent information

¤ *Terilyn Milke 1997, WM'99*

Grandmothers' Council Medicine

The spirit Grandmothers hold council deep within the body of Mother Earth to discuss the current state of our Earth. They ponder how to awaken the women who are the warriors, protectors, and daughters of Mother Earth.

© *Leah Marie Dorion 2004, WM'09*

Santa de los Chilies
© Carmen Rodriquez Sonnes 1993, WM'98

The flowers,
sage,
and beeswax candles,
the medicine cards,
poems
and sacred texts—
these are windows
flung wide
to the soul.

excerpt ¤ helen laurence 1996, WM'98

© Deborah Koff-Chapin 1995, WM'98

Chamán

Like every good Chamán
I have my Mesa (table)
In my kitchen

The Mesa of the Chamán
Is the altar of her Work
There she gathers Energy
In the necessary Manner

The Chamán Works
On two Spheres
The Spiritual Sphere
And the Material Sphere

For Purifying
I take out my sacred Herbs
Cedar, Sage and Copal
The Mesa and Body are
Cleansed

Prayers of Thanks are Given
For sacred Life
For the new Day
Another day Begins

She mixes Herbs with Prayers
She gathers her Ceremonial Tools
In this way she Heals
In this way she does Magic

Good day Fire Spirit
Flame of Life and Death

Good day Water Spirit
Black Iron grill and Water Pot
Of my Grandmother
Are put on the Fire

In this Way
We begin to Prepare
For our daily Bread

There on the Mesa
Is Mortar and Pestle
Volcanic Rock
Strong and Enduring
Guardian of Ancient
Earth Mesas
Old from years used
In my Kitchen

There I grind the Herbs
From the Garden
Fruits from Seed
By hand Planted
In moist Earth

Allowed to Grow
They Mature
By Hand
They are Prepared
Into Meal

Again I Gather
My helpers unto me
Herbs of Cumin and Garlic
Green, Black, Red Peppers

Always at my side
The Three Sacred Sisters
Corn, Beans and Squash

The Chamán
Prepares Food
The Medicine of Life
For her People
In this Manner
Ancient and Sacred

She mixes Herbs with Prayers
She gathers her Ceremonial Tools
In this way she Heals
In this way she does Magic

Always united with the Spirits
Her Mother Earth
And Life's Energy

Always Following
The Red Road
Of My People

Siempre unida
Con los espíritus
Su Tierra Madre
La energia de la vida

Siempre Seguiente
El comino Colorado
De su Gente

© Maria Christina Moroles DeColores 1991,
WM'98

Rainbow Warriors © *Marcia Diane 1993, WM'98*

The smart teacher knows her job.
The clever teacher knows her employer.
The intelligent teacher knows her subject.
The brilliant teacher knows her students.
The wise teacher knows herself.
¤ *Carolyn Gage 1996, WM'98*

While Living Within Patriarchy

Wise Wimmin help wimmin—
Wise Wimmin nominate, vote for, and support wimmin;
Wise Wimmin hire, promote, and give credit to wimmin;
Wise Wimmin mentor, recommend, and advise wimmin;
Wise Wimmin seek policies that protect wimmin,
          fight policies that hurt wimmin.

Wise Wimmin follow the path their soul invites them to;
Wise Wimmin find and do meaningful work;
Wise Wimmin love those it is given them to love;
Wise Wimmin never stop learning who they are;
Wise Wimmin never stop taking the risks of
          becoming themselves;

Wise Wimmin live their lives so that when dying
          they will not regret not having lived their lives.
excerpts ¤ *Inés Martinez 1997, WM'98*

Wisdom Unmasked
© *Katheryn M. Trenshaw 1994, WM'98*

Witch's Brew

Nettle, devil's claw, garlic too,
skullcap, vervain and feverfew,
dandelion, clover, lavender blue
they all go into a witch's brew!
¤ *Sandra Spicer 1996, WM'98*

Old Woman Sleeps Good and Grandmother Moth Wing Woman
© *Carolyn Hillyer, Back Cover Art, WM'98*

WE'MOON '99

GAIA RHYTHMS FOR WOMYN
LUNAR POWER

Moondance
Lynda Hoffman-Snodgrass, Front Cover Art, WM'99

the moon, psyche, spirit, intuition, blood mysteries, lunar goddesses, left side, right brain, creativity, chaos, lunacy, labyrinth, veils, shadows, secrets, night, inner light, meditation, magic, mystic, mythic, transformation, reflection, ocean, tides, cycles, phases, feelings, flow...

What we call *lunar power* comes from the circle dance of Moon, Earth and Sun, casting a veil of light across the moon's face in regular monthly rhythm.

Lunar Power is a force in the repolarization of earth energy working to restore wholeness, reclaim parts of our experience/consciousness that have been denied, and shift the power balance to honor all beings. While the moon cycles through the months, thousands of we'moon around the world are opening this book, looking into the sky and into our own psyches, appreciating our lunar nature. We are casting a vast circle of we'moon around the earth with La Luna in the center. As we come to know Her power, may we come to know our own. Blessed Be.

excerpt, Introduction to the Theme

Full Moon Insomnia

The moon is like a jewel
under my pillow
like the princess and the pea
I can't sleep

I'm trying to sleep
but the moon has other plans
I follow the bouncing ball poetry
like reading subtitles
in a foreign film
Wake up and write it all down
before you lose such good reception . . .

I'm a nightshift stenographer
hired by the muse
to take down the moon's business
¤ *Coleen Redman 1997, WM'99*

Moonspinner ¤ *Nic Beechsquirrel 1997, WM'99*

The power of the moon was recognized and revered in human culture by the earliest peoples, as we know from artifacts, mythologies and from surviving indigenous societies. She was worshipped as the Mother Goddess, creator and destroyer of all life.

As priestess of the night, she rules the inner dimensions of the unconscious and is an ally in our journeys through the unknown. By her continuous act of transformation, she reveals the oneness of Spirit that is not bound to fixed limits of form. In "drawing down the moon," we link up with a powerful alternative energy source. To bring this energy into the world is womyn's work—crucially important in this time of great change where life on earth hangs in the balance. We are learning to go between the worlds.

excerpt, Introduction to the Theme

Time Dancer © *Jakki Moore 2008, WM'10*

Invocation
Moon, Moon, Moon, Moon,
Tara, Hina, Isis, Chandra,
Triple Goddess
Changing Woman,
journey with us 'round and
'round
from dark to light,
from light to dark.
from ebb to flow,
from high to low,
embrace us in our differences.
Moon, Mena,
Lillith, La Lune,
Mama Quilla, Akua'ba,
journey with us 'round and
'round,
though the 13 Moons of this year,
Io, Soma, Chang-O, Al-lat,
teach us how to live as one
Umoja, Karuna,
Aloha Lokahi
through 1300 Moons to come.

◻ *musawa pualani radha drolma 1998, WM'99*

© *Schar Chear Freeman 1998, WM'00*

Moon Dancer

The Moon © *Cathy McClelland 2006, WM'09*

The Forces are Many to Reckon With Flying Between the Worlds

Seven nights without sleep
I walk the shaman's edge
fighting, through the fear,
to hold on
to each reality

A fissure opens, deep within
slowly it widens
splitting
then
cracking in half

Like a rock face
hit, just so
by the sculptor's hammer
the old self falls away

What emerges is yet to be named.

excerpt © NíAódagaín 1996, WM'99

Starry Starry Night *© Sudie Rakusin 1984, WM'99*

Moon Garden

It's the full moon that usually brings my bloods, and in such a tidal wave, that I must rely on brick thick layers of torn-up old flannel sheets. When I first began this practice, I was in a bit of a quandary as to what to do with these blood-soaked rags afterwards. Since I didn't have a washer, I threw them in an old canning pot and left them to soak in cold water for a couple of nights. I felt inspired to take the canning pot of brilliant deep red blood-water to my garden. I poured it onto the earth and watched it soak into the roots of my flowers. One day, as I was pouring my blood on the earth, I imagined a big round "moon garden" of all white flowers. It would shimmer and glow in the night, sending messages of love from me to the moon. I started digging the next day and by the following full moon, I had completed my first raised bed moon garden. I planted every variety of white flower that in some way reminded me of wimmin I have loved: friends, lovers, my mother, grandmother, the Goddess . . .

Every month, as I pour my blood onto my moon garden, I think of women. Women who long ago ritually bled on the earth, women who honored cycles, the mother, themselves and each other—women for whom connection with the earth was a tangible focus central to life. I like seeing the deep red of my blood soak into the rich brown of the soil. I like imagining cells from my body being received by the earth, cycling, moving up into the flowers of my moon garden. Gazing into the face of the tall, graceful, fire-white lily, I see a reflection of myself, the earth and all women—centuries and centuries of wimmin connected by blood, fire, resistance, love, and moonlight.

□ *Christine Pierce 1997, WM'99*

Sacred Hands
□ *Nic Beechsquirrel 1996, WM'99*

Mama Luna

Let the moon have
her shadow.
Midnight is a mother,
it's true.

"Child,"
she says,
"it ain't nothin'
but the dark."
© Laurel D. Sager 1997, WM'99

Full Moon in Virgo
© Carmen Rodríguez Sonnes 1985, WM'99

Silver Strands

The moon is my ally
she slips under my covers
and into my bed at night
weaving her silver strands of wisdom
into my hair.
□ Barbara J. Raisbeck 1997, WM'99

Mama Luna
© Marsha A. Gomez 1997, WM'99

So, yes,
I am
moonstruck,
surely
a luna-tic
of purest form
a woman
walking home
with the Goddess
in her eyes.
excerpt □ Karen Misbach 1997, WM'99

***Ishtar/Innana, Queen of Heaven and the
Underworld*** *© Monica Sjöö, Back Cover Art, WM'99*

101

We open this book this year, this century, this millennium, this moment with the theme, Open . . . . In our Call for Contributions, we invoked an "open theme" and/or the theme of "open(ing)." The very sound of '00 ("oh-oh"), and what happens to your mouth when you say it, introduces our theme, Open!

And so begins We'Moon '00, opening the door to the 21st century, where cataclysms on the planet and in We'Moon's world have shaken the foundations.

In the early morning of February 18, 2001, the Main House at We'Moon Land, including the We'Moon offices, burned to the ground. No one was injured, but other damage was total. Computer systems, archives, and every piece of art and writing submitted for We'Moon '02 were destroyed, along with all record of the selections we had made, edited and proofed for the next datebook. All that work was consumed by Pele, Goddess of Fire, in a roaring blaze. We are grateful that She spared the nearby trees, resident spaces . . . and our lives.

In order to priestess this edition, we had to travel into the underworld of unconscious process to re-member her. With the technology gone, and the poems, stories, slides, prints destroyed, the four of us serving as the Creatrix had to dive deep into the ocean of memory, fishing for images and sentences which would help us recall the We'Moon pages we now saw only in our mind's eye. A partial list of contributors and a pile of charred wet release forms were the only clues we had for reconstructing We'Moon '02. With our systems in collapse, we were forced into the old way of remembering: the oral tradition. The art and writing had already been tendered and imprinted, on many levels—through our grassroots Weaving Circles, our communications with the far-flung web of We'Moon contributors, and the collective process of the Creatrix whereby every piece of art and writing is passionately argued and lovingly placed in the calendar pages. The extensive interactions involved in creating We'Moon were all grist for the mill of memory, grounded in the magic of community.

By New Moon in Gemini, there was a renewed tapestry of calendar pages woven together. Out-pouring of love and support from wemoon all over the world held us in our labor as we midwifed this We'Moon.

Adapted from Introduction to the Theme, WM '02

Risen from the ashes, We'Moon continued to grow and harvest new fruits. We began publishing the covers in full color in 1992. In 2002, we published our first full color wall calendar—We'Moon on the Wall. Next came notecards, originally in Lunar Power packets of 13 postcards, then Solstice Cards and Greeting Cards. The burst into glorious fruit happened with We'Moon 2004: our first datebook in full color! In 2009, we branched out to publish a children's book by Starhawk, *The Last Wild Witch*, with illustrations by Lindy Kehoe. 2011 brings an even more diverse harvest: We'Moon 2011 is our 30th edition; this Anthology is our first collection of We'Moon material, and we are now publishing a condensed electronic version of the datebook—an E-We'Moon application for smart phones.

As the 2000s unfolded, We'Moon once again weathered some profound internal crises. Mother Tongue Ink was outgrowing the capacity of the small womyn's land community at We'Moon Land; staff turnover and difficult personnel dynamics took a heavy toll.

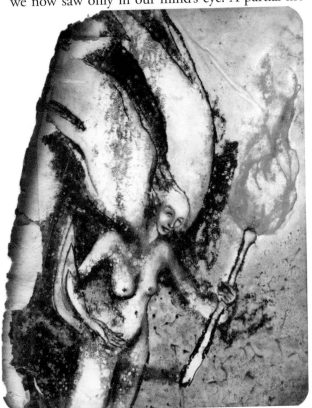

art salvaged from the fire © Deborah Koff-Chapin 2000, WM '02

After 25 years of carrying We'Moon, I decided that was enough: I was no longer willing to continue being the one to hold it all together. I completely turned it over to the Goddess to do with it what She would. We decided to proceed as if We'Moon '07 were going to happen, without commitment to outcome. With the Chariot card as our guide, and the Goddess in the driver's seat, we hung on tight as the We'Moon vehicle traversed sharp corners, hard bumps and well-worn ruts while we focused on healing the rifts, and the work at hand.

I found myself connecting with our extended community of womyn on land in Southern Oregon. I wanted We'Moon to stay close to her roots: womyn's lands have long held the drum beat for earth-based womyn's culture, from which We'Moon springs. Twice before, womyn on land had stepped in to carry the ball when my energies flagged. Now again, womyn steeped in we'moon land culture stepped forward, willing and able to take the reins and steer the course. The Goddess provides!

Musawa, adapted from "We'Moon Crossroads," WM'09

Tree-Mendous © *Wendy Page 1996, WM'11*

Barbara Dickinson: I first visited We'Moon Land in 1996—my first stop on a year-long journey to explore intentional communities. I was excited to meet the women who produced the datebook I had been loving. There, I met Beth, Amy, Lori, Musawa, and other We'Moon landers. It was here I learned that you hold the crescent of the waning moon on your left hand, and waxing in your right. I learned then that We'Moon was looking for wimmin to work in the company, as Musawa was hoping to retire. My interest was sparked, but I was fresh out of school and on my journey to discover community—this was a foreshadowing of events to come.

Flash forward 9 years: I find myself living in the middle of Southern Oregon—a hotbed of intentional Women's Lands. I arrived here with a passion for community, and a degree in fine art and business. Tina, my partner at the time, and I stitched ourselves into the local community, and resurrected WomanSource Rising, a local long-standing non-profit organization. With Sequoia as graphic designer, we began publishing a bi-monthly newspaper, and grew together as a team. We became known as dependable gals who followed through on our commitments, and when Musawa was putting out feelers for We'Moon staff, we were there. In the next two years, we created a We'Moon office at our home and helped set up a new accounts and shipping office in Portland. We'Moon company was transplanting her roots, still in the rich soil of womyn's community. I found myself having come full circle. Sometimes life just fits like a puzzle piece, the stars align, and the great Goddess sets you down in the way of grace.

I love working for We'Moon. I am production coordinator and co-moonager. My passions for art, community, organization—are all satisfied in this work that I do. It's challenging and inspiring. I work with the most wonderful, intelligent, kind, loving women one could ever hope to work with, and we are growing together as a team. Working with Musawa and Bethroot is such an honor, and in the making of this Anthology, I have grown to appreciate them even more for the heart-work they have put into We'Moon, and for Musawa's perseverance and hunger to understand the cosmic world.

Sue Burns: My first We'Moon was a gift from a dear friend. We were grad students studying Women's Studies back in 1991. The feelings I had while reading that first one were powerful, as if I had been invited into an actual, active circle of magickal women writing and creating to save the planet and our souls, or as if i had been invited then to work here now. In between, I taught English and managed women's bookstores, but when this job presented herself to me, I felt called. I work at my home office in Portland as co-moonager and accounts manager. And I am called to continue to deliver this amazing collection of women's art and writing back to that circle. Thank Goddess, I must have done something right.

We'Moon in Prisons

We'Moon has long had a freebies program for channeling surplus We'Moons into the hands of women who might not otherwise see it, primarily through friendly social service organizations. Some time in the 1990s, We'Moon began sending datebooks to imprisoned women—women's spirituality groups who made requests for donations, as well as to women we knew who were either behind bars or working with incarcerated women. Over time the word spread to institutions throughout the country; we now send hundreds of datebooks each year in response to requests from women in prison.

We wanted to include their voices in the Anthology, so we asked some of the women who participate in this program a few questions. Here are excerpts from responses and from letters we have received over the years.   —Lou Chain, coordinator of the We'Moon prisoner program

---

I am a 3rd Degree High Priestess working towards my ordainment…I am a solitary practitioner at this time so We'Moon has been useful in my daily meditations and served as a source of my intentions for Pagan Holidays.   —Nancy Pliefke

When I read material that promotes women's spirituality I am inspired and hopeful to find the journey that the creator has in store for me.
—Marisella Zamora

"Aditi, Goddess of the Luminous Void" by Beth Beurkens (We'Moon 09: At the Crossroads, pg. 156) has become something I read every day. Aditi has become my Goddess. When I read about her and how all your trouble can dissolve into an emptiness that is beyond your wildest imagination if you just let go, I cried until my shoulders shook.
—Linda Donahou

I absolutely love We'Moon stories, poetry and artwork. I read it and dwell on it, discovering an inner peace.   —Karleigh Delayna Arundel

When I look at the art and read the writings, it gives me a chance to dream. It opens my mind…it's the only thing I will be taking when I leave here.
—Deborah Senkir

I use We'Moon to help others when they are down. I choose which writing I feel will help them come to peace inside.   —Andrea Marie Crum

I use We'Moon to track the moon. I have noticed that full moons in prison are exceptionally wild and crazy.   —Caren Hill

In We'Moon 09: At the Crossroads, pg. 40, there is the most moving poem called "I Cry Too." When I read it I felt my soul opening up to a new understanding.   —Roshanda S. Melton

We'Moon has helped me keep up with the moon phases and keeps me tuned in to my body, spirit and soul to enhance my rituals.   —Patti Perkins

I know it is time for women to rise and show our strength and beauty in a positive light.
—Kristal Vibbard

Because I am a strong, opinionated, outgoing woman, I have been labeled by society (men) as a dominating, outspoken feminist. That's great. I love my title.   —Holli M. Conklin

I am a long time feminist…now with my experience of being incarcerated, I can more clearly see the consequences of our patriarchal society on both men and women.   —Anonymous

I have been a feminist all my life dating back to W Magazine, Gloria Steinem and bra burning. I work as a Dominatrix and believe that women should take their place in society as Goddesses and dominants.   —Sinthya Whitney

I use We'Moon to input all good dates, troubled ones too, and above all else—my release date.
—Jennifer Coker

I do believe as a woman I am strong, independent, and can achieve my dreams on my own.
—Karleigh Delayna Arundel

Soul Revival
© *Wendy Page 2005,*
WM'09

For Mimi In Jail

Brave as you were, you will only get braver
Just as colors ring and deepen in the dusk
Keep out an ear for the wild voice inside you
As you sit up steeping in the city's musk
Narrow, the walls, the locked walls that surround you
While they're taking your time for breaking their rules
But wide is the sky, and it's all hidden inside you
Like a file in a pie, starry dome of your mind
And don't mind the doubt and keep to your counsel
Don't you worry about all that wasted time
'Cause day in day out with your hands tied behind you
You touch more than you see, you are working our way free
And narrow, the path, it is wished we would follow
Looking neither up nor down
Enlightened horizon or dim bloody hollow
Just swallow, just swallow
But wide is the sky, and it's all hidden inside you
Unexplored, unconfined, starry dome
of your mind

Radar Birds
© Myshkin 2008

from the CD "Corvidae" © Myshkin 2002, WM'10

Meditation on women in prison

I'm thinking hard,
like rocks, like lead, like the heaviness of boulders and planets
about the lives of women, caged goddesses
I'm thinking of the families that get crushed to glass dust
when their mothers, daughters, sisters, lovers
are systematically stolen from their lives
placed in roughness and a cold structure
designed to tear away their sense of life, connection, power
I'm thinking of weighty thoughts
about my freedom being pitted against their isolation and pain
thinking of how white supremacist capitalism
tells me i can't quite have my freedom
if poor and working class women
and women of color have theirs.

I'm thinking hard
ishtar and kali thoughts, medusa thoughts
of throwing off the behemoth lies and greed
turning to stone the real criminals
I'm thinking of how to build a movement
where people can feel the rage of being made unwittingly
into racists, into materialists, into imperialists
I'm thinking of how women are soul and dance
I'm thinking women are power
and I'm moving to tear the walls down
and know the gorgeous stories of women free.

◻ *Elizabeth Page Roberts 2001, WM04*

A Letter of Appreciation:

I was released from prison last year after completing my sentence. For several years you sent me your wonderful datebook free. I cannot tell you how much I used it and appreciated it. I'm a breast cancer survivor and I had to keep track of medical appointments, medicines and communications. You provided me with the tool to do that.

Prison was a journey I wouldn't wish on my worst enemy but one I wouldn't trade. It gave me my purpose and passion. I now work for a non-profit that brings life skills programs into the women's prison here in Arizona to help them prepare for release. Our goal is to take this program nationally, eventually. We keep hope alive behind bars by giving them tools for a new life.

I just wanted to thank you for all you do for the forgotten population behind prison walls. There is a constant reinforcement behind bars that you are a worthless human being that no one cares about. It means more than you can ever know to receive something like your beautiful book. It also provides hope to many who may be on the verge of losing hope.

—Sue Ellen Allen

WE'MOON '00

GAIA RHYTHMS FOR WOMYN
OPEN

Shakti © *Lynn Dewartt 1996, Front Cover Art, WM'00*

Earth loving peoples have always known what Y2K scenarios anticipate: that we and all beings of Gaia, the living earth, are profoundly interconnected. Technology, for all the ways in which it isolates and fragments people, can serve to link us through vast electronic networks, sparking with information, communications and interaction. But technology has tricked us into dependence on and interdependence though machines, endangering our connection with the planet, our selves and one another in the body, here and now. The trick may now be on techno-patriarchy: the man-made webs are fragile indeed, flawed by design, and they may snap—oh oh! Maybe the Joker who brings us the Y2K bug is a Goddess in disguise, trying to shift consciousness of those who refuse to hear the message in the cries of Mother Earth.

excerpt, Introduction to the Theme

Blackbird

My shadow is a blackbird,
she eats silver fishes and steals time.
She twists chronology
into ellipses that open like windows.
Blackbird flies through windows
dressed up in poems.

excerpt © Julie Weber 1997, WM'00

Birthing Self © *Mimi and Dolphin WM'00*

Birthing Self

This is the private core of a spirit based life:
little moments when we stand heart naked,
head bowed and say to Spirit,
"Well. . .OK, then. . .I'm back."

excerpt © Christina Baldwin 1998, WM'00

Whale's Eye
© *Marja de Vries 1994, WM'00*

0. The Fool

The Fool is a character known in many cultures. In Native American traditions, Heyoke is the sacred clown, and Coyote or Raven are tricksters. The Hawaiian mischief-maker is called Kolohe. Baubo is a lusty greek female clown who made Demeter laugh in her grief. Baubo also appears in ancient Japanese myth. Traditionally the Fool combines the spontaneity and innocence of a child, the power and surprise of a wild animal, the crazy wisdom of a clown. In Tarot, the Fool is an androgynous figure, pictured as a playful child walking on her hands, a disgruntled jester with a dog pulling on the seat of her pants, or a romantic visionary wandering with her head in the clouds about to walk over the edge of a cliff.

The Fool, with her brave and innocent spirit, invites us to leap into the 21st Century and into leap year 2000. Using her guidance, we engage the mystery of life wherever we meet it, to become all of who we are. She asks only that we follow the path of heart and be true to our Spirit selves. With Fool as our guide, we get to raise questions; we do not have to know the answers.

excerpt, Introduction to the Theme

Riddler *© Nancy Watterson 2008, WM'10*

There is a term, "Divine Chaos." I am sure you have heard it before.

It would be a great gift if we could teach our children the gift that chaos brings. That when you get a flat tire and you have to be somewhere, that life just gave you a nice pause in your day. *Not* that life hates you and is out to get you. This is your gentle reminder that you are not in control, that someone is looking out for you, wanting to get your attention—and, most importantly, that when life does *not* go as planned, it *is*, always *is* a good thing. It has changed your perspective; it has given you an open door to meet someone new, let someone help you and reconnect you to life.

So, next time your day "falls apart," pause, say thanks and enjoy the ride.

excerpt ¤ Kasha Ritter 2005, WM'07

Wood Song   *© Erin Cooper 2002, WM'09*

Stepping into the unknown
Imagine it as stepping
onto a glass bridge
A supporting structure
you can't see

© Jenny Weston 2005, WM'07

leap
The trees are whispering to me
The leaves are waving me to stop
Leave my car in line at the red light
Leave the pressed, starched policy-infested road
and leap

¤ Elizabeth Kelly 1996, WM'07

©Lilian de Mello 1998, WM'00

What will I do with the rest of my life that I'll be able at the end to call real living? Simple being, blissful simplicity, every second. Peace and quiet and *knowing* . . . meditate on the wonder and impossibility of life and the illusion of everything but Nature . . . to live among trees in the woods.

I want to ask old, old Nature. She might show me how to part with myself. Like a mother.

© Moon 1997, WM'00

Ancient Ways © Diana Bryer 1997, WM'00

Healing

The life of a dreamer is not easy.
The dreams keep you awake.
Essie Parrish, Pomo Indian Healer

Dream your hands
like twin suns rise
to flower in the heat,
each hand, a perfect
five-petaled blossom.

Dream your hands
emerge from wounded earth
like animal teeth of trees
cut for timber. You will
itch to reforest city lot.

Dream your fast hands swat flies
Your cool hands kill fever
Your piano hands kiss tusk
Your angry hands slap back
Your thieving hands steal time
Your dragon hands melt doubt
Your blind hands see
for the first time
the aura above my skin—
And in the single motion of the flock
your hands swoop down to release me
from my cage of worry—
flowing cloud hands
spilling over the whole thirsting Earth—

Imagine what will be
when our fluttering, drumming,
smoking, laboring, twitching
snapping, scarred, bitten, broken, pale,
dark horse hands
thick with clay
shape down—

Yes, dream
Imitate your dreams
until you become them.

¤ Ann Filemyr 1998, WM'00

108

The Fool

do I appear ridiculous
turning handsprings
and somersaults
leaping into things,
the way I do?

but smell the breeze
feel the rain on your face
laugh at the wrong time
or nothing at all
unravel the lines
on your palms
do everything backwards

any minute now,
it will become clear

□ *Michèle A. Belluomini 1998, WM'00*

Opening © Musawa 1998, WM'00

Playing Goddess
© Anna Oneglia 1994, WM'00

Leap of Faith *© Linda Sweatt 1995, Back Cover Art, WM'00*

Self Portrait □ *Julia Butterfly Hill 1999, WM'00*

The Eco-feminist

For the love of a tree,
   she went out on a limb.
For the love of the sea,
   she rocked the boat.
For the love of the earth,
   she dug deeper.

excerpt © Charlotte Tall Mountain 1998, WM'00

WE'MOON '01

GAIA RHYTHMS FOR WOMYN
MAGIC

Priestess 9 © *Ulla Anobile 1996, Front Cover Art, WM'01*

Her Magic

Are you bathed in Her beam?
Are you dazed in Her glance?
Are you drunk in Her scent?
Are you shocked in Her chant?
Are you thrilled in Her cry?
Are you crushed in Her dance?
Are you cooked in Her fire?
Are you wrecked in Her storm?
Are you lost in Her game?
Are you freed in Her joy?
Are you drowned in Her sea?
Are you cleansed in Her peace?
Are you healed in Her arms?
Are you saved in Her grace?
Are you waked in Her love?
Are you found in Her light?

© *Janine Canan 1999, WM'01*

'01 Theme: Magic

Do you believe in magic? Magic happens, whether we believe in it or not. But have you ever noticed that when you are open to it, it seems to happen a lot more?

Human life has been guided by magical worldviews from the beginning of human consciousness. People living close to the earth have maintained the sacred web of life by understanding that we are participants in magic: mystery greater than we can fathom or control. Ancient spiritual traditions of every culture pass on teachings, often in coded form, with keys to the magical workings of life. The Tarot is one such ancient set of keys which we now use to divine the themes of each year's We'Moon. We took our cue for We'Moon '01 from The Magician card, number one (I) in the Major Arcana (the 22 archetypal images in Tarot that embody aspects of spiritual empowerment).

excerpt,
Introduction to the Theme

Witch by Moonlight
© *Kim Antieau 1999, WM'01*

The principle of magic is not to enslave the universe to our individual will. It is to transform the self to recognize and respond to the limitless opportunities to grow, which are always offered to us.

excerpt © Selina Maria di Girolamo 1999, WM'01

Dewi II ¤ *Gyps Curmi 1998, WM'01*

1: MAGICIAN

Over the last thousand years, magic itself became a disappearing act, unless sanctioned by ruling patriarchal institutions. Folk magic was forbidden. Powerful wise women, midwives and healers were burned as witches. Indigenous people, cultures and lands were taken over. Esoteric traditions went underground. Tarot, for instance, became an ordinary deck of playing cards, with its four suits dimly reminiscent of the original symbols representing the four elements and the Major Arcana reduced to Jokers. Magic became associated with trickery. Reason and empirical science became contemporary culture's means towards truth.

By the beginning of this millennium (technically January 2001), magic has come full circle. The ever-new wonders of technology have us spell bound; even the complexity of machines we use every day is mystifying to most people. Scientists go between the worlds of inner and outer space, where the stuff of reality is neither particles or waves but both, and the keys to mystery are now terms like quarks, quantum leaps, black holes, super strings. Yet technology can only imitate nature, not replace her. The genetic code may be cracked but the life force remains a mystery. Mother Nature is the greatest Magician of all—we may learn some tricks from Her, but She always has another card up Her sleeve.

Witch II © *Judy Springer 1990, WM'92*

Witchy wizard, bruja brew
Mystic, medium, source-erer, too
Mystery, miracle, ritual, spell
Coven, altar, circle, well
Alter, healer, familiar, muse
Affirmation, charm, power to choose . . .
excerpt, Introduction to the Theme

Birth Dance © *Theresa Sharrar 2002, WM'06,*

CASTING A CIRCLE / Wicca Ritual

✧ Holding hands in a circle is one way to "cast a circle"_ visualizing together a cone of white light all around you (or meeting in a tipi), is another. In the <u>Wicca</u> traditions of the Craft (pagan, faery, witch) as well as in most religions, there is always a formal opening of the circle at the beginning (and the end) of each ritual. Here are the basic ingredients which you can fill out with your own magical fantasy ... according to Wicca Craft:

✸ Walk around the space you will do the ritual in, visualizing it and circling it in light.

⚐ Invoke the spirits of the four directions and the elements associated with them (East-air; South-fire; West-water; North-earth) as you go around. Call out to them to come and be present and protect the workings of the circle_ meet and greet them with beauty.

△ purify and charge the energies in the circle by sprinkling salt water and burn some cedar or rosemary to clear the air, or pass some sage around.
Let the four elements be present on your altar or somewhere in the circle ... swords (or any kind of cutting edge) and incense for air, wands and flames for fire, cups and water (or herb tea, fruit juice, wine) for water; pentagrams and salt or rocks, clay earth) for earth.--- possibly a ♀ could represent each of the elements in the ritual.

〰 the circle is always clearly opened at the beginning and at the end of the ritual, being careful to ground the energy first each time.

Pass a kiss around the circle or say something to seal it, affirming that each one enters and leaves "in perfect love and perfect trust".
WM'85

Protest Magic in Seattle

What the police were truly unprepared for was the power of nonviolence—not to mention Magic! We were working magic on every level: from rituals we offered before the action to meditation and trance work in our circles, to the WTO spell—an ice sculpture on our altar that melted throughout the ritual. We worked magic in jail: we sang songs, told stories, shared meditations and learned to ground and call on the elements. About fifty of us held an impromptu ritual while waiting in a cell for arraignment and later danced the spiral dance. The guards, the threats, the violence and the concrete could not keep out the love, commitment and joy we shared. The women in jail with me were mostly young, amazingly strong, caring, thoughtful, intelligent and politically aware. There were also older women whose courage and humor were an inspiration to us. I was hungry, sick and in pain a lot of the time, but I was never for a moment unhappy to be where I was. I experienced a depth of almost radiant happiness like a pure current in a roiling river that I could tap into whenever my spirit started to flag.

Connecting the Circles
© Melissa Harris 1999, WM'01

We won. The World Trade Organization will never, now, be able to quietly assume power and consolidate its rule outside public awareness. And a new generation of young activists has been through a life-changing experience. A few uncomfortable days in the company of heroic and beautiful women seems a small price to pay.

excerpted from An Open Letter to the Pagan Community from Starhawk after the WTO protests in Seattle, November, 1999
© Starhawk 1999, WM'01

Inside the Psychic's Tent
© Cynthia Ré Robbins 1996, WM'01

Night Vision
¤ J. Lilith Taylor 1999, WM'01

Change

Change armory into harmony
Change artillery into art
Change war into worship
Change nuclear into new clear
Invasion into vision
Conquer into concur
Change bombs into bonds
Change end into mend
¤ Colleen Redman 1999, WM'01

Magical Passages © Donna Goodwin 1997, WM'01

There is Magic
when I choose to see you
as Spirit having human experience.
excerpt ▫ Claire Johnson 1999, WM'01

Grandma's Remedy

"Soak your feet in a bowl of moonlight," my grandma used to say, "The moon will soothe what ails you in an effervescent way."
▫ *Rhea Giffin 1998, WM'01*

Temple Spinner

I am dreaming back my sisters
Whisper-worn footfalls on the Temple steps
Skywalkers
Storm dwellers
Heavy-breasted cauldron keepers
Songweavers
Snake sisters
Darkmoon dancers

Labyrinth builders
Star bridgers
Fiery-eyed dragon-ryders
Wind seekers
Shape shifters
Corn daughters

Wolf women
Earth stewards
Gentle-handed womb sounders
Dream spinners
Flame keepers
Moon birthers

Come home sisters, come home

© *Marie Elena Gaspari 1999, WM'01*

Corn Spirit © Diane Rigoli 1998, Back Cover Art, WM'01

WE'MOON '02

GAIA RHYTHMS FOR WOMYN
PRIESTESSING THE PLANET

Gaia & Daphne © *Sandra Stanton, Front Cover Art, WM'02,*

'02 Theme: Priestessing the Planet

When we chose the theme for We'Moon '02, we wanted to honor work that women are doing all over the world to heal and tend Mother Earth, to empower women and to make the world safer for all beings. We shaped the priestess word as a *verb*, in order to focus on women's activity, small scale or grand-gestured. The priestess is not only the one who conducts ritual, she is also the one who sweeps behind the altar (to use an image from a poem that was lost in the fire). She is not only the woman who takes visible leadership in the public eye, challenging exploitation and making waves that impact national and global policies, she is also the woman who makes quiet revolution mending the broken in everyday life, in her backyard, her neighborhood, her community.

"We invite you to share ways in which you priestess the planet. Life on earth is endangered on so many levels that the creativity of women is especially called forth for the transformations needed at this time. Who and what moves you to action? Who are the womyn you know whose work changes the world?"

from WM'02 Call for Contributions

Priestess Dreams

I dream of Temples—thousands, across the world—sprouting up from Mother Earth like new Spring Buds, providing spaces for womyn to re-awaken, re-member, and re-turn to their Sacred Goddess Selves.

▫ *Phoenix B. Grace 2000, WM'02*

Ceridwen © *Tina Smale 2000, WM'02*

The Calling

Sisters, what if it is true? What if there is a Calling? What if we are WAKING UP? Maybe there was once a tribe of priestesses whose oracles foretold this time of grave danger, and they made a pact. After the Goddess religion fell away, maybe the priestesses slipped into the background, promising to return if they were ever really needed again. What if we are starting to remember magic and each other? Starting to re-member our True selves?

Maybe *we* are the Priestesses, reborn in this time, and we will make the changes needed for our survival. What if it is now our responsibility to change the world? To truly change, we must have a new vision. Really new. A change in worldwide consciousness. And how does one do THAT? Maybe *one* doesn't.

If We are the cells of the Earth, the Goddess, we are being asked to remember ourselves, come together, create true magic and save the planet.

What if it is true, and there is a Calling? Have you heard it? Will you answer? It is time. We can change the world. We are the Priestesses. I hear the Call. Any of you hear it, too?

excerpt © Kim Antieau with Jeanne Hardy 2001, WM'02

11. The Priestess

Priestesses are women attuned to Spirit in ordinary life, dedicated to life-affirming values, extraordinary in a global culture driven by profit and disdain for biosphere survival. Priestesses can skip right over conventionally-drawn boundaries between the political and the spiritual, between art and politics, the personal and the global, worship and play. In traditional Tarot imagery, the High Priestess is often depicted between opposite pillars, holding keys to the gateway of Mystery that leads beyond duality. Her authority comes from her wholeness, drawing on the source of oneness rather than being drawn into opposition. Her sanctuary is the whole earth.

excerpt, Introduction to the Theme

Sacred Visitors © *Schar Chear Friedman 1998, WM'01*

Synthesis © *Mara Berendt Friedman 2000, WM'02*

To own the word Priestess,
I am becoming more brave,
beside my thousand thousand
priestess-sisters.

I see the Goddess is returning
through our troubled skies
through wars and violated children,
through land raped
into angry dust
and I will priestess Her,
call her healing love
through ritual
and my daily living;
I know in all her many names
she spells the flame of hope.

excerpt © Rose Flint 2005, WM'09

You are one of the miracles of creation.
Address yourself with respect and wonder.
excerpt © DV Trimmer 2009, WM'11

The Temple of Sekhmet

Located on Highway 95, forty-five miles north of Las Vegas, Nevada and fifteen miles south of the National Nuclear Test Site, a statue of Sekhmet, ancient image of women's power, sits regally inside her temple. She faces the test site to heal Mother Earth. The temple, rising in the middle of the Mojave Desert, was built in honor of Sekhmet, the lion-headed Egyptian goddess of birth, fertility and rage.

¤ Monica Sjöö 2001, WM'02

This beautiful space serves the peace and spirituality community as a place for gathering, centering and meditation. The sand-colored stucco temple is open to all the elements of nature. In the center of the temple is a sacred fire pit for ceremony. The temple provides a calm space of refuge for opponents of nuclear weapons tests. Peace and reverence live within the temple along with a quiet sense of self-empowerment. A full Wiccan calendar of events honoring the Wheel of the Year is celebrated.

Because the desert is fragile, when you visit it is requested that you look where you walk. Every animal, every plant, every rock and every grain of sand is our spirit.

© Patricia Pearlman and Genevieve Vaughn 2001, WM'02

Invoking the Directions
© Marj Greenhut 1993, WM'02

Bitch Goddess *© Anna Oneglia 1995, WM'02*

Women are bitches now. It's a fact. Bitches know how to live, and we are raising up a flock of small bitches. Be ready.

excerpt ¤ Lana Mareé 2001, WM'02

Grandmother Cedar, Grandmother Pine

She has faced the ax. She has been leveled for cornfields.
The golf course is her deathbed.
She has been chopped down,
piled end to end in choking rivers,
split, stacked, nailed, pounded and
burned for fuel, burned for heat,
burned by the careless cigarette.
Her body made the rugged piers, made the ships
which were loaded down
with tea, cotton, sugar, cotton, men.
She made the wealthy, made the wheel, made the wagons
as the wild was beat back against the mountains.
And still she persists in being
despite lightning, mud slides, chainsaws,
the sprawling growth of the city crippling her limbs.

I hide inside my home wearing her body like a box
to protect me from the cold, prying eyes of strangers.
She stares back at me from these walls
fixing me to the map of wives with my lemon-stained rag.
I bury my sweaters in her chest
to keep them from the gnawing moths;
I dance across her spine pointing my toes and leaping
to give form to my howling pleasure—
and in the gesture of the hopeful,
I bundle up the roots of a small one,
dig a hole, soak it, place the sapling into the mud,
its sweet spicy branches brushing against my sweat.

Remember the trees who make this life possible,
who some call grandmother,
because they, like us,
have parents, ancestors, live in community.
I have seen them dancing in their ceremony
of bending low
when the wind rushes in from the north.
Trees are made from all things holy:
rain, soil, sunlight, bogs, bees, and centuries—
do I honor them properly
when I put another log on the fire,
when I decorate holiday branches with tinsel,
when I pick my teeth with a toothpick
when I jot down notes for a meeting?
Even this page
which you hold in your hands as you read
is made from their lips
giving my voice a place to rest or rise up keening—

© Ann Filemyr 2001, WM'02

In India, Amma has created for the poor, especially rejected women and children, dozens of schools, colleges, orphanages and hospitals; to 50,000 people, she has given houses, pensions, food and clothing. Around the world, she has built hundreds of spiritual centers and temples. In 20 different languages, books and magazines offer her simple yet profound teaching of compassionate consciousness.

Amma's incredible life is a heart-shattering example of true Love, Beauty, Sacrifice, and Supreme Consciousness.

excerpt © Janine Canan 2001, WM'02

Sacred Thread Mandala
© *Cynthia Ré Robbins, Back Cover Art, WM'02*

Pervasive as air, resourceful as earth, life-sustaining as water, transformative as fire, Great Mother is as subtle as a paradigm shift, and as earth-shaking. In the patriarchal equation, Woman and Nature, once held sacred, became the negative "other," the wild and instinctive shadow side of existence, to be controlled and exploited. She does get wild! Her stormy elemental extremes (hurricanes, earthquakes, floods, volcanoes) command occasional attention in a world transfixed by violence and bad news. Her devastation—the destruction of whole peoples, cultures, species, habitats—is the worst news of all. Her sacred power is not to be denied, however. The extent of Her dominion is obvious when attempts are made to replicate what Mother Nature did perfectly before human intervention. It takes enormous effort to restore ecological balance, to support the self-healing human body under siege, to eliminate artificially induced toxins. For Her, and for our survival, we must commit to fundamental recreation of planetary health. As cells of Her body, we mobilize in Her healing response. Great Mother's resilience is greater than the death-culture's violations. She is larger than life, larger than death.

excerpt, Introduction to the Theme

WE'MOON '03

Gaia Rhythms for Womyn
Great Mother

Mother of Life
© *Frankie Hansberry 2001, Front Cover Art, WM'03*

The Source

We know she lives.
She is the voice of the newborn
and the Ancestor,
the gaze of the last white tiger
and the flower
that breaks through the road.
She is the red thread
of life in all of us;
she is tomorrow
and we cry for her:
Mother free us.

excerpt ¤ Rose Flint 2001, WM'03

Gaia's Cry
© *Katherine E. Schoelkopf 2000, WM'03*

118

The Great Mother is celebrated here as the Earth, Source of all life. She is the ancient rock of being, blessing Her creation through the ages, through the cycles of seasons and generations. We'moon encounter Her in Nature, loving Her with naked feet, immersing themselves in Her forests, meeting up with Her wild animal Self. They tell stories of Her healing powers and worship Her as Goddess-in-Body through sexuality, pregnancy, childbirth, creativity of all kinds. The Moon pages resonate with Love as the heartbeat of Great Mother. Sometimes Her gift is elusive, and we'moon struggle to feel connected to Goddess-presence. To embrace Her is to embrace contradictions and mysteries. She gives death as well as life. Gaia is invincible; She is also wounded. We'Moon '03 cries out on behalf of this precious Earth, invoking the Great Mother's power to liberate the planet and all Her creatures from devastation.

excerpt, Introduction to the Theme

The GrandMother is the Maker
© Denise Kester 2007, WM'11

Prayer

Hail Nerthus! Anti-war Goddess of old. Where are You, Nerthus? Come. Come now. Come running
　with your red wagon bumping over the battlefield.
The battlefields have become supermarkets, restaurants,
　bus stops, refugee camps, churches, temples, mosques.
Hurry! The soldiers have become children.
Just say the word, and guns will not fire. One glance from You, grenades will not explode, bombs will fall flat.
Come, with Your holy force field,
　turn landmines into fruits for starving peoples.
Lift one finger, mighty Nerthus, and trigger Peace.
Monkeywrench the machines of war with Your Love,
dull the blade, catch the missile, grab the detonator.
Pile Your wagon high with dead weapons,
cart them off the edge of earth.
Charm bullets into rain for thirsty ground.
Goddess! Send us Mercy, irresistible.
Flood the halls of power, the tents of the dispossessed with Mercy.
Still with Mercy the command to shoot, bulldoze, launch.
Inspire with Mercy the passion to mend.
Pour out Mercy, O Nerthus, to the ends of the earth.
Hurry! Nerthus, Hurry!

excerpt © Bethroot Gwynn 2002, WM'03

And So . . . the
Great Forgiving Goddess
mulches, cooks,
boils, and churns,
composting patriarchy
into a fine, fertile soil.

excerpt © Diana Tigerlily 1999, WM'03

from Wickedary *by Mary Daly*
© Sudie Rakusin 1985, WM'91

Ix Chel

Mayan Moon Goddess, Mother, Grandmother of Change.
Serpent of the Heavens, endlessly recreating
Yourself. Old Woman Spider, center of the world's web, eternally
weaving and reweaving the fabric of life itself.

You sit at your loom, sing with your nesting weaver bird,
stroke each soul between your fingers,
weave us together in all our differences.

Healer and renewer, you send refreshing rain,
watch over women in childbirth
and with your sacred rabbit, scribe of lunar calendars,
compose herbs to ease and mend us,
welcome us to your sacred island, Isla Mujeres.

Oh, solitary and independent wanderer,
lover of nocturnal creatures
in your ever changing constancy
touch me with your light,
be my midwife for creation.

◻ Antonia Matthew 2001, WM'03

No I Can't Go Back Yet

I need to lie here.
I need to immerse myself.
I need to see nothing but green
for a little while.

I need to nourish my soul
to stroke it gently to life.
I need to lie on this ancient log
to soak up sky latticed leaves.
I need to wander my eye up
up up a trunk till I can't see.

I need to be here by the creek
to give my body to the ferns.
I need to breathe rich air
to receive my taste of soil.

Wilderness is no longer a luxury:
Just as my child
needs milk from my breast,
this I need from my mother.

◻ Nirav Sumati 2001, WM'03

Mother Nature's the cure,
Take at least
Three times a day!

excerpt ◻ Lorye Keats Hopper
2001, WM'03

Kaite © *Megaera 1995, WM'03*

Is This Heaven?

Is this heaven,
where God
greets everyone
with a big Motherly hug
and a romping laugh of joy?

© *Janine Canan 2001, WM'03*

SHE CREATES ALL
SHE IS AGELESS
SHE CHANGES
SHE HEALS
SHE LIBERATES
SHE EMBODIES
SHE CONNECTS
SHE GIVES BIRTH
SHE ABOUNDS
SHE NURTURES
SHE INSPIRES
SHE GIVES DEATH
SHE IS ALL LOVE
SHE IS YOU!!!

© *Musawa and Bethroot 2002,*
Titles for the 13 moon themes of
We'Moon '03

And she saw that she looked like the Goddess Mothers she had just seen. The thousands of little fat gals unearthed were not meant as a singular idea of reproduction or menstruation, but they represented creativity, abundance, renewal, bounty of Earth and self. She left the museum juicy, full, and ripe with possibility.

excerpt ¤ Deb-RA Sawers 2001, WM'03

Holding the World
© *Corey Alicks Lie-Nielsen 2000, WM'03*

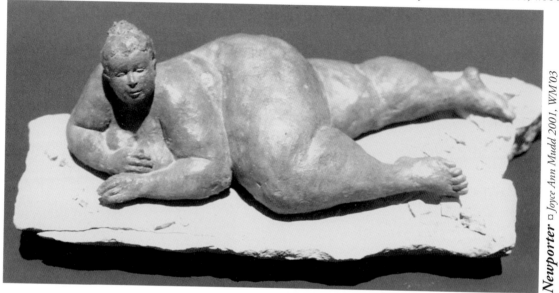

Newporter ¤ Joyce Ann Mudd 2001, WM'03

Wear Your Dragon

Wear your dragon like you wear your clothes.
Don't convince yourself you are the clothes—
Just be seated in them.
The great mother is already inside you,
Already clothed—
Just be seated in her.

¤ Tatiana Blanco 2001, WM'03

Mountain Weaving
© *Durga Yael Bernhard 2000. Back Cover Art, WM'03*

WE'MOON '04

GAIA RHYTHMS FOR WOMYN
POWER

Sueño Dorado (Golden Dream)
© *Cynthia Ré Robbins 2002, Front Cover Art, WM'04*

In We'Moon '04 the focus is on the nature of power. Nature embodies exquisite powers of diversity, balance and interconnection. The interaction of elemental powers—air, fire, water, earth—create, sustain and transform the living planet.

When control over others is the only power people know, we are caught up in endless power struggles. The cost, in terms of human and planetary destruction, is enormous. In a world where abuse of power is so prevalent, we look to womyn to redefine, model and practice power in life-affirming ways, reaching for empowerment that connects people with one another, balancing individual needs with community spirit and honoring the interconnected web of life.

We are especially delighted to show, this year for the first time, the full power of We'Moon art in living color! Sky indigo, ocean blue, fire red, sun yellow, forest green enrich the natural cycles that carry we'moon through the year with the full spectrum of elemental power. Refracting the subject of Power itself through the metaphor of color, we are inspired beyond black and white thinking about the nature of power.

excerpt, Introduction to the Theme

Kali © *Hrana Janto 1995, WM'04*

Calling Down the Power

of the moon
the night
the dakini who dance
creation to chaos
the gopi who dance
the universe into being
mother earth
her dance among the stars

I am
she says
power of volcano
and beast
and storm and love and land
lightning, lamp, bubble, cloud
and girl and woman and man
and all things
living and passing

I am
tidal wave
and orgasm

and delight
and ten million clouds
and ten billion stars
the energy
the center
the dynamo

I am
the push behind
being and begetting
existing and enduring
I am the great axle
on which the stars rotate

come join hands with me now
in this circle now
while the drums play
and may every breath
you breathe
bring you
power
© *Mary Mackey 2002, WM'04*

IV: Empowerer

The Power theme ('04) is based on the Emperor card (IV). In reclaiming power as a potentially positive force in the world, we stretch to embrace a womyn-inspired rendering of "the Emperor." We re-envision Her as an Empowerer whose strength transcends the polarity of "Emperor" and "Empress." Rather than construe these two energies as male or female, patriarchal vs. matriarchal, we claim both as complementary aspects of a greater power. The Empowerer balances both left and right brain, yin and yang, heart and head, receptive and active, being and doing. We are most in our power when we come from wholeness and create balance from the dynamic tension between polarities.

excerpt, Introduction to the Theme

I Overcome, Not Without Help
◻ *Sophia Kelly Shultz 2009, WM'11*

Oya © *Hrana Janto 1992, WM'04*

Sometimes

Sometimes I need to feel
like I can move mountains and
I'll grab something heavy to heave, shove or pull.
I wanna prove I'm strong like—
I wanna prove I'm useful like
You know, to carry one grain of sand from
here to there, and then another, and then another
it aint gonna ever satisfy me like—
it caint never ring my bell like
it sure as hell won't float my boat.

You see these boulders?
You see these troubled lives?
Sometimes the futile feel
of the slip-slop endless process of
my immoderate unenlightened life
totally terrifies me like
when I encounter a mountain
and know the thing needs moving and

can feel my hands are tied
and can see the money's almost gone then
I despair—
that my wee pea-size intelligence
is inadequate after all.

The ensuing squirm is pure pathetic like
a loud fly stuck-dance angry
in a spider's wiggling web
But sometimes
when I smack into a mountain
I can re-member myself in time
and I can get out of my own way
long enough and
I can plant my flat feet firmly on the floor and
I can put my freakin' hands together and
I can set my blazing beating heart behind them.
Then my belief begins to MOVE my mountains.

© *Rosemary Wyman 2008, WM'11*

123

Left to Right, Top to Bottom: **Mother Nature at the Age of Three** ▫ *Robyn Waters 1993, WM'04,* **Rethinking Red Riding Hood** ▫ *Robyn Waters 1992, WM'04,* **Wild Women Protect the Forest** © *Amarah K. Gabriel 1996, WM'04*

124

The Womyn of "La Vida Nueva"

I met Pastora, Violeta, their grandmother, mother and three sisters in November 2001 when we gathered in their dirt floored, thin bamboo-walled home, to introduce my travel group to the womyn's cooperative they had formed five years earlier. Living in a womyn only household, in the Zapotec community of Teotitlan del Valle, in Mexico's southern state of Oaxaca, is a radical act in itself. This indigenous community is ruled by tradition, strictly reinforced by male dominated authorities, who are given complete control.

La Vida Nueva is a weaving cooperative of womyn who have been singled out for ridicule, humiliation and personal violence because they have acted on their own collective strength and power. They are determined to stand on their own, to sell their rugs directly to the consumer, thereby avoiding the exploitation of the male store owners.

As they displayed their 100% wool, handcrafted, beautiful "tapetes" (rugs), they shared how they begin by cleaning the wool of twigs, then taking it to the river to wash. In the mountains they collect herbs, bark and insects used to concoct the natural dyes. It is they who collect the firewood they need for their wood fires for cooking. It is they who sell gelatins, rice puddings, etc., at the market to earn the little money they need. It is they who maintain their "milpa" (corn patch), where they grow the food they need for the year. There was no holding back how PROUD they were to be living independently.

¤ *Juanita Rodriquez 2003, WM'04*

The Summer I Discovered Power

The summer I discovered power
the ink flowed dark and freely from my pen
like a river of moon's blood.
I discovered what was between my legs,
wore no undergarments
and made peace with chin hair.

The summer I discovered power
I only read books written by optimists,
only ate what came out of the ground,
spent enough time outside
to truly know my insides.

The summer I discovered power
I left the sunscreen
off
because I wanted the fiery lips of the sun
to seduce my skin
into wearing Her erotic afterglow,
left the deodorant
off
because I wanted to breathe the sweet smell of
my body's own ripeness
rich like Sumatran coffee.

The summer I discovered power
I discovered strange and impossible
places
deep wells and live wires.
I went straight to the Source
and plugged in.

© *Catherine Wilcox 2002, WM'04*

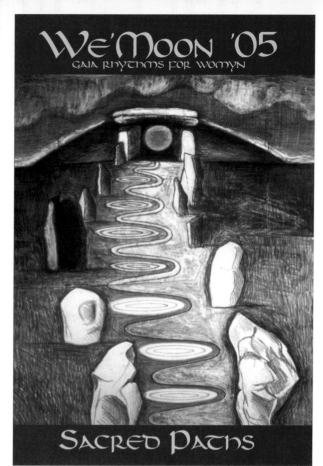

We'Moon '05
Gaia Rhythms for Womyn

Sacred Paths

Avebury Stone Avenue
© Monica Sjöö 1992, Front Cover Art, WM'05

Nana

It's hard to find the path now.
Because I was following her.
I was following her ways without knowing
And now she is gone . . .
Gone, with all her wisdom . . .
No longer up ahead.
No more silver streams
Of healing things she said.
She can't tell me again.
I have listened for the last time.
Now I have to own it.
Now I have to know it.
Now I have to carry, and pass it on.
Remember it.
Look after it.
She can't tell me again.
It's hard to find the path now . . .
But I must search amongst the roots.
Because I know that . . .
I can sense that . . .
Someone is following me.
Waiting for her wisdom.

© Sioux Patullo 2003, WM'05

We call sacred any pathway that connects us with Spirit. How we stay connected with Source is unique for each of us. To speak of 'sacred path' opens a way to the meta-level of our deepest inner journeys—where Spirit is alive in us and seeking expression in whatever we do. This awareness encourages us to look for signs of spirit in the midst of our everyday lives and not to lose sight of the forest for the trees. It reminds each of us: there really is a path I am on and my life journey reveals it.

This We'Moon on the theme of Sacred Paths offers an antidote to increasing desperation on the planet in these times; it gives gentle, vibrant inspiration to wake up and get back on course, individually and collectively.

Imagine: women walking our sacred paths, connected to each other and to Source, in parallel, entwining, spiraling journeys empowered by Spirit—we will turn this world around! This We'Moon is dedicated to the life-affirming paths of women everywhere. May we walk our talk on the sacred paths that most inspire us—for the benefit of all life.

excerpt, Introduction to the Theme

Darkest Night © Toni Truesdale 2003, WM'05

Our cue for the theme comes from Major Arcana Tarot Card #5, The Hierophant (or High Priest). We puzzled over how best to extract positive essence from what is otherwise a patriarchal image. In most conventional Tarot interpretations, this card has to do with religious hierarchy, control and dogmatic orthodoxy—not the values we cultivate in free-spirited We'Moon work! We honor more empowering images of spiritual leadership: priestess, teacher, guide, mentor, one who helps us open the doors to our own spiritual authority. In We'Moon '05, we reconfigure the Hierophant: each we'moon who shares word or image in these pages is Authority, speaking guidance from her own spiritual adventure, reporting to us the treasures she is finding on her sacred path.

excerpt, Introduction to the Theme

A Bee Whispers What It Knows
© *Sudie Rakusin 1984, WM'93*

She Searches the Distance
© *Megaera 2002, WM'09*

Make room in your heart for yourself.
You are the path.
excerpt © Eleanor Carolan 1996, WM'00

Traveling The Gypsy Switch—A Terrestrial Zodiac

The Gypsy Switch is a traditional year-long journey round England and Wales. It is roughly egg-shaped, centered on the stone-circle Arbor Low in Derbyshire—also egg-shaped: the cosmic egg in the womb of Albion, White Goddess Motherland, England, just after Appleby.

As we physically move around the land, we move round the year, marking out a giant zodiac; reflecting the heavens; turning the wheel of the year; marking and celebrating the fire festivals, equinoxes, solstices, phases of the moon, and making the journey within ourselves also. The macrocosm *is* the microcosm.

Ancient nomadic peoples did not wander aimlessly, they followed traditional patterns and routes through the land. These patterns are still followed in some lands—notably by Australian Aborigines—not as much a healing as a keeping well—of people, earth and universe—a fine balance which we have lost and need to find again. We need to open up the old paths: sacred place linking to sacred place. Maybe now we need to create new paths.

Blessed Be.
© *Jill Smith and Taliesin, May 1985, Wales, WM'86*

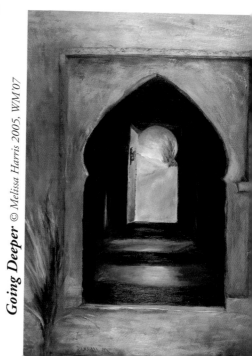

Going Deeper © *Melissa Harris 2005, WM'07*

Raven Woman
© Sandra Stanton 1993, WM'05

Irrigation

I love poems infused with history past
worked into the present day topic

Like rocks overturned we return to our worms
unearth our wounds for good irrigation

Burrowed in journals are rich story castings
lineage lines that link generations

Like mineral veins of precious inheritance
I'm mining the evidence of my ancestral descent

I'm leaving my fingerprints on poems written down
like roots taking hold in a plot thickened

I'm turning the pages like turning the soil
to know what is growing in me

¤ *Colleen Redman 2003, WM'05*

Solace

a woman who feels emptiness
notices a wing outside the window

raven offers solace

every morning they converse
bird, in the clucks and caws
plucked from branches

woman, with words
collected from dreams
where she too can fly

what do they talk about?
maybe the ten thousand ways of green
of loopholes in time and the taste of sky

raven knows the woman's grief
and when she sleeps in past sunrise
she wakes to wild cackles
and finds a feather in her heart

© Crystie Kisler 2003, WM'05

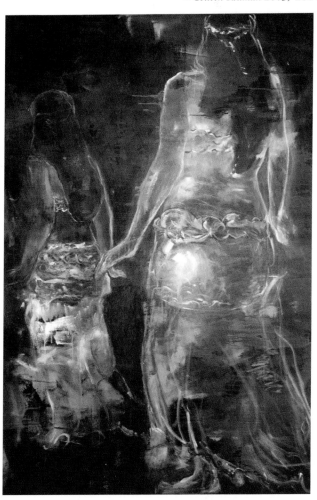

Sikinnis *© Ginger Royal 2003, WM'05*

128

Guadalupe Tonantzin

Guadalupe Tonatzin, speak to us now,
Guadalupe Tonatzin,
dark mother of the Americas,
la diosa oscura,
mother to the Chicanos and Latinos,
Protector of those who died in Chiapas,
the nuns killed in Guatemala,
los niños in Rio.
Mother of the working poor,
with tacos, tamales, sweet
pan dulce for the people.
Coatlicue, whose serpent skirt
eats the Sun each evening,
bringing it back in the morning;
whose sacred flower opens up
from her holy thighs,
to birth her children;
whose headband of skulls and dark mask
consumes the universe
Guadalupe Tonantzin, obsidian butterfly,
we place marigolds at your feet,
rose petals on your breast.
Guadalupe Tonantzin, speak to us now,
ignite us with your fierce compassion.

¤ *Marcia R. Starck 2003, WM'05*

Matriotism
¤ *Kjersten Hallin deGaia 2003, WM'05*

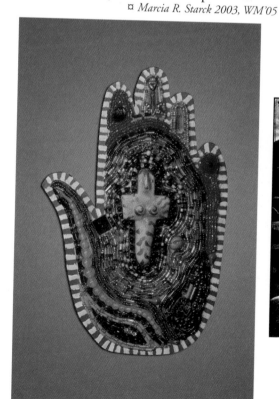

Goddess Hand © *Sarah Teofanov 2003, WM'05*

The Journey Om © *Robyn Waters 1993,*
Back Cover Art, WM'05

25TH ANNIVERSARY EDITION
WE'MOON '06
GAIA RHYTHMS FOR WOMYN

IN THE SPIRIT OF LOVE

Stream of Compassion
© Mara Berendt Friedman 2002, Front Cover Art, WM'06

'06 Theme:
In the Spirit of Love

Each year, Tarot tradition gifts and challenges us with the next card in sequence for our We'Moon theme: VI for the 2006 edition. "The Lovers" card is traditionally about intimate relationship: issues of partnering, passion, merging and boundaries, the dynamics of relating to self and others. This We'Moon is about relationship in the broadest sense: whatever we do "in the Spirit of Love."

The practice of love—kindness, connection, compassion—is offered as guidance for our lives in community with others, and as medicine for the world. The Spirit of Love animates wemoons' impassioned concern for global justice. They urge us with visual and verbal images toward solidarity with peoples, most acutely women and children, who are suffering under industrialized patriarchy. The Earth Herself is tendered by these healing impulses, with prayers for Her protection from toxicity and pillage of Her resources. Nature is embraced with erotic sensibility; Earth is Lover, Mother, Healer—holding all of us in Her generous lap.

excerpt, Introduction to the Theme

Words of Love

Oh, do not hurt my beloved.
Do not march across her
With your wars and weed-whackers,
Your tanks, your bulldozers,
your bug-spray.
Do not send weapons
Across her beautiful sky
Where only the constellations
should travel.
Listen to her promise,
Observe her mysteries,
Give her your words of love.
It is enough.

excerpt ▢ Alix Greenwood 2003, WM'06

Solstice Aloha *© Robyn Waters 2000, WM'06*

130

VI: The Lovers

With the LOVERS as our cue (Major Arcana Tarot card #6), we inquire deep into the heart of love. We'Moon '06 explores that profound and joyful energy which connects us to other beings, to our own True Self, and to the source of life. A world awash with antagonisms cries out for love.

from the Call for Contributions for WM '06

© Deborah Koff-Chapin 2000, WM '06

✤ *Katya (Nina Sabaroff) Taylor 1973, WM '06*

Union

Our union
should have blown the tent to bits,
should have set off sirens, whistles, and bells.
Instead,
there was just a steady glow,
the tent floating in the darkness
like a giant firefly.

© *Kala Wright 1999. WM '00*

Two Hands Touching © *Tee A. Corinne 2005, WM '06*

Artichoke on a First Date

First:
look at her from the corner of your eye
the way she catches the leaves
between her tongue and teeth
letting them slip in and then out.
Second:
listen as her lips linger
slow as they circle the leaves
pulling, pulling on the artichoke's flesh.
Third:
smell the garlic and basil, butter and lemon
on her fingers
as they unravel the leaves
carefully from the stem
Fourth:
taste dusk, purple and dark and briny,
as it falls through the window
and over her hand uprooting the thistle
with one fast tug.
Fifth:
feel your bones shift and your pulse sweeten
as she offers you
a bite of the heart.

© *Amy Schutzer 1998, WM '00*

Love Trees (Source) ¤ *Christina Smith 2000, WM'06*

© *Eleanor Ruckman 2004, WM'06*

I am lovers
with what hasn't a name:
the inside of wind,
the stutter of rain
on leaves.

excerpt © Amy Schutzer 1998, WM'06

Love Greater

When you fall in love
it's like a ripe coconut—
You get all the good sweetness, the milk,
the juicy love that makes love so appealing.

But after awhile, the coconut
goes past ripe and begins to harden.
All the love juice becomes thick,
not so easy to swallow. You have to chew
on the hardened fruit to extract the juice.

There's a lot more work to be done.

Once the coconut is beyond milk,
You have to grate the coconut to get
to the pulp of it all—
the relationship has matured.

You have to pour boiling water over it,
making the coconut milk you once had so easily.
But that's a lot of patience and muscle,
and you have to own a machete.

When you fall in love,
you must really love someone,
if you're willing to ripen with them.

© *Celeste Labadie 2004, WM'06*

She Loves Her Mare © *Megaera 2002, WM'06*

132

Women Heart ◻ *Lisa Seed 2004, WM'06*

Attention

We must work in the soil,

planting healthy seeds to nourish.

We must work with the children,

planting seeds of love to nurture.

We must work with the elders,

harvesting wisdom of experience.

We must work together

to create a garden of heaven.

Every thought a seed,

every word a prayer to feed,

every action a display of possibility.

We are the waking possibilities

of tenderness, compassion,

truth and love.

The beneficial moments

are in every interaction with life,

eternally

This love will set us free

excerpt ◻ Chaslynn Watts 2004, WM'06

All the Wild Womyn and Me

Sometimes I Ponder My lovely life,
And realize It's so Full.
Full of wonderful Women, Beautiful powerful Womyn,
Strong and joyful Wimmin.
    So full of You.
I have watched you and Learned so much.
Watched you joining hands hearts and Souls
To build houses, communities, raise children,
Make better Tomorrows.
Fill bellies with bread, Roses in your hair, Smiles on Faces,
Wisdom in your eyes, Love in your embrace, Reaching out,
Holding me, Giving me endless Support, Information,
Example. Nourishing my soul and growing body.
Celebrating, showing me Beauty, Yours and Mine.
Listening to Who I Am. And I want to be like All of You,
But would settle for being like Any of You.
The spunk of my Grandmother.
The contemplation of my Nieces (young open-eyed)
The beauty of my Mother. The strength of my *Tías*.
The laughter of my Best Friends.
So overjoyed to BE with you…all…
Where would I be Without you…
I think I would still be a fierce, beautiful, wild soul child.
Someone once told me Love and Strength
Are the base of all that is Me —I got That from You,
Wild Wonderful Womyn.

◻ *Galloway Quena Crain 2004, WM'06*

Sisters © *Theresa Sharrar 2004, Back Cover Art, WM'06*

WE'MOON '07
GAIA RHYTHMS FOR WOMYN

ON PURPOSE

Women Breaking Through
© Toni Truesdale 1998, Front Cover Art, WM'07

What lessons and imperatives call to us in our personal and planetary work? For 2007, we see a pressing need to be "on purpose" in how we direct our life energies.

How do we effect change in the world and in our personal lives? There is the outer path of purposeful, outgoing action to change our external circumstances. Goal-oriented, externally directed purpose focuses on "taking aim and shooting the arrow at a target." We work to be effective through technique, strategy, form. We problem-solve, make decisions, remove obstacles, construct new possibilities. There is, then, the inner path: a state of oneness which underlies purposive being. Being on purpose can involve inner alignment with Source. From spiritual disciplines that deepen mind and spirit in meditative contemplation, we learn the still point, "the place from which the arrow takes off." We cultivate an inner-centered, receptive space, alive with openness to the present moment.

excerpt, Introduction to the Theme

Where mindfulness is,
purpose flows
through every act.
Life resacralized.
© *Mimi Foyle 2005, WM'07*

Simmering in a warm
soup of evolution,
I am, as you are,
Cooking up
the Goddess's plan.
excerpt ▫ Celeste Labadie 2005, WM'07

Cup of Sweetness
© *Shiloh Sophia McCloud 2003, WM'07*

11. The Chariot

We chose "On Purpose" as We'Moon '07's theme, inspired and informed by the Chariot, Major Arcana Tarot card VII. The Chariot symbolizes our ability to direct the forces of our lives through balanced personal power, clear intention, guidance, focused wisdom and action. Tarot imagery usually pictures the Chariot as a vehicle drawn by horses (or other powerful animals) of different colors, representing polar forces that must work as a team to pull in the same direction. A strong skillful driver holds the reins, carefully balancing the dynamic tension between opposing tendencies, guiding the movement forward with single-minded purpose. With the theme "On Purpose," we explore a vision of embodied spiritual power that aligns personal will with Greater Purpose, uniting heart and mind with Spirit in moving through life's journey.

excerpt, Introduction to the Theme

Athena © *Hrana Janto 2000, WM'07*

Perseverance © *Eleanor Ruckman 1996, WM'05*

I am the goddess
who has watched and waited
for you to be ready
to run with it.

excerpt © *Denise T. Barry 2005, WM'07*

Purpose Persists

Multiple modest choices, delicate as butterfly wings
Wreathe the daily routine, shrouding angst in gentleness
Determination is not always dramatic, sometimes
She guides fates with a soft and common hand.

© *Helen Prinold 2005, WM'07*

Saving the Planet Takes Sacrifice

I take my own bags to the store—even the small plastic produce bags. I've come a long way from "I'll remember next time" to feeling so guilty if I forget my bags that I precariously juggle my items in my arms. When the bag-pusher asks for the third time, "Are you *sure* you don't want a bag?", I respond loudly "NO! I don't *need* a bag!" or "Plastic is Evil." When they've seen their maximum use, I recycle them all. I've progressed to using canvas bags. I've trained myself: when I'm done putting away my groceries, I hang the bag of bags on my front door to remind myself to put them back in my fuel-efficient little car for the next time. This extends in all my actions. If I forget my travel mug and I'm longing for a hot soy mocha, I go without or carry that recyclable paper cup all the way home. I've probably saved at least one tree this year. Imagine how many resources could be saved if everyone did this! Give new meaning, beginning with yourself, to the 3 Rs: Reduce, Re-Use, Recycle.

© *Amber Amanita Darkwood 2005, WM'07*

Breezes at Dawn
© Lupen Grainne 2000, WM'07

Sometimes the goddess wears a cloak of urban chic.
excerpt © Marni Norwich 2003, WM'07

She Makes Choices © Mira Michelle 2001, WM'07

The Power of Now

If I'm not loving this,
why am I doing it?
If I am doing this,
why aren't I loving it?
¤ *Pam Adams 2004, WM'07*

I am impeccable.
I am your teacher.
You will become impeccable also
and you will wonder how it is
you have lived so long without this skill.

Impeccable means absolute economy of energy.
There is precision and care in all action
and tremendous presence without depletion.
There is depth of knowing from within
and this is expressed with ease and simplicity.
There is order and purpose in this skill
and the function is to create a pattern
that promotes wholeness and health
with expansiveness of vision.

Take responsibility for your life!
Impeccable means cut out
what you don't want
and put into yourself what you do want
with every thought, word and deed.
excerpt © Denise T. Barry 2005, WM'07

Visual Haiku © *Jenna Weston 2005, WM'07*

136

Sometimes when it seems
the world is moving towards an end
and chaos is waiting just outside the door
I sing to my sisters:
Come! Let us dance!
Let us whirl through the dark night
till the morning dew washes our feet
till the warm sun finds us
asleep on her bosom.
Come! Let us dance a new world into being!

excerpt © N.V. Bennett 1999, WM'07

The Great Turning   *Black Dove* © Gael Nagle 1998, WM'07

The Great Turning is a name for the essential adventure of our time: the shift from the Industrial Growth Society to a life-sustaining civilization. The ecological and social crises we face are caused by an economic system dependent on accelerating growth. This self-destructing political economy sets its goals and measures its performance in terms of ever-increasing corporate profits—in other words, by how fast materials can be extracted from Earth and turned into consumer products, weapons and waste.

A revolution is underway, because people are realizing that our needs can be met without destroying our world. We have the technical knowledge, the communication tools and material resources to grow enough food, ensure clean air and water, and meet rational energy needs. Future generations, if there is a livable world for them, will look back at the epochal transition we are making to a life-sustaining society. And they may well call this the time of the Great Turning. It is happening now. In countless localities, like green shoots pushing up through the rubble, new social and economic arrangements are sprouting. Not waiting for our national or state politicos to catch up with us, we are banding together, taking action in our own communities. Flowing from our creativity and collaboration on behalf of life, these actions may look marginal, but they hold the seeds for the future.

excerpt © Joanna Macy 2001, WM'07

The work of
a woman visionary
is to know the past,
dream the future
and take action in
the present.

*© Shiloh Sophia McCloud
2003, WM'07*

Sisiutl *© Gael Nagle 2001,
Back Cover Art, WM'07*

We'Moon '08

Gaia Rhythms for Womyn

Mandala for Peace

Betty LaDuke 2000

Mending the Web

Mandala for Peace
Betty LaDuke 2000, Front Cover Art, WM'08

Themis, Maat, Kali, Memesis, Durga!
O Goddesses of Justice!
Spider Woman, Changing Woman,
O Great Mothers of Creation!
Please attend to us and our precarious world.
There is so much disharmony and imbalance
in and around us.
We easily despair.
Open us to perceive and trust in Gaia's self-healing.
Help us to energize right relations among Her peoples
and within Her Precious bio-matrix
of creatures and plants, water and winds.
Help us to mend the sacred web of life.

© Bethroot Gwynn 2006, WM'08

2008: **In Perspective**

We have known for a long time that Mother Earth is in crisis. Many of us have lived for decades with a sense of foreboding, a hint that a future time of intense change and challenge was on the horizon. Now the time of change has come. Either we make major and difficult choices that will bring our lives back into balance with nature, or we proceed with the warming of the earth, the assault on her life support systems, the waging of wars and the suppression of human dreams and opportunities. What world do we want?

Only a just world can be sustainable. Only a world where the needs of all are balanced and met fairly can attain ecological balance. Only a world in which all people are valued, where every mind is nurtured and every spirit cherished, can muster the creativity and sheer intelligence we will need in the coming times. To work for balance, to work for survival, is to work for justice.

To face the crisis before us, we need to relinquish a very powerful story, the story of progress, which tells us that we humans have transcended nature, are no longer bound by her limitations and constraints. We can fly across a continent in half a day, email instantly to friends on the other side of the world, cure diseases and light the darkness. And yet with all our technological knowledge, we are still dependent on the elements of life—the air, the water, the living soil, the sun's energy, the genetic heritage of our crops and seeds, and our mortal, animal bodies. To save the world, we must accept that we are part of the world, and come back down to earth.

Do we have the time to make the changes we know we need to make? I asked this question once in deep meditation, and the answer came back, "No." But before I could panic or despair, I got another message. "You're a Witch. Part the curtains of time and plant the seeds of change in that timeless place where change has already happened."

excerpt © Starhawk 2007, WM'08

Sewing Myth *© Toni Truesdale 1999, WM'08*

138

In the Motherpeace Tarot Justice image, the three Norns, or Fates, are in active commuication with natural forces: the Tree of Life, animal energy, crystal, flowing water. This imagery reflects the deep Justice that comes from attunement with the Mother and unity with all life, (from the Call for We'Moon '08).

excerpt, Introduction to the Theme

Justice

Earth Restoration Song

There's women in the kitchen they're cooking up a stew
There's women in the boardrooms they know what to do

So raise your voice and sing along
Join in this Earth Restoration song

There's people in the cities turning concrete into fields
creating local markets so the people can be healed

There's elders in the classrooms
they're teaching what they know
They're teaching little children
how the earth is going to grow

So raise your voice and sing along
Join in this Earth Restoration song

There's lovers in the bedroom
and they're making love
Joining the earth to the heavens above

There's children in the gardens
and they're talking to the plants
There's children in the gardens,
they know how to dance

So raise your voice and sing along
Join this Earth Restoration song

There's soldiers on the hillside
planting out the trees
Dismantling the bombs
because they're guardians of the peace

So raise your voice and sing along
Join in this Earth Restoration song

▫ *Margot Henderson 2002, WM'08*

'If Only' (over a cuppa)
we women could set the world to right . . .
© *Gloria Ojulari Sule 2006, WM'08*

The Snake That Bit You

If something hurts you really bad
make an icon of it and put it in your sanctuary
hang it from the mirror of your car
or tuck it next to the pillow of your bed

Record the sickening thud and play it
until you fall peacefully asleep
Recall the heat of that searing shame
until it wells up in you like a cool breath

And if a poisonous snake should bite you
make a bronze cast of it and put it in a high place

Then raise your eyes to it considering well
that you are still alive, though changed

See the gaps where you have bled and
take the stitches from your closed wounds
weaving them into a mantle that you wear
for your morning and evening prayer

And if grace and goodness should require
that you look into the eyes of certain death
recall the transformations you have known
and go there knowing well . . .

□ Anne Benvenuti 2006, WM'08

Om Shanti
© Jen Otey
2006, WM08

New Orleans Blues

It's time to sing the Blues,
It's time to sing the Blues for New Orleans,
where the dead floated in their wheel chairs
past the old French Quarter partly underwater;
where the graves of great jazz players
sit in sewage alongside their best albums;
where the broken glass of store fronts
reflects the rays of the scorching Sun

where a wild woman named Katrina
was blamed for breaking two levees;
when, in fact, the wetlands had disappeared,
oil rigs hugged the coast,
and the engineers' budget had been slashed

where people speak French, Creole, English,
make succulent seafood dishes,
where passionate spirits overcame poverty
playing music, dancing till dawn.

Now we all sing the Blues
for this exotic city
buried under slime and water,
whose myths and magic continue
to haunt our dreams.

© Marcia Starck 2005, WM08

Empyrean Earth
□ Rosemary Lloyd Freeman 2006,
WM'08

Re-membering the Web
¤ *Selina Maria di Girolamo 2006, WM'08*

Remind Me

Darkness always births the light. There is no insanity without surfacing reason. Apathy can give way to conviction and action.
Remind me.

There is no suppression without eventual uprising. Public silence unleashes individual voices. Where there is death, there must be life.
Remind me.

Where there is waste, growth will be forged. Narcissistic leaders incense empowered communities. Censorship spurs collective voices.
Remind me.

Senseless occupations cause people to question. Unjustified spending arouses investigations. The pendulum always swings.
Remind me.

Hopelessness, despair, intolerance and fear can debilitate. Belief, anger, purpose, education, and faith can facilitate. What can I do?
Remind me.

© *Diane Bergstrom 2006, WM'08*

Witching Hour

We'll walk the windswept corridors
of midnight, go stepping generations back
to find the huddled bones of those
whose hurt still resonates in living hearts

and we will give
such healing balm and solace
in our kiss of peace.
We'll do whatever it may take
to mend this world's history,
bring fresh hope
to the next seven generations
following our path.

excerpt ¤ Rose Flint 2006, WM'08

Sacred Seed Pods
¤ *Greta Boann Perry 2005, Back Cover Art, WM'08*

141

We'Moon '09
Gaia Rhythms for Womyn

Wonder □ *Jeannine Chappell 2006*

At the Crossroads

Wonder © *Jeannine Chappell 2006,*
Front Cover Art, WM'09

In Tarot terminology, the Hermit or Crone card (IX for We'Moon '09), represents the one whose intensive inward-turning brings power to light the way through the darkness. Given the critical choices confronting us in these challenging times, we named our '09 theme: At the Crossroads. When you come to a crossroads and know not which way to turn, stop and ask your inner voice—and thank the goddess she speaks the same language as you! (an old German saying from an early We'Moon). With the theme of We'Moon '09, we invoke sources of guidance and inspiration that connect you with your center, opening the channels of heart, mind, body, spirit and soul to your truth. We need all the help we can get to make wise choices at this crucial turning point—in our own lives and for continuing life on earth.

The traditional Crone Goddess standing at the Crossroads is Hecate, the Triple Goddess of Past-Present-Future, who in Her wisdom looks all ways at once.

excerpt, Introduction to the Theme

Dream of the Crossroads

Someone in the dream said, "You're at the crossroads," as if answering a question. It startled me, because as I looked around I realized it was nothing like I had ever imagined this archetypal "place." In my mind, "The Crossroads" has always conjured an image of some flat, dry, dusty abandoned place, one simple intersection of two roads, a choice to make alone. No turning back. But in my dream, there were countless roads converging on this place, each the road of many travelers who were arriving constantly, each in their own time, from the road that had called them. At the center was a great celebratory gathering, nothing but love among these strangers, all celebrating their arrival here. So great was this energy that emitting from the center

Crone © *Motherpeace: a pseudonym for Karen Vogel and Vicki Noble 1981, WM'09*

was a bright white-golden light, and all who entered into it became pure energy. People walking out of the center were transformed in some imperceptible way, and were meeting and hugging each other, and having lively conversations. In pairs, or clusters, or alone they walked off, choosing one of the many roads. I had come to the crossroads and I was not alone! I felt the most ecstatic relief! As I ascended out of my dreaming state, trying to hold on to this image in my waking mind, I heard the Great Mother laughing gently at my surprise—"You didn't really think I'd leave you stranded did you?"

□ *Christine McQuiston 2007, WM'09*

One day I shall say to myself,
This is the way of being
you have shaped,
and the vastness of the view
was worth
the climb.

excerpt ¤ Veronica M. Murphy 1982, WM'04

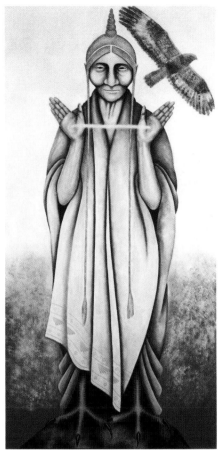

Vwalâ: Long Flight
© Carolyn Hillyer 1997, WM'01

© Marja de Vries 1998, WM'04

This will be no silent spring
her chant   her stare   her secret from
the void will blaze a brilliance
a wildness   a wail so total
the Goddess trembles

excerpt © Nell Stone 1981, WM'00

Hecate, Crone Mother
We seek your great wisdom.
Planet on the edge
Chaos in our lives
How did we get here?
How do we go forward?
The road is unclear: which way?

We are still.
We listen for the clarity of your voice.
The inmost whisper
The ancient lessons
The roaring imperative in crisis-time
to choose! act! come together! touch
Source now—
Center us, step by mindful step.
Be with us each and all.
Blessed Be.

© Bethroot Gwynn 2007, WM'09

Village Crone: Thailand
¤ Angie Coffin Heiney 1998, WM'00

We, the International Council of Thirteen Indigenous Grandmothers, represent a global alliance of prayer, education and healing for our Mother Earth, all Her inhabitants, all the children, and for the next seven generations to come. We are deeply concerned with the unprecedented destruction of our Mother Earth and the destruction of indigenous ways of life. We believe the teachings of our ancestors will light our way through an uncertain future. We look to further our vision through the realization of projects that protect our diverse cultures: lands, medicines, language and ceremonial ways of prayer and through projects that educate and nurture our children.

Agnes Baker Pilgrim (Takelma/Siletz, Oregon), Margaret Behan, Red Spider Woman (Cheyenne/Arapaho, Montana), Rita Long Visitor Holy Dance (Oglala Lakota, S. Dakota), Tsering Dolma Gyaltong (Tibetan), Flordemayo (Mayan, Nicaragua), Aama Bombo (Tamang, Nepal), Beatrice Long Visitor Holy Dance (Oglala Lakota, S. Dakota), Julieta Casimiro (Mazatec, Mexico), Clara Shinobu Iura (Santo Daime, Brazil), Maria Alice Campos Freire (Santo Daime, Brazil), Rita Pitka Blumenstein (Yupik, Arctic Circle), Mona Polacca (Hopi/Havasupai/Tewa, Arizona), Bernadette Rebienot (Omyèné, Gabon, Africa)

13 Grandmothers

© *Marisol Villanueva 2007, courtesy International Council of Thirteen Indigenous Grandmothers, WM'09*

***Asia: Building
Community Leaders***
¤ *Betty LaDuke 2007, WM'09*

144

Rooted in Reverence, Seated in Spirit
© *Mara Berendt Friedman 2006, WM'09*

Another World is Possible

Another world is possible.
We can dream it in, with our eyes
open to this Beauty, to all
that Earth gives each of us, each day
those miracles of dark and light—
*rainlight, dawn, sun moon snow, stormgrey
and the wide fields of night always
somewhere opening their flower-
stars*—this, this! Another world is

possible. With river and bird
sweet and free without fear, without
minds blind to harmony, to how
we can hold. We have been too long
spoiled greedy children of Earth,
life of rocks and creatures
slipping out of our careless hands.
We must stand now and learn to love
as a Mother loves her child, each
cell of her, each grain of her, each
precious heartbeat of her that is
ourselves, our path and our journey
into our dream of future, where
another world is possible
cradling this one in its arms.

© *Rose Flint 2005, WM'09*

the earth i love

you are the earth i love. hillocks,
ravines, arches, tangled underbrush.
i billow over, gently sweep you cool.
fall into your upturned fronds, fill
your rose-mouths with rain. softly
i speckle you with snowdrops, then
lie upon you, thick and gold as sun.
your misty scent rises: berries and peat
moss, pinesap and stream. i curve to
your contours, eddy in nooks, rush
up to bend back your grasses, tumble
your stones. i circle your roots and
climb. you lift. bend. spread. open. i
build and swell, headfirst to part your
branches, tremble the limbs, sway the
nests. birds startle up. your hundred
beating wings embrace the sky.

© *Natasha J. Bruckner 2005, WM'09*

Crossroads © *Tina L. Freimuth 1996, Back Cover Art, WM'09*

2010 Theme:
Reinvent the Wheel

Firedancer ¤ *Teresa Wild 2007, Front Cover Art, WM'10*

We'Moon 2010 is a wake up call. In recent years, our themes have honed in on womyn's creative response to the planetary urgency of these times. Now as life-support systems continue to break down and reel out of control on a global scale, we are called to *Reinvent the Wheel* to restore balance for survival of life on earth.

As of this writing, the international economy is in collapse; global war, terror, poverty, hunger, disease, the threat of nuclear and natural disasters are on the rise; and the ability of the planet to support life is breaking down all over.

And at the same time. . .

The rise in ecological awareness, green technologies, environmental justice, holistic healing, natural foods and medicines, earth-based spirituality, indigenous and women's wisdom traditions, leadership by and for the people—all these energies are seismic shifts in consciousness. The polarity is beginning to shift back toward a more life-affirming stance with a growing commitment to clean up our act on a global scale. As the ground shifts beneath us, we are being called to create a new way of being that supports a whole and healthy planet.

Where will the spin of the wheel stop? Can we hold the balance? Only time will tell which way the tide is turning.
excerpt, Introduction to the Theme

I speak of total revolution
and must therefore
turn around.
excerpt ¤ Elizabeth Page Roberts 2008, WM'10

find
the womyn
who goes back
to change
the future
¤ *Patti Sinclair 2007,
WM'10*

Pua Mana
© *Lisa Seed 2007, WM'10*

Reaching Hands
¤ *Janaia Donaldson 2002 WM'10*

O Goddesses of The Great Round!
Gaia, Mother Nature, Changing Woman
We are in awe of your mighty spinning
Your Great Cycles of Life/Death/Re-birth
Up and Down and Around
Fortuna and Tyche—Mothers of Destiny
Norns and Moerae—The Three Fates
Arianrhod—Keeper of the Silver Star-Wheel
Kali—Time Dancer, Goddess of the Karmic Wheel
Help us repair the world
Reinvent the human spin
Even as we swing round toward the unthinkable
Help us to trust in your Wholeness.

© Bethroot Gwynn 2008, WM'10

La Fortuna *© Luz-Maria López 2007, WM'10*

The Beginning
© Jeannine Chappell 2003, WM'10

Be the Goddess

In this time of the Great Shift,
Let us make love without regret
No love is wasted.
Let us sing the old songs again.
Let us remember how to be
Magical creatures,
Animals of light,
Creating new life
In the spirit of our ancestors who loved us.

excerpt ¤ Silvie Jensen 2007, WM'10

Arch Dancer © Clio Wondrausch 2004, WM'10

Hold me, rock,
in the sacred shape
of compassion.

Help me remember
I am only Light
borrowing this flesh
for one brief moment,
one brief life.

*excerpt © Wendy Brown-Báez
2005, WM'10*

Infinity © *Lindy Kehoe 2005, WM'10*

Relationship Advice

It works really well to see your lover—
new lover or partner of 10, 20, 30 plus years—
as a young deer   or a bandicoot
some animal small and wild but curious enough
to stop and sniff the air in your direction
willing in complete stillness
to come close to your outstretched hand

    DO NOT REACH TO PAT OR PET OR STROKE
stay in unknowing
stay in surrender
stay in the soft rhythm of breathing wonder

It also works well to imagine you have become lost
in a country where no one speaks your language
Be utterly grateful for a smile
for the tender weathered hands
offering you a bowl of something unrecognizable
    that steams scents mysterious and delicious

You will be a child again in this country
    watching all the things you cannot understand
    amazed that you have landed in beginning again
Don't make believe that the story is about you
    that you are chosen to be on a quest
    that there are dragons of which you need to rid this kingdom

No   instead take in the syllables offered to you
    hold them with your tongue   lumpy and awkward
    like stones or pieces of stew
You may gag a little   we all do
Accept kindness and coaxing
and a gentle clean cloth soaking up inevitable tears
Soon   you will speak   whole   words

© Miriam Dyak 2008, WM'10

Shattered Mirrors

i will turn to meet my destiny,
   reflected in shattered mirrors.
heart broken open,
   i will pick up the pieces
no matter how sharp
   to reflect
   what is neglected
   in dark corners.
wounded, light-deprived,
   with prayerful hands i'll
   recycle devastation to
   nourish new life.
art, like gardening,
   is an act of faith and healing,
   shining for the world.
as Mystery's greater
   than the sum of all suffering,
   i will trust to Love.

¤ *Mimi Foyle 2008, WM'10*

Pema's Garden © *Beth Lenco 2005, WM'10*

Estrella at Home ◻ *Dolphin 2008, WM'10*

Bicycle Solutionary © *Emily Butterfly 2008, WM'10*

Letter from Gaia

In your living spaces, watch
for the mirror movements
of global breadth. Respond

as if every small movement
of twig or feather
mattered to every being. This

is the way
of all of my moving:
all effects and constructs,
all destructs and rebuilds:
ant hill, turtle egg,
avalanche.

And what will you birth?
For you, I will open
my deep chasms of fire
and microbial pools, groan
my mothering womb
chorus of species
song to bring the you
of all you are
into Be.

Wear green, spring green
thoughts, eat green at every
meal, bleed green blood,
photosynthesize
the green shift of life
into your deepest cell.

Sleep green in and under
green. Feed your eyes
with green. Breathe
the new of green.
Tell others.

© *Kate Rose Bast 2008, WM'10*

Spirit of the Mustang
© *Cathy McClelland 2008, WM'10*

Mothering the Fire Egg
© *Lisa Noble 2004, Back Cover Art, WM'10*

We'Moon 2011

Gaia Rhythms for Womyn

From Small Seeds   © *Anna Oneglia 2000*

GROUNDSWELL

From Small Seeds
© *Anna Oneglia 2000, Front Cover Art, WM'11*

2011 Theme: Groundswell

The Groundswell theme is inspired by Tarot card #11, Strength. A shift in consciousness is happening worldwide, a tectonic shift of great consequence—people are drawing on strengths that come, not from powers at the top, but from the suppressed. The emerging leadership of women, girls, elders and indigenous wisdom traditions marks a return toward the divine Mother in all her manifestations. A universal cry is arising from the deep well of unmet needs in the world—crying out anew for Mother Earth/Mother Nature, Great Mother of All!

A New World is Coming! The groundswells toward sustainable innovation are palpable, in city and countryside, around the world. People are raising bees on rooftops in New York City. Urban farms are sprouting; restaurants, schools, prisons are growing their own organic gardens. The emerging focus on local food and traditional farming methods is re-connecting people with the soil from which our nourishment comes.

We'Moon 2011 celebrates upwellings of strength and hope rippling throughout the world. Art and writing in these pages remind us how precious is the natural world, how it sources us in our work to preserve it. We highlight groundswells of innovation: e.g., village women solar engineers in India, Wwoofers learning permaculture, creative protests against the war machine. Ancient goddesses are springing out of the museums to join in the dance of Liberation!

We'Moon's 30 year legacy is rooted in these kinds of movements for radical change, and in a depth of Spirit which leads with the heart. Our artists and writers remind us of the fierce strength of Motherlove, of loving relationship, the connections that hold true beyond life, the embrace of Mother Earth.

excerpt, Introduction to the Theme

Crossroads of Consciousness

There's a great wave rising
I feel it climbing
up my back, through my spine
exploding the once
closed doors of my heart

I'm preparing to take flight.
The winds are adrifting
shifting my sight
I see through old eyes
these new times.

excerpt ▢ Lena Moon 2004, WM'11

Endless Surge
▢ *Jeanette M. French 2008, WM'11*

Strength © Angie Lazaro 1997, WM'00

Oh Mother Earth!
We feel the groundswell
of your mighty changes.
We are grateful to be carried along
on the current of your embrace.
We pledge our own momentum toward
harmony among all your creatures,
and restoration of this precious planet
and her life-forms.

© Bethroot Gwynn 2008, WM'11

Prayer © Cathy McClelland 2009, WM'11

My Tribe Through Darkness Comes Shining

When all is covered with dark lies
thick like debris from fallen towers
my people pick up hearts.

When all that is shown is tinted
with black greed and stained with blood from false wars
my people wipe away tears.

When even food is fake and whole forests fall like leaves
and great ocean whales can barely breathe
my people still sing from the beach.
They sing a humble song with full voices
crying out for the wisdom any creature will share.

My people are reapers of the waste of humankind,
willing to take anything tossed aside
and build with it a temple.

My people see in every scrap
a glimmer of the miracle
of creation to be brought forth through their hands.
Bring it on then, I say, let it all fall down
into our laps, into our receiving hands,
into our welcoming hearts.

We'll make a new world out of anything
You give us.

© Carol Bridges 2004, WM'11

Jennifer Loves Her Kids
© Anne-Rosemary Conway 1998, WM'07

Woman of Spirit © Dorrie Joy 2007, WM'11

This World

This is Feminism now:
becoming Sisterhood—
politician, priestess and
protester working together,

sharing what it means
to be Woman, everywhere.
Our linked hands and
strong hearts are a power:
the Goddess is returning
through each one of us

and we are bringing
deep changes.
We are dreaming in
a future that gives hope
to the World, we are
women's voices rising:
strident, beautiful—
and heard.

excerpt © Rose Flint 2009, WM'11

The Bordercrossing Starchild Mission

we are the bridge constructors
the ones who stand between!
between the old and the new

we are the edge dancers
and strong bridges we shall be;
to hold the world
between the stars

I want to be a bridge
over the roaring floods
between the countries
of yesterday
and the future lands
I see the coming change
ah—it gonna be furious!

come!
you unborn children of us
set over!
—and call us home
from the other side.
we need to get grounded
to build the bridges—
for you to walk straight
into safe lands

we are the edge dancers
and bridge constructors
we shall be!
we gonna take responsibility
for our unborn children's
future.

◻ *Lela Engels 2004, WM'11*

Fire © Monika Steinhoff 1998, WM'11

Sub-Saharan Children ▫ *Bethroot Gwynn 1962, WM'11*

Give Her an Inch, She'll Take a Mile!

Offer a girl schooling, and she'll likely take home more than an education. According to reports in World Pulse magazine, investing in schooling for girls in developing countries creates exponential growth for her and her community. The educated woman invests 90% of her income in her family (compared to 35% for men). With 7 years of schooling: she'll likely birth 2.2 fewer children and marry 4 years later in life. For each extra year of primary school, her earnings can rise 20%.

In the words of Sejal Hathi, 17 year-old founder and president of Girls Helping Girls, "… a girl possesses the key to her community's development and an extraordinary power to effect social change. Girls are the Movers and Shakers!"

▫ *Barbara Dickinson 2009, WM'11*

Wwoof!

"Wwoof! Wwoof!" was the greeting barking at my inbox all last year. I fielded over 200 requests from potential volunteers who found us through WWOOF (World Wide Opportunities on Organic Farms), and by the end of October, some 50 women had passed through our land. Some were students, some travelers, many had lost jobs or were looking at bleak recession-time work options. All had found a way to change their current circumstance into an opportunity for learning about sustainable living. They arrived in ones, twos or threes, pitched tents and settled in for a few weeks of hard work and big joy. Each had their own skills, interests and challenges. Sherri was good with a hammer, wanted to learn about building with earth. Melissa got poison oak-ed, skunked, and somehow transformed. Gin gifted us a magical holy tomato mural, Lucie stole everyone's heart. Sam canned gallons of tomatoes in every imaginable form, and mistook clay for flour,

making for some very sculptural muffins. Cricket kept returning, always quietly on task.

Days we worked in the garden, on natural building projects, fencing and irrigation. Nights we made amazing meals, music, art and laughter. No one left unchanged; for many, working in a predominantly female space was new and hugely empowering. As for me, I now hold a precious optimism for the groundswell of young folks willing and able to tackle the future's challenges with the tools of permaculture, serious about living in balance with the earth.

▫ *Myshkin 2009, WM'11*

Women Mend the Earth
© *Toni Truesdale 2009, Back Cover Art, WM'11*

In the Herstory of We'Moon, we started conjuring We'Moon themes in terms of Tarot in the '90s with each edition's named theme. Following We'Moon chronology, WM'90 was paired with IX the Crone card in Tarot (which also corresponded numerologically with WM'09). This overlapping of themes in We'Moon numerology (based on the last two digits) also occurred between WM'01 and WM'10 (X) and between WM'92 and WM'11 (XI). These three years of doubling up on We'Moon themes meant that in the 22 years we have been using We'Moon Tarot, we have missed three of the 22 cards in the Tarot Major Arcana. Ironically, We'Moon themes only got as far as the Moon card in Tarot (XVIII)! That leaves the Sun (XIX), Judgement (XX) and the World (XXI) cards still to be explored. . .with many years to go before we get there! Looking into the crystal ball of the Tarot oracle, it looks like there are some challenging transformations coming up in the meantime, starting with WM'12 (XII The Hanged One), which we are translating as "Chrysalis," the theme for We'Moon 2012, followed by We'Moon 2013 (XIII Death), which we might translate as "Letting Go" or "Trance End Dance."

The sequel to this 30 year romp through We'Moon Tarot is an open question. You might have to wait until We'Moon 2019, 2020, and 2021 to get to the Sun (XIX), Judgement (XX) and the World (XXI) with us! Drawing from the first 30 years of We'Moon, here are some clues about how we might read the final three cards in this cycle of We'Moon Tarot:

XIX. THE SUN:
Center/
Life force/
Energy
Source

Women of the Earth
© Leah Marie Dorion 2008, WM'11

XX. JUDGEMENT:
Lightning
Strike/
Rainbow
Vision/
Heart Songs

Oya *© Sandra Stanton 1999, WM'10*

XXI. THE WORLD:
Jumping
Through
the Hoop/
All One

Embrace
© Deborah Koff-Chapin 1992, WM'04

111. Gaia Rhythms for Womyn
- Wheel of Life
- Wheel of the Year
- Wheel of the Heavens

Born to Drum © *Annie Ocean 2008, WM'10*

The Dance of Changing Woman

Goddess of the seasons, of the constellations turning above, of sunrise and sunset, of moon's waning and waxing—she governs all of the mysteries of death and rebirth. She is the spring becoming summer turning towards fall and dying into winter's cold, the continual dance of birth, growth, death and the restoration to rebirth again.

She is the eternal rhythm and cycle of the moon, the hanging of the seasons, the ebb and flow of the tide. We live in a universe where everything changes. We are Changing Woman.

excerpt © *Beth Beurkens 2008, WM'10*

Life Cycles

Go deeply and remember the web of creation
that holds us all in fluctuating harmony
one moment as every moment
holds the force of ancient filaments
weaving light through and in and out your soul
as oceans of time take tide below the moon

¤ Emily Rebecca Tool 2004, WM'08

Through the Rabbit Hole

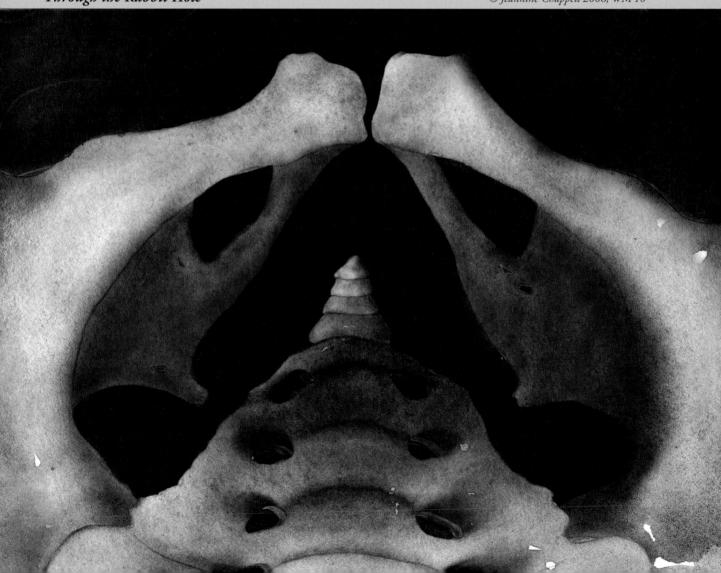

Birthing a Dragon

She walks
> with the moon
> in her belly

Along the
> river's edge
> before dawn

Lifting a
> dragon from
> folds of skin

She moves
> low and sweet
> her tail on the wind.

¤ *Tami Lynn Kent 2001, WM'03*

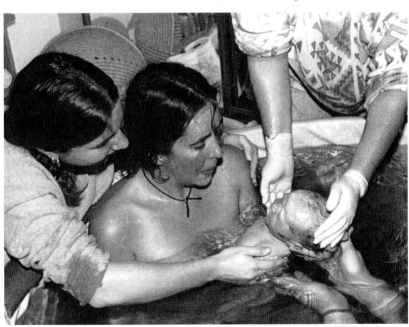

Veiled © Annie Ocean 1989, WM'89

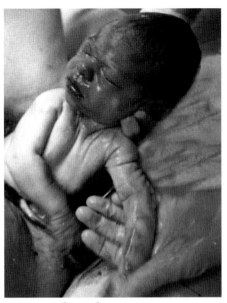

She Who Emerges
© *Annie Ocean 1989, WM'90*

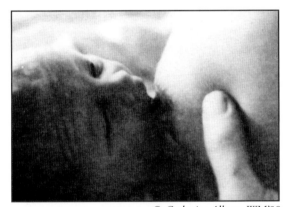

© *Catherine Allport, WM'89*

For Eva

You were born underwater
surging from me like a wave
into a world between
the secret dark ocean of my womb
and the atmosphere
of the world without.
Serene, you looked up at me
through the water's surface,
your mother in a world
you had not yet entered;
the pearly umbilical rope
still linking you to my depths,
No longer curled
in your amniotic sea,
the infinity of water
still cradled you,
was still all you knew.
So we made it gentle,
your incarnation, your transition
from ocean to ether,
spirit to body, within to without;
welcoming you
with warmth and water
in hushed darkness and firelight,
while a comet blazed above us
like some holy star
telling the world of your birth.

© *Corey Alicks Lie-Nielson 1999, WM'02*

Dawn Unfolding © *Carrie Gaylord 2001, WM'02*

Left to Right Top: **Arungi** © *Lindy Kehoe 2005, WM'09;* **Nelle** © *Sharon Hart 2000, WM'02;* © *Nancy B. Holley 2002, WM'11*

Middle: **Neeram Salem** ¤ *Eve-Marie Roy 2007, WM'10*

Left to Right Bottom: **Pen Pal to my Soul** © *Joyce Brady 1997, WM'06;* **First Fish** © *Laura Irene Wayne 1993, WM'94*

Watch Me Fly © *Catherine Rains 2001, WM'05*

Ways of Seeing

In the car after the operation my niece,
not yet three, notices my tears. *You crying*
she asks. I nod, try to smile.
I'll make you laugh she tells me as she sticks
her fingers in her mouth and pulls her lips wide,
sticks out her tongue, crosses her eyes.
Despite the incision,
despite the babies I'll never bear,
I laugh. *Don't worry* I hear as I close my eyes.
There's an angel beside you. "There is?"
Yes, she says in that *of course*
kind of way only 3 year olds can manage.
"Where is it?" Frustrated now she groans,
Right there and points to my left side.
I smile. We ride along in silence.
Oh, It moved over there, pointing
now over my shoulder. *She's blue,*
Chloe states with absolute faith.
Her mother and I exchange glances.
My heart, itself exploding and blue,
beats to the rhythm of a three year old,
reflecting a world in which everything
is common, everything possible,
everything a promise.

         ▢ *Joyce Hayden 2007, WM'09*

The Girl Effect

The Revolution will be led
by a twelve-year-old girl.

         www.GirlEffect.org, WM'11

Walking Tall © *Modupe 2000, WM'11*

meditation for growing

and then walking in a small short stepping dance
and not just turning my back
but waving and pogo hop hop
dancing and growing big and bigger
until I feel my skin on the sky and my hands
palm up touching each star from under the night
part that is dark and deep and even bigger
than the end of my skin
pulled silky and tight
even bigger than i thought
i was

         © *Nancy Blair, WM'90*

Path to the Heart of the Woods
© *Paige Sullivan 1994, WM'07*

Courtney, Age 3, and Pippy, Seaside
© *Deb Meadows-West, WM'90*

159

Sisters (mural detail) © Robin Corbo 2007, WM09; **Urban Priestess: Cultivating Self-Love** © Mira Michelle 2004, WM'07; **Juggler** © Anna Oneglis 2004, WM'11; **Earth Mother** © Cola Smith 2007, WM'09

160

Clicking Stones

i move through fogs of mystery
with tiny steps
on the way to meet myself
in a clearing between woods,
out we step into
springtime,
swollen with life.

with a deep bow,
i hand myself four stones
from the river bottom
water worn and round,
achingly smooth.

i hand myself back,
a string of corn, red corn,
with a slow smile
and look long in my face
to see who is there.

i see myself
from child to mountaintop.
i see myself
covered in a blanket woven
of wildflowers and feathers
that i watched myself make.

i am holding babies
and riding horses,
i am holding palmfulls of ocean.

i am moving with myself,
running together
quietly and quickly
through the forest
to a place where the creek rushes
and the sun sings on our
bodies
as we promise
to be sisters always,
connected at the heart
with tangled curling
deep green vine
so that we can always
find each other.

and then we walk
through the forest
clicking stones.

© *Pandora Cate Judge 1993, WM'94*

Urban Priestess:
To Leave Your Mark
© *Mira Michelle 2004, WM'07*

Heart

It has to do with heart.
Her life is different because she is different.
She makes up her own mind.
Her life births a fresher start.
Old wave delusion shatters.
No time to borrow.
No more straight line dancing.
No more angry days.
Death of separation.
She lives, escapes suffocation.
Freedom from new age world, old world cage.
Freedom from new world order, old world lie.
Freedom from delusion.
What she takes is hard to do.
What she does is hard to take.
It has to do with heart

© *Gentle Doe 1992, WM'95*

Amazons/High Risk © *Max Dashu 2001, WM'02*

"Labor is like a woman's journey . . .
to find her dream,
her power,
to unravel the mysteries
of her own birth.
She goes there with courage
and then with fear
utter despair
pain and sorrow . . .
and then, intense joyous powerful.
personal emergence, ecstasy,
She is her own child.
She is the fiery river
through which the new soul flows.

We, who are called to attend her,
are bound by sacred duty and ancient tradition
to sooth and protect and reassure
in these places of power and pain.
Our hands on her body . . . our eyes, fully open to
her eyes, deep as any ocean.
Our songs reflect the rhythms of heartbeat . . .
the music of uterine contraction expansion
of breath
of awesome beauty
of fetal silence . . .

Valerie Sonnenberg, WM'89

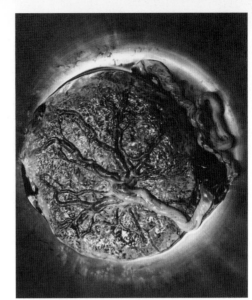

Placenta, Tree of Life
© *Annie Ocean 1989, WM'89*

Placenta Means Cake

Placenta, the original birthday cake, was eaten by early birthers. The placenta, full of nutrients, nourished and sustained the mother—nine months of feeding the fetus from her body—and revitalized her after labor.

The long-established ritual of having a birthday cake has been subconscious to the modern womon. By symbolically eating our placenta every year, we celebrate womon giving life through her body.

© *Annie Ocean 1989, WM'90*

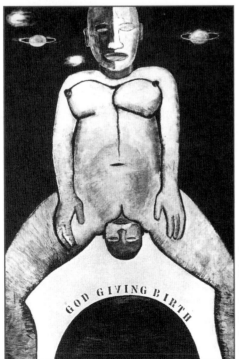

God Giving Birth © *Monica Sjöö 1968, WM'94*

© *Dwayne Campbell 1988, WM'90*

162

Mother and Daughter
© Megaera 1993, WM'06

Ma

The word for mother, world wide, is based on *ma*. *Ma* is the earliest form of the Indo-European root-word for mother, *mâter*, which is reflected in the Latin, *mäter*; the Greek, *métèr*; and the prehistoric Germanic, *möthar*. These, in turn, have become *madre* in Spanish and Italian, *mére* in French, *mae* in Portuguese; *mite'ra* in modern Greek; *mutter* in modern German, *moeder* in Dutch, *moder* in Swedish, *mör* in Danish, *mör* in Norwegian, and *mother* in English. Mother is *mat'* in Russian, *matka* in Polish and Czech, *majka* in Serbo-Croatian, *mayka* in Bulgarian, *anya* in Hungarian, *ema* in Estonian, *mate* in Latvian, *nana* in Albanian, *ima* in Hebrew, *anne* in Turkish and *omi* in classic Arabic. In the many languages of Sub-Saharan Africa, too, *ma* is prevalent; *mama* in Ibo and Hausa, *mma* in South African Sotho, *mbuta* in the Congo and *inate* in Ethiopian Amharic.

The similarity holds in Asia as well: *aamaa* in Nepali, *mae* in Thai, *nanay* in Philippino, *omoni* in Korean, *chomo* in Tibetan, *moqing* in Mandarin and *mama* in Cantonese. In the Telgu and Tamil languages of India, mother is *amma*, and she is *mata* in Hindi. In Pakistani, mother is *man*, which means "moon" and "wisdom."

Mmmm, Mmma, mmmaa, mmaaaaaa. *Ma! Ma*, as in "maternal." *Ma*, as in "mammary." *Ma*, as in "mammal." *Mama* means "mother's breasts" in many places, and *ma* refers to "milk" as well as "mother."

It is interesting to note that our galaxy is not only named for milk, it actually *means* milk. Galaxy is from the Greek, *gala*, "mother's milk," referring to Gala-Tea, the Milk Goddess, the galactic mother in classical Greek mythology.

excerpt © Mama Donna Henes 1992, WM'03

Mother
¤ Kit Skeoch 2001, WM'03

The Kiss © Margriet Seinen 1999, WM'11

Mother Dance

Small toes bruise my knees
Tangled together we sleep
Seed and husk.
Until star fish fists climb my hair
And monkey grasp pinches the back of my hand.
Love bites my fingers with two new teeth.

I am here for you to push against,
Sometimes shattering as you grow
Breaking my shell
Excavating dawn
To the tune of wonder hatching.

© Selina Maria di Girolamo 1998, WM'00

Rowan and Red Thread

If I think back into my emergence
from my Mother's womb I feel the miracle
in the centre of my body as if I held within me
a chalice filled with fire. My daughter flamed out
on the red life thread, as I had done,
as my Mother did, and beyond her all the mothers
in the clan—some clear and close and others gone
into the mists—reaching back into the land,
passing on this fine red cord that binds us,
turns us inside out.

And what we make between us down these years
of generations, passing on the gifts—strength,
red hair or black, love of cats, second sight,
a need for making art or policy or healing—
is a chain, each link as intricate as Celtic knotwork
or the stepping reel of a circle dance that turns
the wheel of inner space, the centre, where we hold.

Red cord of life: mother, daughter, mother
Red thread wound between the rings of stone,
the wells and hillsides of the birthing land;
our bloodline winding back and going on
beyond the distance, beyond the patterned dance
we name our lives within this time, this space,
this tiny moment of the world's destiny:
mother, daughter, mother—red thread
strong as mountain, deep as earth's bright heart.

¤ *Rose Flint 2006, WM'08*

In Full Bloom

Our single purpose
is to magnify that
Light
we share between us.
© *Mimi Foyle 2005, WM'08*

Let Us Run © *Janet Pearson 2006, WM'08*

164

I am my own sure

I am my own shore
I am my own solid ground
I am my only ocean

I alone am filled
With all forms and color
All glistening edges and phantasm

I will carry my own weight,
I will bear time
I will be my own light
To see with and grow by

I will be my own water
soothing my burning wants
And dissolving my salted drops
Of worn and outgrown sorrows

I will be my own earth
and hold the promise of birth,
Cradle the tender growing seeds
Of my flowering days
Crooning from soil,
Dark and holy,
An inevitable surging of renewed life

Priestess © *Carol Wylie 1998, WM'01*

I will be my own air for sacred prayer of breath
A chance or two for flight
And when grounded merely by gravity
A soaring heart's place

I will be my own fire, a force to burn down hatred
And clear the way for hope
I will blaze for freedom
And with endless heat and orange rage
Raze the killer constructs
And kindle kindness, fuel justice,
From flame, make peace.

¤ *Liz Roberts 2005, WM'07*

It's Written All Over Her
© *Sierra Lonepine Briano 1995, WM'09*

Seneca Women's Peace Encampment
© *Shoshana Rothaizer, WM'86*

First Hot Flash

l couldn't have chosen a better moment—sitting around after dinner at Fly Away Home, with two matriarchs and two maidens, talking. We have just finished our first day of We'Moon Weaving Circle, where we'moon in the community help choose art and writing for the **Cycles!** issue of We'Moon.

We are talking about E-waves and ears and forests and follicles—I interrupt the hot discussion with a hot flash. "Is anyone else feeling really warm in here?" I have already taken my shirt off and am sitting at the table barebreasted. Everyone else is fully clothed. It is the first night of Spring. There is no fire in the wood stove. The question dangles in the air for a moment before the answer slowly dawns in smiles: "hot flash!" We are all kind of thrilled—like when a daughter shows her first bloods. How appropriate, with all this We'Moon cycles material fresh like sugar plums dancing through our heads.

It's almost like dessert. We get up from the table and go into the Inner Below—the circle sanctuary center of this round house (where our extended community of womyn on land gathered just last night for a Spring Equinox ceremony). I lie down. Someone lights a candle. Someone hands me a flower—fresh daffodil. For an instant, I feel like a corpse, laying there with my hands folded on my chest holding this flower. I pull out a piece of lava flow fresh from Kileaua that I received as part of a Candlemas initiation ceremony in Hawaii. It is to remind me that I am a priestess of the sacred fire, and that my job on earth is simply to help tend the flame of life. I put it on my womb and ask them to lay their hands on me and feel my fire.

Goddess of Pentacles
© Selina Maria Di Girolamo 2000, WM'02

They hold their hands above my womb, as if warming them over a fire. For what seems like a long time, we sit there in silence, just feeling the fire inside. I can feel the energy emanating from me and being nurtured and acknowledged by them. It's as if I now have my own alternative energy source that is self-sustaining—after 33 years of renewing it each month with my bloods. We sing: "I am woman Giving Birth to Myself," over and over, rising and falling in waves—the birthing song of a Matriarch. I am bathed in the affirmation of sound and touch. I begin to feel this circle of we'moon around me as a womb. . . and I am in it. I am in the womb of the Great Mother. I am being held by her, taking nourishment through my center, I am connected to Source.

◻ *Musawa 1993, WM'94*

Laksmi: Goddess of Abundance
© Hrana Janto 1995, WM'09

When friends of mine turn 50 and start calling themselves Crones, I want to say, Wait! When do we get to celebrate the full flowing of our power as mature womyn? Somehow, the stage between "motherhood" and "old age" has been skipped! No wonder the "mid-life crisis" or "empty nest syndrome" or the "menopausal years" can be so difficult for womyn. At the very time that men are supposed to be at the height of their career paths in the patriarchal culture, it is supposed to be all over for womyn. When the average womyn's life cycle ends at 40 or 50, it makes sense that one becomes a Crone at that age. Now that the life cycle may be extended an average of 30 or 40 more years (varying greatly according to inherited or environmental factors, class, race, culture, Earth orientation, etc.), wemoon have more freedom to develop independently of our place in the reproductive cycle.

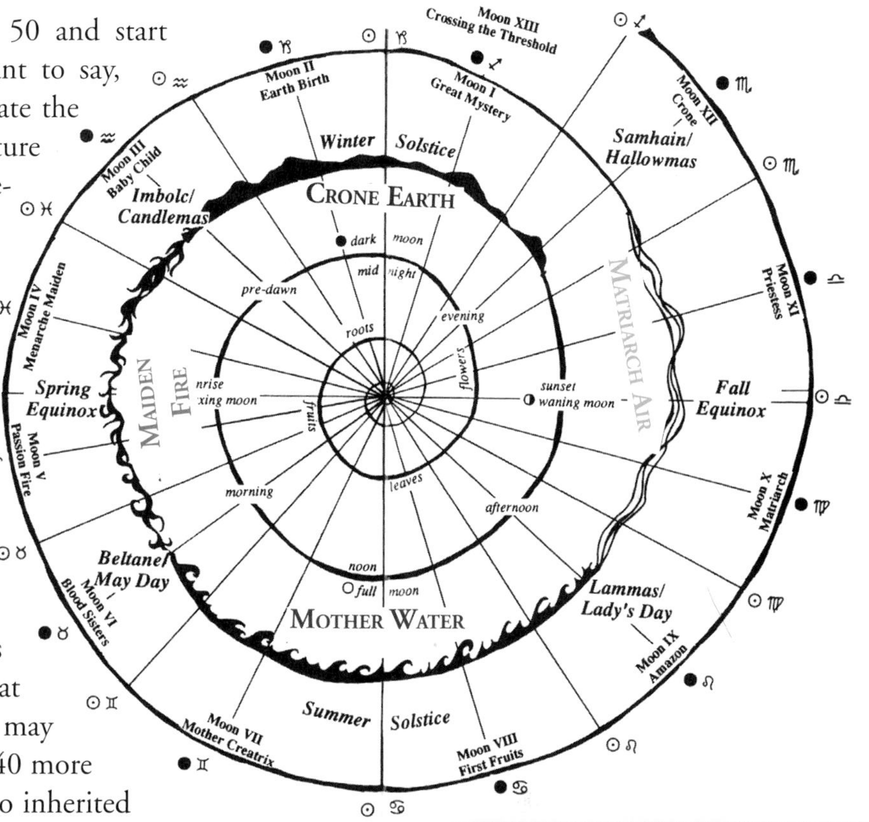

The triple goddess does not disappear in this model—she reappears in each of the four stages, allowing for more depth of development in each. A "Maiden" is not just a sexual being—she is also a baby, she has a childhood, and she grows into her identity which includes, but is not limited to, her sexuality. A "Mother" is not just "with child"—she may also be a lover and a creative being who works and is fruitful.

I Must Be Dreaming
© Stephanie Gaydos 1989, WM'97

We need to find our own names for a womyn becoming whole, living her truth, and being in her power. We call her "Amazon" for her strength and independence. We call her "Matriarch" for her ability to shape the world she lives in. We call her "Priestess" for her work on the inner plane. A "Crone" is one who is wise in going between the worlds. She also manifests in three phases: she is an old womyn aging, she journeys into the unknown and death, and she becomes one with the Earth, the source, the void—the great mystery from which comes renewal.

© Musawa 1994, WM'95

Blood Keeper
© Clio Wondrausch 2005, WM'07

Diagram labels:

CRONE EARTH — Winter Solstice — MAIDEN FIRE — MATRIARCH AIR — MOTHER WATER — Fall Equinox — Spring Equinox — Summer Solstice

Moon I Great Mystery — Moon II Earth Birth — Moon III Baby Child — Moon IV Menarche Maiden — Moon V Passion Fire — Moon VI Blood Sisters — Moon VII Mother Creatrix — Moon VIII First Fruits — Moon IX Amazon — Moon X Matriarch — Moon XI Priestess — Moon XII Crone — Moon XIII Crossing the Threshold

Samhain/Hallowmas — Imbolc/Candlemas — Beltane/May Day — Lammas/Lady's Day

dark moon — mid night — pre-dawn — roots — evening — flowers — sunrise — rising moon — sunset — waning moon — fruits — leaves — morning — afternoon — noon — full moon

Village Elder, Thailand
© Angie Coffin Heiney 1998,

The Seriously Pissed-Off Grannies

The Seriously Pissed-Off Grannies organized to protest the surge of U.S. troops in Iraq in 2007. A group of "seasoned" women, all grandmothers or grandmotherly age, handcuffed ourselves to the doors of the Federal Building in Portland, Oregon, in nonviolent civil disobedience.

The Furies, Seekers of Justice
© Bedo 2002, WM'11

We were outraged that our government was sending still more of our grandchildren to kill still more children of other women. TV cameras filmed security officers leading silver-haired women off in handcuffs.

Enlivened by our experience at the federal building, we added a few grandpas and began picketing a military recruiting office. We blocked doors with our rocking chairs, rode our bicycles up and down the sidewalk, used pre-school paint to put red handprints on windows. Police cars carrying our rocking chairs made the evening news.

When our case came to trial, we educated a room full of potential jurors about why we were protesting war. The prosecutor was caught off-guard by four highly-skilled attorneys from the National Lawyers Guild who gladly volunteered their time. When the jury quickly found us not-guilty, we made front page news.

The Seriously Pissed-Off Grannies train younger generations in civil disobedience, support nonviolent struggles for justice, and work to end wars.

¤ *DeEtte Beghtol Waleed 2009, WM'11*

What is a wise woman? One who knows how to sit out a squall. One who knows that a squall will get worse and the rain wand wind will be fierce but then it will taper down and with patience on the part of the wise woman the squall will stop momentarily. This will give her a short break so that she can go where she plans to and get there before the next squall begins. Patience, endurance, and being able to stay the course are attributes of a crone. Having gone through squalls many times before, she knows she can survive. She knows not to go out too soon, that sometimes squalls follow each other in rapid sucession. She is alert to all possibilities. Squalls between friends also require patience. A wise friend will not allow herself to be battered by hard rain, strong wind. She will wait out her friend's anger or walk away, waiting until the anger passes, until the sun comes out and they can talk.

Crones know squalls will pass. That the weather of life keeps changing. Not that the weather can't be upsetting but it's not the end, though it may seem so. From many years of variable weather—storms and sunshine—crones know, and this knowledge gives them a solid place to stand.

¤ *Ruth Mountaingrove 1997, age 74, WM'98*

Riding the Wave © Jakki Moore 2009, WM'11

Roots

Mary, great–grandmother
solid and strong as a rock
supple as roses . . .
I see you stand in your warm kitchen
growing sweet potatoes in jam jars . . .
I cannot remember your voice
only your hands, and your eyes
smiling at me from photographs
or the oven of my dreams
What happened to make the women
who came after you
touchy as hothouse plants,
fragile as greenhouses?
yet they too have survived, as women do,
and I dig my air–roots into your firm flesh
as I did when eight, burrowing for a kiss,
and stare at the calendar in your kitchen
moon–shaped signs dating back
  five thousand years—
   or even more
and wish I too might flower
  and bear fruit

© Ellen S. Jaffee 1996, WM'98

Grandmother Edith
© Kali 1990, WM'98

102 Years and Looking Forward
© Susan Kullmann 2005, WM'09

What will I do with the rest of my life that I'll be able at the end to call real living? Simple being, blissful simplicity, every second. Peace and quiet and *knowing* . . .

mediate on the wonder and impossibility of life and the illusion of everything but Nature . . . to live among trees in the woods.

I want to ask old, old Nature. She might show me how to part with myself. Like a mother.   *© Moon 1997, WM'00*

169

Coming Migration

Deep bowl of winter night sky
arches high and away toward
a rosy stain in the west
pierced by brilliant Venus.
It will be snapping cold later
when the moon sets sail.

Over there my frail neighbor
like a bundled stick
slowly deliberately
performs her small but
important rituals outside at dusk.

Hugging her the other day
felt exactly like
holding a wild bird;
the vivid colors, the bright eyes
straight and softly curved bones
hollow and very light.

Pressing her gently
against me I felt
a rapid thrum;
a strange vibration
of birdlike circulation.

Fluttering she
cocked her head just so
to peer at me.
There it is again!
The tell-tail quiver of Spirit
and her coming migration.

© Rosemary Wyman 2002, WM'11

Crone Tree *© Carolyn Hillyer, WM'93*

Love is the Funeral Pyre
© *Durga Yael Bernhard 1999, WM'03*

Snake Dancing

After coffee,
I discovered a snakeskin
strung like laundry
over the morning glories,
and wondered how the snake
had done it,
this ballet of awakening.

Itchy first, around the eyes,
a blinking,
bits loosening by the nostrils,
a yawn
and stretch.
Then a muscles out of its sleeve
leaving old clothes where they lie.

It occurs to me
how effortlessly it can go.
Once the facial skin loosens,
cheek and
jaw skin shrink away nicely.
The rest just follows.

¤ *Suzanne Ghiglia 1991, WM'94*

© *Katheryn Rosenfield 1992, WM'94*

She Took Chris, Then Julie

Kali is on the prowl.
Watch out!—She springs without warning.
She has tasted fresh, young blood twice now among us.
Appetite whetted, She was not content with one ambush
not sated with one feast on healthy, vibrant woman flesh.
She struck again, aimed again deep into community heart
"Let me see," did She mutter through bloody fangs,
"where is the next, most robust morsel?"
Drunk, and hungry to eat promise again,
She sniffed the scent of joy
spit out the bitter suicide dregs of Her first kill
and, stealthy, crept among us—silent—
skilled in the art of surprise, drawn to pulsing happy vigor.

Not this one, we begged.
But Kali had made Her choice.
She let us touch and carry the body of our cherished friend,
watch irrevocable stillness,
the evolving purple, yellow, mottled bloom of cellular finish.
Then She insisted that we feed Her fiery maw
with this precious woman
who blazed into glory before our eyes.

Kali has only begun.
The two skulls around Her neck are a starter set.
She will be adding to Her necklace for years to come.
Old bones, wrinkled skin satisfy Her well enough,
they are Her staple fare.
But She went out of order,
broke into this clan and took our heirs.
This snatching of bright youth
Is aberration/Is outrage/Is Her prerogative
And we are stunned by her raw power, Her Absolute Mystery.
Shall we say Holy Mother? Can we say Blessed Be?

Ah, She is impeccable—this teacher of fierce lessons.
Now we know, are reminded.
No holds are barred. No one is safe.
The only promise is that we will, each one,
look into Her grinning face
whenever She says, and be taken into Her Joy.
Her Mystery. Her Holiness.
Her Strange Mothering.
Shall we say Mercy? Shall we say Love?

Blessed Be.

excerpt © *Bethroot Gwynn 1998, WM'03*

When I die, give my body to the wimmin
They'll Know what to do.

They'll Know how to hold it
And lovingly wash it
And bless it with herbs and oil.

They'll Know how to wrap it
In a simple woven cloth
And lay it to rest.

They'll Know how to drum out a beat
And chant low and throaty and let
It grow and growl and keen.

They'll Know how to dance me and
Sing me and laugh me into Her arms
And how to celebrate who I was.

They'll Know how to lay me in a
Shallow grave and cover me with leaves
And trace an ochre spiral on my brow.

They'll Know how to call the slugs
And worms to feast on my flesh
And return this which was only borrowed.

Give my body to the wimmin.
They'll Know what to do.

¤ *Rose Johnson 1993, WM'97*

Our bodies change... curve to wrinkle gold to grey. Quick, leaping pushing out to slow, inward seeing breath. Seed to flower to fruit to rot. The earth She is born dying. We are all old and young always learning who we are... That is what weaves us as one.

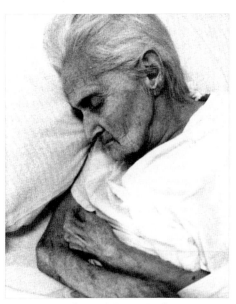

Claire Two Weeks Before Passing On
© *Jeanine Mooney 1992, WM'94*

Respect Death
the Great Relaxer
Nothing is
denied Her succor
excerpt ¤ Jem Mara 2008, WM'10

Matriarcial Grave © *Puma Lichtblau 1994, WM'02*

Silver's Grave © *Sequoia 1999, WM'01*
Grave dug by Southern Oregon wimmin;
grave art by Sequoia with help from Amara.

Mesa Verde Cliff Palace © *EagleHawk 2000, WM'05*

The Ridgeway Song

I walk the oldest road
the ridge to the river
above the tree line

I walk the great divide
blue sky on the one side
grey on the other
I journey through time

I walk the path of the ancestors
carved in memory
the path of the ancestors
carved in memory
carved in stone

time after time after time
layers of time gone by

step after step after step
I walk with the old ones

© *Witchhazel Wildwood 2000, WM'05*

Great Echo

There is a great echo, it is memory
in our bones, the curl of our hair
my grandmother keeps her curls in a box
on the third floor of a Manhattan apartment building
I wear my curls in the wild winds,
turning spirals with salt water
the grace of my lioness, flutter of my wings
I will have long gray curls one day
I will have a little girl with curls one day
we all wear each other's faces interchangeably
in this transference of lifetimes
my old roads are unknown to my new feet
separation is simply us moving back and forth
between parts of ourselves
no ending to the things begun
no answer to the question that propels us
through the beauty of this world
into the illumination of the next
my visions and memories are the same
my life is teaching me the words
to enable it to be a story which can be told
our journey brings us to the meeting place,
origin, the beginning
do not feel lost when you realize
you have made your way home.

© *Lisa Kagan 2009, WM'11*

The Premonition
© *Sara Glass 2007, WM'09*

172

Aditi, Goddess of the Luminous Void

Shamans speak of the void as a place of creation, unlimited possibilities. The Hindu goddess of the void, Aditi, is paradoxically also a sun deity. Her domain is "the nothing," no time and no space. She is the primordial womb from which all creation arises. They say she had no birth herself, yet is the origin of all things.

Aditi, goddess of the empty form, boundless with possibilities. Aditi speaks now from her place of the vast unlimited:

"I am the original manifestrix, the black being, womb of initiation in the luminous darkness.

You are from me. I welcome your visits to my velvety blackness. I am not just a one-time port of call. I am the repeat destination. I hold all and nothing. Stamp your feet. Unburden your heart. Crack open your head. I am the dreaded yet the necessary. Come, meet with me. Pour out all your troubles. They dissolve into the cosmic emptiness. Pick up something else while you're here. How about a little elixir of eternity, some medicine for your soul? Do not worry. That is my healing counsel. From the perspective of void, the vastness of creative forms, all is possible. If one way does not work, another will.

Let's talk about pain. Your fears. Your hollowness. Your loss and loneliness. Look inside me, now. Are you looking? Yes—see, pain is a device that keeps you distracted, keeps you off center. Sure, it tells you something is wrong, needs to heal, needs to change. But pain can

Bush Spirit
© *Durga Yael Bernhard 1990, WM'00*

Crow Mother, Her Eyes, Her Eggs
¤ *Meinrad Craighead 1991, WM'05*

create more pain. Leave it lay. Jump tracks. Get on the healing way, the path of infinite love. Here all things are possible, swimming and floating around in my void. Eventually it's time for labor, birth. You can release your pain in me or you can nurture and feed it. Your choice. There's a lot of life out there. Keep your focus on what you seek. Not on what you are missing.

The luminous void paints creation, breathes with wholeness, spaciousness: it supports and comforts you. It's your sacred well. Drink of the dark vastness and be healed. I am Aditi. I am the unborn who gives life to the world. Vaster than vast. You know me. All your yearnings and future possibilities rest in me.

Pray to me. Light a dark candle in your soul. I will find you. I never miss. Your breath is my trail to you."

© *Beth Beurkens 2007, WM'09*

the sickle moon shows
a crack in the sky
where the breath
of the Goddess
blows through.

excerpt © Erin Dragonsong 1998, WM'00

Spring

first warm day of spring

cantaloupe sky
end of day

standing on a hill
before the wide sea

the rush of day
gently falls off

like silk
from bare shoulders

a blessing of the breeze
a kiss upon my forehead

© Starr Goode, WM'91

Ritual ¤ Abby Mariah Wentworth 2002,

Summer

Nurture the Seeds © Joyce Radtke 1993, WM'03

Date with the Muse

The sun shines
in bright defiance
of the dark horizon
shadows wrestle
with the light
I am showing up
for my date with the muse
she is lounging
in the pear tree
discussing with the blossoms
the anticipated flavor
of the fruit.

excerpt © Lisa Kagan 2009, WM'11

Fall

Shades of Autumn
❑ *Michelle Wilkinson 2007, WM'10*

Today, the market's falling.
Autumn leaves are falling. It's beautiful.
Instructions for uprising
Coming down with falling leaves and
The waiting's almost done.
The second industrial revolution is the one against industry
Freeing us from the wars, the toxins, the domination
Free us like trees into sharing and seasons
And merciful silence.
Seeds: prepare yourselves for yourselves.
Friends: prepare yourselves like autumn silence falling
Walk out into the glittering groves in silence
We're told trust in god
But I swear allegiance to this earth
And the endlessness of life finding her way
Trust in bags of beans and rice
Gardens and gallons of olive oil
Trust in rain, community
In gravity, self sufficiency
We were always each others' social security

excerpt ❑ *Oak Chezar 2009, WM'11*

Winter

Darktime

So the way the lip of night
curls protectively around
starkling moon-grey days
doesn't have to be
evil.
Winter isn't evil.
The Dark gives rise to cusps,
to emergences,
a sweetly nestled
seedling cupped and precious
in the Dark Mother's
cavities.
Warm. Safe.
We revolve too hotly around
the sun,
value the detached
transcendence of
incandescent bulbs and
a certain maleness
   of solar authority
The Dark half of the year
Suits me just fine.
An incubation,
   A percolation.
Winter time.
The Dream Time.
Worms and calligraphy.
A quiet turning under,
the underbelly
A rich velvet basket,
   Stars and fog
tucked around
   the edges.
The Dark, my love, is a
Sweet loamy
Pocket for
Change-lings.

❑ *Shae Savoy 2009, WM'11*

Air © *Dnija Ros 2009, WM'11*

175

The sacred holidays are the eight points of power in the cycle of seasons that define a calendar year: Winter Solstice, Imbolc (Candlemas), Spring Equinox, Beltane (May Day), Summer Solstice, Lammas, Fall Equinox, Samhain (Hallowe'en/All Hallow's Eve). These magical eight points on the circle of the year mark times when the relationships between the Sun, Moon and Earth are particularly powerful and can be felt or experienced by us most profoundly. At these times, whether we are conscious of the holiday or not, we all have stronger experiences, bigger dreams and more intense impressions of the invisible energies and forces. In other words, the holidays exist whether we recognize them or not.

The Sacred Calendar is a visible image superimposed over the invisible structure that holds reality in place in our world. Marking the eight magical spots on the calendar year and celebrating them in some way is part of the Old Religion of the Goddess, which is active again today in the Women's Sprituality movement. These are the witches' "high holidays," and are recognized and honored in addition to the monthly New Moon and Full Moon. The Solstices and Equinoxes are noted in our modern calendars as the beginning days of winter, spring, summer and fall; and the "cross quarter" days that fall in between them are claimed by Pagans and Christians alike—they are included on the Julian calendar as church (and sometimes public) holidays.

A profound way of tuning into the powers and practices of the worldwide culture of the Mother Goddess is to honor her ancient calendar of eight magical sacred holidays. It is not really necessary to "do ritual" on the sacred holidays, since if you simply make the space in your life to observe and pay attention, the holidays will "do" you. Tuning into the "play of the dakinis" will allow them to spontaneously appear in your life as synchronicities and supernatural events, which tend to take place at a higher frequency around the holidays.

excerpt © Vicki Noble 1998, adapted from
Motherpeace and the Sacred Holidays *(Bear & Co., 2003), WM'98*

© Max Dashu 1974

The cycle of the year is created by the relationship of the earth to the sun—the interplay of night and day, dark and light, receptivity and activity. Winter Solstice marks the North point on the wheel, when nights are longest. It is most reflective, yin time of year. Summer Solstice at the South point of the wheel marks the time of the longest day of the year, the most active, yang season.

Thus, the strong polarities on the wheel are the Solstices, while the Equinoxes mark the midpoints in the energy shift from one pole to another. Spring Equinox, the East point on the wheel, and Fall Equinox, the West point on the wheel, are times when the lengths of day and night are at the balance point.

Located between the Solstices and Equinoxes are the points on the wheel called the cross-quarter days. It is at these times that the subtle energy shifts which happened at the quarters actually become visible in nature. For example, the light which is indicated at the Winter Solstice becomes visible with the substantially longer days at Candlemas. (Note: the Northern and Southern Hemispheres experience these cycles as a mirror image)

The time between Winter Solstice and Summer Solstice is a move toward individuation. It is movement toward self-actualization in the world. Then from Summer Solstice to Winter Solstice is a movement toward reintegration into the whole. We celebrate the height of that feeling of connectedness as we gather as families at Winter Solstice only to begin our emergences as individuals again in the spring. This seasonal cycle is the energy cycle of the Earth as she moves back and forth between the polarities of inward and outward activity.

The moon follows a similar pattern in her relationship to the sun. The moon experiences this eight-fold cycle thirteen times during one of the earth's yearly cycles.

excerpt © Sarah Scholfield, WM '90

She Turns Winter into Spring
© Mara Berendt Friedman 1996, WM '98

Imbolc/Candlemas

This is the first of four cross–quarter days marking the high points between Solstices and Equinoxes, high sabbats in honor of the great goddess in her myriad of forms. The names and dates given for them here originate from the Celtic tradition, but are also goddess celebration times in many lands and cultures. Imbolc is a festival of fire, celebrated with flames, symbolizing the moon as the source of fertility, life-giving creative power, new life that is growing again. The days begin to get visibly longer. Torches, candles, and fires are lit in honor of the moon goddess.

WM'94

© Monica Sjöö 1996, WM'07

Earth Mother begins to stir from Winter's sleep, as the sunlight grows stronger with each passing day. The first signs of renewal appear. Seeds that have been resting in the earth crack their castings and send out a root, initiating the discovery of individuation. Hope and faith sustained through the cold and dark have turned to certainty.

Declare who you are! Out of the dark earth, close to the heartbeat of the Mother, define. name and claim your spiritual path. What are your spiritual goals for the coming year? What is stirring inside you that seeks to grow and how will you nurture this growth?

excerpt adapted from Women's Rites, Women's Mysteries
© Ruth Barrett 2004, WM'07

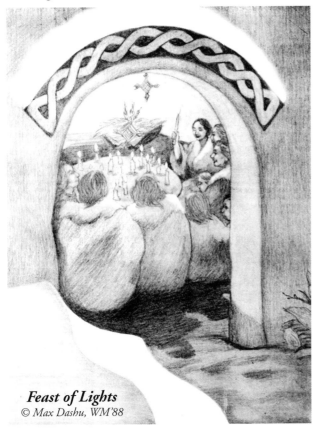

Feast of Lights
© Max Dashu, WM'88

Under the waxing light of the Aquarian sun, we honor Februa, Goddess of Purification, and Brigid, Irish Triple Goddess of Poetry, Healing, and Smithcraft.

This is the time of individuation, when we dare to become our own person. The time of the unpossessed virgin Goddess, expresses through the essential, anarchistic feminine principle of Inner Power. Take time to be alone. Purify a sacred space for yourself.

excerpt © Dánahy Sharonrose 1996, WM'97

Holding the Dream *© Lisa Seed 2006, WM'09*

Imbolc

The feeling in this still dark, unstable, muddy time
that the light at the end of the tunnel is my own soul
staring back at me on the inside
and I'm blind as a mole pushing through
some primal unseen path
with my stubby little snout and inexplicable will

If winter is a wide ocean of night
January is the hollow point, the trough
      that holds visions too deep to fish up into morning
it is a cave too far down for light or even hunger
      life hibernating in me suspended, waiting
and the mind floating free of the body now
like something promising but unborn
      I want to lean over my own self to see if I'm breathing
      I want to regress into a world of fur and blood
      I am as slow as a stone's pulse

Into this no place, no thing
Imbolc comes at the end of forever
and the beginning of all time
Suddenly there is one fiercely yellow crocus open
dreams pierce dense and soggy layers of sleep
      right up into the thin clear air of day
just like the red torpedo shoots of peonies
pierce the ground by my back door
carrying all the courage that weeks later they will need
      to unfurl those painfully delicate new leaves

I am asking for that courage, Mother
I'm ready as I'm gonna be
nothing more to wait for
just hold my hand while my eyes stumble into light

© Miriam Dyak 1994, WM'07

© Carolyn Hillyer 1997, WM'00

Ma-Lekma: Bright Eyes

Candle Gazing:

Light a candle in a darkened, peaceful space where the air is still. Close your eyes. Breathe deeply. Ground and center.

Now open your eyes and let your gaze rest on the brightest spot of the flame—just above the wick. Really **look** at the flame.

Focus on the flame—do not let the image split or your mind wander off. Remember to breathe. Go into the brightness, feel its warmth.

See this little flame transforming matter into energy before your eyes. Watch the fire spirit dancing in air. . .trance dancing.

Let its peaceful radiance fill you completely.

Notice the thoughts, feelings and images that arise. Energize the ones you want—release those you don't want by simply giving them over to the flame with your wish to let it be so.

Your mind is clear now and your body is relaxed.

© Zana 1992, WM'94   WM'85

Spring returns, the sun warms the soil. Seeds awaken, pushing roots into dark earth. Shoots push up into the light, and sap rises as trees break into leaf.

Eostar was the ancient, Germanic Goddess of the spring. Her colorful eggs are the symbols of renewed life. The magical, fertile hare, that leaps up from the fields just as the life force leaps up within us, was her sacred animal.

Day and night are balanced now. Justice means balance—balancing one set of needs against another, balancing what we take with what we give. May justice arise, cracking through the deadening systems of oppression like grass breaking through pavement.

Plant a seed, this springtime. Hold it in your hand, and envision a world in which we live in balance with nature, at peace with one another, where creativity and love can flourish. Place your seed in the earth. Water and tend it as you tend those qualities and take those actions which can bring that world to birth.

© Starhawk 2007, WM'08

Spring at Last © Karen Phelps 2007, WM'08

Mud Goddess #2 © Keely Meagan 1996, WM'00

Hare and the Moon
© Cliodhna Quinlan 2009, WM'11

Spring Equinox

Spring is here. Time to wake up. Break the chains of Winter. Animals come out of caves, shedding their winter coats. Under a first quarter moon, life bursts forth; flowers smile. The Aries sun shines upon the young child Goddess playing hide and seek with the balance of light and dark. It is the time of the Goddess Eostara, the hare and egg her symbols of fertility. Persephone returns from the underworld to be reunited with her mother, Demeter. Joy abounds.

As the wheel turns let us remember our childhood and heal the mother-daughter connection and strengthen the bond of sisterhood. Honor the children; teach them new stories of creation, revering all the peoples of the planet. Become a child yourself. Blessed be!

excerpt © Dánahy Sharonrose 1996, WM'97

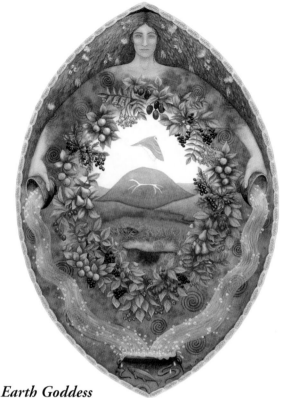

Earth Goddess
© *Meraylah Allwood 1997, WM'08*

Through all time and all space, trans-galactic, immemorial, substantial, in glee bowers of bird and flower, we convene in the bird nest of the year, piping songs. You can cover your altar with flowers—sisters—and sing the song that Earth has sung since first bee and first flower blossomed. Sky shout praises of collaboration, that we may activate and embody earth regeneration.

What is our juiciest sharing and how are we carrying out what is sacred and precious and rubbing the wild thoughts of a thrillion, thrumming species amongst our sacred sisters, calyx and whorl? The Earth is waking up: spring zing! She is dazzling us with celebration. What bud casing are you bursting from, leafing out? What is unfurling in you? What colors and patterns are your wings? What flower is rising in you? Where is your hive and garden, how do you connect with flying and flowering sisters on the move? Like bees, like Melissa, dance your special dance that communicates directions to the nectar—one short flight that will sweeten all the days of Life.

marna © Mother Tongue Ink 2010, WM'11

* Dancing Blue One © *Jen Lashua 2003*

What to Do on Spring Equinox

Compost this poem:
take out all the words that remind you of winter,
words that slip frozen into the heart,
Bare limbs of words
that stick into the sky and shake.
Prune out dead wood;
rough ragged never gonna fruit,
done is done.
Pay attention to what is here,
not what isn't.
Send your roots into another row or field or bed.
Mow. Rake up all the grass.
Layer, as if you're expecting hail or a deep frost;
the end of winter is always unpredictable.
Add manure, plenty of manure
and call in the flies, the dung beetles, the worms.
Soon, there'll be heat. Steam.
The pile will soften, break down, give in, let go.
Compost winter into Spring,
take off those old clothes you've been wearing,
the despair like a hat on your head,
dig into the pile,
into the heat and the heart of what matters.
Plant your garden and remember, each year,
everything will be different,
compost what you can.

▢ *Amy Schutzer 1998, WM'00*

Spring

Equinoxe de Printemps
les jours et les nuits sont égaux sur toute
la terre. Le sol redevient fertile, les créations
se dessinent les jeunes pousses apparaissent
L'énergie de la vie apparaît à la Lumière.

© *Nadine Zenobi, WM'83*

181

Traditionally a fertility festival, Beltane is associated with maypoles, circle dances, bonfires and making love in the fields—ancient rites, encouraging the land to bear abundantly. In our age, while land is forced to bear year-round and unchecked growth eats the earth from under us, we'moon commit to conscious fertility and sustainable abundance.

Celebrate alchemical power with an irresistible seduction of the wild divine. Create a temple of sensual opulence, an altar of earthly delights heaped with love offerings to favorite non-human beings. Call the four directions in their most delicious forms: torch song for the lilting east; snake dance for the smoldering south; sweet nectar for the juicy west; kisses passed round for the embodied north. Light a fire or use the fire of rhythm, breath, pulse. Is it the Moon we most adore or a tenacious weed in an unlikely place or the sea or a spider? Woo each in turn and receive the rising heat of the season in response.

Dedicate Beltane to the pan-erotic: expansive, exuberant, joyful or fierce, let crackling passion take the night. In the red coals of morning is the warmth that endures, the fiery flower that soon becomes fruit.

by Jessica Montgomery © Mother Tongue Ink 2003, WM'04

The Cosmic Mother
© Amarah Gabriel 2002, WM'05

Forepray: to the Great One Invocation to Ignite Desire

Shakti! Your fiery yoni
rouses. Wake us!
Kameshvara! Mother of Desire
For the sacrament of the body,
claim and consecrate us now.
Kali and Pele! Prepare us
to erupt—to stream.

Artemis, Ishtar!
May we who would
penetrate your mysteries
dare dissolve in you.
Sex Goddesses you
dance and carouse
as One. Infuse us
with your fever heat.
With your revels, Great One,
charge the body of creation!

◻ *Susa Silvermarie 2001, WM'03*

Screw the Picnic © Lucy Calhoun 2004, WM'08

Beltane/May Day

Beltane is the dawn of desire. Fingers of sunlight sink heat into moist earth. Responding in a blush of apple blossom fragrance and frogsong, soil opens. Hard buds expanding. Silken petals part to a glowing golden core. With the passing motion of a green snake, a glistening reservoir of dew held suspended on a blade of grass is released. Running down the stem into the sweet dripping wetness of the earth.

◻ *Peggy Sue McRae 1993,*
reprinted from Earth First! Journal (Beltane 1993), WM'96

At Beltane, we dance the Maypole.
The twining ribbons of many colors
remind us of the many aspects of love.

excerpt © Starhawk 2007, WM'07

1914 Swingout ¤ *submitted by Marlene Permar 1999,*
photographer unknown, WM'00

© Max Dashu, WM'88

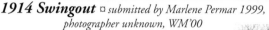

Beating Heart © *Gael Nagle 1996, WM'07*

© Shoshana Rothaizer, WM'84

May Day: May 1

This is the second of the four high sabbats in honor of the great goddess whoever she is for you. Traditionally celebrated with flowers and dancing around a Maypole with ribbons of color. It is a festival of rebirth and the fertility of the earth, the creativity of women, and of young girls growing up. Days are getting longer and warmer, the light is stronger, all of nature celebrates.

Mai anfang: 1. Mai

Das Zweite der vier hohe Sabbat zu ehren der grossen göttin, irgendwer sie ist für dich. Traditionell gefeirt mit Blumen und Tanz um einen bunt geschmüchten Maibaum. Ein Fest der Weidergeburt und der Fruchrbarkeit der Erde, die Kreativität der Frauen und jungen Mädchen wächst. Die Tage werden läner und wärmer, das Licht wird stäzker, die ganze Natur feirt.

WM'84

183

Summer Solstice marks the peak of the solar cycle. In the midst of the longest day of the year, we simultaneously begin our return to the dark half of the year. Summer Solstice is active: it's about doing and expanding, living the dream envisioned in the dream-time of Winter. The Earth is fertile, and the womb of the Earth Mother grows ripe with Life.

In the mythic cycle of the Goddess, the Maiden Goddess experiences the joy of union with Her creative, sexual, sensual Self and begins to manifest Her creations. Thus, this holiday begins the Maiden Goddess's transition to the cycle of the Mother Goddess as Maker/Creatrix.

Honor and celebrate the many ways you manifest the creativity in your life. Regardless of whether a woman physically gives birth, she becomes "Mother" when she nurtures, sustains and protects life, human or other species, through her life's work and activism. Where is your passionate energy focused in your life? How do you feed your creative fire? How are you a "Mother/Maker/Creatrix"? How do you nurture, sustain and protect your creations?

excerpt adapted from Women's Rites, Women's Mysteries
© Ruth Barrett 2004, WM'07

Amigas del Sol
© Lisa Kagan 2005, WM '07

When we work for justice, when we take action and try to change the world, we may experience bright periods of fiery energy and radiant hope. If we're not careful, explosive phases of energy are followed by burnout. Big changes take time. The Solstice reminds us that we, too, need time to turn inward, to nurture what is under the surface, to dream as well as act.

© Starhawk 2007, WM'08

Hartland, Raymond Mississippi
¤ Emelie Hebert / Deborah Wyatt 2005, WM'08

le jour le plus long. L'expiration de la terre, le soleil est à sa puissance maximum, forte échappée de l'énergie primaire. Tout se développe. Attention nécessaire.

□ *Nadine Zenobi WM'83* **Solstice d'Été**

Dancing with the Sun
© *Mara Berendt Friedman 1994, WM'05*

Summer Solstice

The longest day of the year lights our ability to love and connect in community. Summer Solstice corresponds with the full moon and to the mother ocean. It is the time for hand fastings, wish making and dancing in fairy rings. Litha, the celtic Goddess of abundance and Yemaya the African orisha of the ocean, are honored with offerings of honey and roses.

As summer flourishes around us we are reminded of the interconnectedness of all life. No being is alone on this planet, we exist in relationship to each other. The artificial barriers we impose to keep us from nature and our communities are a loss of our power. Racism, sexism and other social divisions within the human family can leave us weak and isolated. Modern inventions such as television, computers and automobiles box us away from the sun and fresh air we need for life.

As summer reaches her peak, let us reclaim the wisdom of the bee, the tree, the web and the spiral. Get outside and meet your neighbors. Have a community ritual or potluck. Source yourself in nature by walking in a forest or on the beach. Join hands with family and friends around a fire. Celebrate diversity.

© *Ginger Salkowski 2002, WM'03*

Urban Agriculture
□ *Beth Ferguson 2005, WM'08*

This is the time when the Goddess withdraws into the mounds, the Earth, the Fairy hills with the coming of Autumn. She is transformed into Her Earth Mother aspect in the mounds and tombs. The forces that began to rise out of the Earth at Imbolc, return now to enter the earth womb at Lammas.

Fires were lit on Lammas mounds (like Silbury Hill in the Avebury Cycle), the largest monument of the great goddess built in northern Europe, being Her pregnant womb, where people gathered to watch the mound/womb/mother give birth to the Harvest child in conjunction with the Moon and the Waters. Harvesting took place with the Waning Moon, the cutting of the corn, and the first fruits were offered to the Goddess or Earth Mother. Great Lammas Fairs were held with games and celebrations. Fermented alcohol/beer—seen as the essence of germination of a kind of watery fire of life—was used as a ritual element in the Lammas feast. Cooking fires were honored as the transformative power of fire and water together. Lammas is harvest time, when the fruits of the earth are abundant and there is a surplus of grains and vegetables.

© Monica Sjöö, WM'86

Lady Day
© Max Dashu, WM'88

Gathering the Future
© Schar Cbear Freemn 1998, WM'00

At Lammas we have reached the midpoint between Summer Solstice and Fall Equinox. It is the feast of first fruits and a celebration of the bountiful earth. Traditionally, breads were baked with the first grains and were offered to the Mother Goddess asking for protection on the harvest to come. Bonfires were built on the hilltops to ward off bad spirits and the ground was blessed with beer and moon blood.

The harvests of today differ from any the world has ever known. Huge "agribusinesses" produce tons of a single crop with the use of chemical fertilizers, pesticides and genetic engineering. This intensive food production is a major source of pollution. In spite of this mass production however, for most people in the world, food is still a scarce resource. 35,000 children die of starvation every day.

For Lammas this year take some action on the issue of food. If you planted a garden, offer some of your first bounty to a needy person in the name of the Goddess. Buy your food as organic and local as possible to support sustainable agriculture. Call your congress person and ask for labeling of genetically engineered foods. Go vegetarian.

© Ginny Salkowski 2002, WM'03

artwork: **The Sower** *© Agnes Nyanhongo 2001 photo: © Cora Greenhill 2001, WM'03*

Enclosed Garden □ *Meinrad Craighead 1984, WM'05*

Habondia (Lammas)

The goddess is ripe and swelling with life. The earth puts forth her bounty. First fruits are weighing down the branches of the trees. Farms and gardens yield their summer harvests. This is a time to give thanks for the goddess for her many blessings and celebrate the gifts life brings.

In this day and age there are truly many things to be thankful for. As women many of us have incredible numbers of choices. In this age of information and growth, many more of us have access to choices that were not always available in the past. This indeed is a kind of abundance that we sometimes overlook. In realizing our abundance, we must also come to terms with the different levels of privilege that still exist in the world. Habondia's day is a good time to reflect on issues of privilege and class: to send energy and support to those who have less than we, to give thanks and appreciation for that which we do have, to invoke increase with our magic as needed for ourselves and others, to pray for the end of hunger and homelessness in the world and the dissolving of all such inequities.

© *1991, excerpted and reprinted with permission from* Aridne's Thread *by Shekhinah Mountainwater 1991, The Crossing Press: Freedom, CA, WM'98*

Storm the Drummer
© *Carolyn Hillyer 2003, WM'08*

At Fall Equinox the balance begins to tip from light to dark, drawing us inward. "*Breathing in and out,*" she says, "*be mindful. Balance amidst change.*"

We watch the last light dance violet mauve across the mountain to the East. A young woman calls in the Spirits of East, "*Breath of life: Ha!*" she chants, and we join her, "*Ha!*" calling in the element of Air. We face each direction in turn, calling in the element and the qualities we associate with it. "*Spirits of the South, element Fire. . . of the West, Water . . . of the North, Earth . . .*" We invoke the Goddess in the center, all one. The circle is cast. Chanting Her many names, we raise the cone of power and begin our magic work: releasing all obstacles within and without, we invoke Peace.

excerpt by Musawa © Mother Tongue Ink 2004, WM'05

Her Giveaway Dance

Now this miracle: flower to fruit. Such a production to offer so casually. When an apple strikes and rolls from the roof, her rhythm of deliverance slaps the edge of a djembe. When one thuds to the earth: bass from the drum's center. Her Giveaway Dance goes on for weeks. We gather red bounty every day. We eat apples for breakfast, for dessert. In fever we eat them to become summer. Still she dances apples down. Each gesture, a cupped breast. Again and again until her mothering's done.

▯ *Susa Silvermarie, WM'00*

Fools in Balance ▯ *Martine Paran Palmiter 1998, WM'00*

Softly a whistle rises in the wind, gently the dust broom sweeps. Leaves rustle against the Earth. She rises, growing stronger, standing taller, pushing farther, yielding more. The Winds of Change dance through our lives, hurling lightning, spitting fire, torrential rains fall. We reap the harvest, we grab the shafts of wheat and rip them from the soil. There in Her garden the Goddess Oya leaves and seeds fly; Death and Life rustle in the Wind. The season changes and we who are the dead reborn must worship Her. We harvest pumpkin, corn, and grain; we are reminded of our morality—the continuing cycle of reap, rest, and sow.

© *Luisah Teishuisah Teish 1997, excerpted from* Carnival of the Spirit, *reprinted with permission from the author, WM'98*

In this time of balance, we enter the portals of timespace and hear the chitter-whispers of our great-grandmothers, who bless us with courage, fortitude, ease and faith. We hear the great-grand-daughters' song, coaching us clearly how to navigate disaster. Reaching out, in this time, across equal sunrise, equal sunset, an even point in a world about to topsy-turvy, the interlinking circle fires write out across Gaia globe, words of blessing. We are the letters of an alphabet and grammar of blessing, our sisterly magic an incantation to balance and peace. Sip tea, light candles, savor darkness, breathe peace. What is your incantation of blessing and balance? How will you share it?

excerpt, marna © Mother Tongue Ink 2010
WM'11

In Her Hand © *Qahira Lynn 1997, WM'10*

Leaf Goddess
▢ *Nadine C. Butterfield 2003, WM'05*

For me it is a time of introspection and taking stock, similar to Jewish Rosh Hashanah, a day of self-examination. I review mistakes, request forgiveness from anyone I may have offended, and make future resolves. Turning leaves, turning inward: I look deep into my soul. My altar broom sweeps out internal debris, acknowledging my faults and weaknesses, relinquishing grudges, forgiving others and asking myself: have I shared? Loved enough? Been unkind? Judged others? Adhered to my own standards? Grown as a human being? The personal really *is* political: we change the world when we change ourselves.

excerpt, Ffiona Morgan © Mother Tongue Ink 2009,
WM'10

Fall Equinox   Sept. 23

days and nights are equal all over the world — the sun's path crosses over the equator going South — she rises and sets at the midpoint on your horizon between her northern and southern extremes at the solstices, harvest time, gather and store, recycle and review, enjoy the fruits of your labor, appreciate a time of plenty and prepare to shift over to more inside work. Balance goddess celebrations:
festival of Demeter, goddess of the harvest, joyfull celebration in thanks for work done, Persephone goes underground.
other holidays of the season:
Rosh Hoshana — Jewish New Year

Herbstanfang   Tag und Nachtgleiche   23. Sept.
Tage und Nächte sind gleich lang auf der ganzen Erde, Erntezeit, sammeln und lagern, erfreu dich an den Früchten der Arbeit und der Zeit der Fülle, bereite dich vor auf den Übergang zur inneren Arbeit. Balance
Feiern der Göttinnen:
freudvolle Danksagungen an Demeter, die Göttin der Ernte, Persephone geht in den Untergrund
andere Festtage der Jahreszeit:
Rosh Hoshana — Jüdisches Neues Jahr

WM'83

Known as the Day of the Dead in Latin America, Hallow's Eve is sacred around the world as a time to honor the ancestors who are said to "walk abroad" when the veil between the worlds is thinnest. Ancient European women prepared "Hekate's Suppers" to leave at the crossroads and gathered herbs in cemeteries to practice their powerful regenerative magic. In Sumer (ancient Iraq), Inanna descended to the underworld to meet her dark sister, Ereshkigal; at Candlemas she will be reborn into her power. The most powerful symbols of this holiday are representations of the Death Goddess and her retinue of witches, spiders, spooks, jack-o-lanterns, black cats, goblins and ghosts.

Vicki Noble © Mother Tongue Ink 2008, WM'09

Hecate © Catherine Larsen 2005, WM'09

Hallomas Black Cat

You remind us of the ancient ones,
the women who walked the earth
in goddess form.
You invite us to re-enact the mysteries,
to know the goddess in ourselves.

□ Hawk Madrone 1987, WM'88

HALLOWEEN

★ Halloween is the last round in the earth's dance of lights and shadows for the year -- the growing cycle goes underground. It is the Witches' New Year, "the night when the veil is thin that divides the worlds." ★ Hecate, goddess of the underworld, is the spirit of this time ... the dark side of the moon, the witch, the crone, the one who stands at the crossroads.

♐ The Sun is in Scorpio ♏, fixed sign of the water element, unconscious emotional depths, ruled by Pluto, planetary power of total transformation through death and rebirth.

Ritual is one way to go between the worlds, by acting out our link with the unconscious spirit realms directly.

* adapted from The Spiral Dance *by Starhawk, WM'85*

Light candles, or go by the dark. Lay your belly down in direct contact with the Dirt. Ah, Mother Earth. Rain, slush, sleet, snow—no matter. Feel the power of earthquake, power of thunder, power of fecund, fallow depth, upswell of Earth's belly to yours. Everything that was too big for you, or toxic, the Earth devours and instantaneously transmutes to nourishment for flowers. This is the umbilicus of the year, the dark moon of the solar cycle. Our ancestors surround us always and now we feel their blessing. Take a pot of strong coffee or tea (or whatever forebears drank) laced with honey and, with a heft of basil as wand, spill three times by your hearth (stove), your front door and your back, singing a welcoming, blessing song. Sing loudly, this is how those who have come before like it. Time of augur, time of descent. Entering time of silence and source. Sit with sisters in the black moon time, bellies dark with dirt, in fallow, electric silence, and be Earth.

marna © Mother Tongue Ink 2010, WM'11

Ghost Dance *© Lilian deMello 1999, WM'01*

Heyoka Dances on the Bones of Yesterday's Sorrow
© Joyce Radtke 1996, WM'98

Request

What will be left is
mineral and water only;
spirit is light. When it's
in flight, lay the rest
above the tideline, arms
stretched wide. Place

a tear in each of my palms, then
keep your distance. This
is a matter now
between the gulls and
otters. Do not come near

that place for three
seasons, till your
sadness is smoothed
over and my flesh
is gone. Carve

my name on a small
piece of ivory. Give
it to your daughters; say,
she was a poet; say,
she sang a song.

© Oiseau 2003, WM'05

Snow Ravens
© *Catherine Molland 2007, WM'09*

It is the longest night of the year, the shortest day. We meet to honor the darkness at its peak, reclaiming the night sky and the dark womb as source of light and life. We rejoice in the return of the sun as the light begins to grow. The Goddess is the newborn baby. We honor the birth of the Sun Goddess, Lucina, coming with her crown of lights to disperse the darkness. Amateratsu (Japan) comes out of the dark cave, sees her reflection in a mirror, and lights the world with love from the beauty she sees. Yemaya (Africa) creates the world anew from her womb.

Burn many candles. Light the Yule log. Allow yourself to be still and quiet. Let the darkness bring forth new idea. Make wishes for the new year. Stay up all night and greet the morning sun. Blessed be!

excerpt © Dánahy Sharonrose 1996, WM'97

Winter

Night comes early in Winter; the Dark is deep and long. Yet in the stillness of sleep and death, Yemonja gives us Her song. In Her quiet dreaming the hum of the Ocean is heard. In the rushing waters Olokun gives us the Word.

I was there in the beginning
and I'll be there till the end
In my depths new life is teeming
all that dies shall live again.

Winter begins on December 21st. It is the Solstice, the longest night of the year. Winter is celebrated by lighting bonfires or Yule logs to entice the Sun to return. Evergreens are decorated to symbolize the Tree of Life, people kiss under the mistletoe, visit each other's homes and share food. Much of the ancient symbols of the Winter Solstice has been absorbed into the rituals of Christmas.

© *Luisah Teishuisah Teish 1997, excerpted from* Carnival of the Spirit, *reprinted with permission from the author, WM'98*

Winter, on de la nuit la plus longue, l'inspir de la terre, mort et re-naissance de la lumière, première étincelle d'une nouvelle et profonde vie intérieure, pousse embryonnaire et besoin de protection. Solstice d'Hiver

□ *Nadine Zenobi, WM'83*

ice flakes dance in breathy air

what in this world perceives
the longest night of the year
when spirits dance in black emptiness

in this dark space of the cycle
outside, the cries of the world pierce the stillness
yet the earth turns toward the light

deep in the familiar
there is a place of knowing
all things are possible.

excerpt © Kathy Abromeit 2003, WM'08

Samovila *© Sandra M. Stanton 1996, WM'08*

At This Time

At this time we stand
upon the earth as winter trees.
We are called on to release.
To strip our branches
and to shed our leaves.
Till we are naked
bare unto the bone
naked yet rooted
in the soil of the soul
So we know
we do not stand alone
Seeing our leaves
suffused with light
their form can no longer hold.
See them turning
red, umber, ochre, copper, gold
Till we are left reaching
our bare branches to the sky
surrendering.
only then
can the emerging buds be seen
only then can we bring light
to our unfolding dream

© Margot Henderson 2004, WM'09

Earth "four elements suite"
© Josslyn Meyeres 2002, WM'09

193

Wheel of the Heavens

If the year is a song . . .

. . . the Moon is the drum beat
marking rhythm in phases,
changing mood with the signs,
waxing and waning thirteen times
as she circles around.

    The Sun carries the song
changing keys each season
in her relation with the Earth,
singing ever new verses
of the Zodiac's twelve tunes.

    Star signs shape melodies
that all circling orbs play—
each planet an instrument
intoning harmonies
in her own time and way.

    It is we who experience
the song of this year
in the notes and melodies
we are learning to hear.

    We play with the Moon,
we sing with the Sun,
we join in Earth's dance
to the music of spheres.

© Musawa 1984, WM'94

© Sudie Rakusin, WM'93

Dream Messenger *© Cathy McClelland 2002, WM'11*

Sing to the moon
when she is round
and luck with you
will then abound.
Spells done now
will soon come 'round

Wish upon the moon
when she is new
and kiss the hand of her
times two,
and grow with her
your wishes do.

And when the moon
is waning old,
and she is small
and pale and cold,
sing your sorrows,
sing your woes,
and with her fading
they too go.

¤ Robyn of Entropy 1992, WM'94

Reflect

Reflect on the darkness,
where fear is lost.

Reflect on the darkness,
Where light begins,

Reflect on the darkness,
where gold is dancing.

© Janine Canan 1997, WM'99

© Katheryn M. Trenshaw 1992, WM'98

Moon Signs and Moon Transits

The Moon changes signs every 2 ½ days and sets the mood and tone of the time. The Moon's placement at our birth describes our relation to our home, soul, family and emotional lineage; it symbolizes our inner spiritual river and our lifetime mode of operations.

Heather Roan Robbins
© Mother Tongue Ink 2009, WM'11

Lunar Calendars

Cultures with a lunar calendar are as varied as Hindus, Arabs, Arabs, Jews, Celts, Hawaiians, and wemoon who use this one.

The 13 moons of The Druid tree-calendar are the basis of their alphabet as well—beginning the new moon before Solstice/Capricorn and ending with the new moon after the next Winter Solstice.

The old Hawaiian calendar has a name for each phase of the moon, and they called the days by these names—an intimate way to live with and come to know the moon through all her changes.

The Jewish calendar also traditionally starts each month with the new moon (Rosh Chodesh), and major holidays are celebrated on the new or full moons around Equinoxes and Solstices (Passover, for example, is the first full moon after Spring Equinox.) Christian Easter is always the first Sunday of the first full moon after Spring Equinox.

In matriarchal societies, and among all people who live close to nature, the moon is greatly respected, and her changes are closely followed in the rituals of daily life. Moon time is cyclical, revolving around Mother Nature. Patriarchal time is linear, arbitrarily divided up by man-made events. They represent totally different approaches to life: in societies where people are cut off from nature's rhythms, we are generally encouraged to live flat, straight lives in fixed roles, where differences are seen as a source of conflict and oppression—and change is threatening.

When we live with natural time, we are more able to live with change in a positive way, accepting the ups and downs, the ebb and flow, strengths and weaknesses, and the differences between us more easily—as the moon shows us with her changing faces.

Musawa 2010

Sol-Luna ¤ *Beth Ferguson 2005, WM'08*

Astrology/Cosmic Cycles

Star Thrower
© Marion Cloaninger 2001, WM'04

We'Moon has been an astrological moon calendar for all of its 30 years, presenting specific information about astrological signs, planetary positions, aspects and more. The introductory section in each We'Moon contains a primer of astrological information, deeply informative to novices as well as to those who are facile with astrology. The calendar pages display precise astrological data, as wemoon track their days under the Wheel of the Heavens. And many rush first to the Year at a Glance articles to find what astrologer Gretchen Lawlor has to say about the year ahead for women born under each sun sign! In the following pages, the 12 zodiacal signs are featured, introduced with voices of the Rouvenac Womyn who channeled this imaginative story for natal sign qualities. We include snippets from one of our astrologers, Heather Roan Robbins, with a big picture glance at how energies shift as the sun moves through the signs.

Gretchen Lawlor: Back in early days of We'Moon, when I was creating my own Moon Calendar in New Zealand, Musawa and I would correspond, commiserating over the annual birthing labors of our respective publications. When I left New Zealand I passed mine on to friends, Creative Cronies—who continue to produce an extraordinary Australasian calendar/datebook. Musawa invited me to join her in creating We'Moon—and I leapt at the chance to focus upon my passion—writing the annual Year at a Glance predictions.

Every year I spend a month deep in the oracular caves, surrounded by sky maps, notes, candles and bells, plotting the trajectories of lives for the year to come. I lay out huge zodiacs on the floor and walk around in them, lie down and even sleep in them. I place metaphoric collections of people at each sign and sit with them in council, listening to their stories.

I place symbolic objects to represent the evolving planetary scenarios upon the zodiac wheel to ponder their impact. Currently Pluto is a potato peeler, painfully stripping away layers to reveal deeper truth. Uranus is a three plug electrical adapter—channeling the wild electricity, hard to predict exactly where or how. Jupiter is a hopeful, uplifting bottle of bubbles with a bubble wand, Saturn a 12-inch ruler measuring out clarity and structure.

Now the deadline comes earlier; it used to be that I could write about the year ahead, now I gaze several years into the future. This puts me into a strange otherworldliness, making it difficult for me to return to the present. There's always the transitional phase, where I experience poignant, frequently disorienting hindsight about things that haven't happened yet.

Ah, and the true alchemical work comes when I have to distill down all that I see into 275 words, so you can open to your sign in We'Moon for a glimpse of your own way forward.

Thank you We'Moon readers all over the world for the messages of appreciation you send me, for your fascination and delight with how I manage to be talking directly with you about your own precious lives.

Astrological Year at a Glance

In these times, when so much is shaking and unraveling, the orderly procession of planets and the predictable cycles of the Moon provide both comfort and context for our earthly experience. The sky maps ways to optimize the best of the year and mitigate the challenges.

excerpts and wheel: Gretchen Lawlor
© Mother Tongue Ink, WM'10 & WM'11

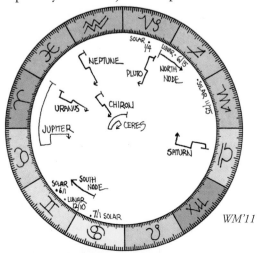

WM'11

The Medicine Wheel
by SunBear & Wabun, WM'94

Therin, 2010:

I never learned the cipher,
The maze of tables
other wimmin read and fathom;
Yet still I open eagerly
to see the year before me,
I read my loved ones,
Carefully comparing
where our pathways intersect.
I watch the moons.
I let their symbols
guide my breathing.

The great mother
had called her twelve daughters together
and said:

Now the time has come
that you have to prepare yourselves for your
travel through life.
To each of you I will give a special
gift with a seed of life ~ so each will have
a different task than the other.
Sometimes you will not have it
easy on your ways, and you might get
dissatisfied or jealous of each other.
But you will learn to see that each of you
is WHOLE, when you will have found out
that all twelve of you are ONE.

And you should never forget
that I will always be
with all of you,
because
our circle of thirteen
is the dance
of LOVE

Rouvenac Women's Land, S. France, WM'85

Anthology Astrology

This Anthology reflects the collective consciousness that has been evolving over the past 30 years. We'Moon is a guidebook for explorers into the inner and outer heavens that inspires us to use natural rhythms of planetary cycles as allies and guides, opening ourselves to live a symbolic life. The passage of Pluto/Persephone through Libra, Scorpio, Sagittarius and Capricorn during these years, uniquely symbolizes the path of We'Moon's evolution.

•Pluto/Persephone was transiting Libra in 1980 when a small band of women from the fringes of feminist consciousness began We'Moon. With Libra's emerging dynamic, all our relationships were challenged, redefined and reformed.

•The Scorpio era (1983–1995) fed our instinctual urge to explore life's mysteries, and to confront and transmute our shadowside in the deep process of personal and social transformation.

•Pluto/Persephone transited Sagittarius (1995–2008); those vulnerable depths we experienced in Scorpio fueled the expression of our insights, understandings and aspirations, and freed our voices, our art and our truth.

• In this era of Capricorn (2008–2023), we are learning how deeply our human legacies are intertwined. Even though patriarchal thought forms perpetuate linear views, we are rediscovering the many faces of Gaia, and honoring our interconnectedness. *In the Spirit of We'Moon* is an excellent Capricorn contribution of accumulated wisdom and an offering for future generations to build upon. Let the Mother's Tongues speak out for all of We'Earth, and collective mindfulness guide our steps forward.

© Sandra Pastorius 2010

. . . and to **AQUARIUS** she said:

To you, my eleventh daughter, I give the energy of <u>fixed air.</u> You don't need structures anymore, you can cross the borders. You will bring the dream to the others, that everything is possible; you are open for the future. This makes you free and unbound—but for others you can sometimes be distant or superficial. At the same time your universal mind thinks of everybody, so you will be always a good friend: playful, helpful and gentle. You can fly very high and see everything, but you can also easily lose the contact with your surroundings.

WM'85

MoBoko © *Toni Truesdale 2001, WM'04*

WM'85

≋ Aquarius:

The Fixed Aquarius Sun asks us to honor the collective experience. It's time to cultivate allies and take our philosophy into political and cultural action.

excerpt, Heather Roan Robbins
© *Mother Tongue Ink 2006, WM'08*

KUMBHA – POT

art by Minerva © Creative Cronies,
Moon Calendar Productions 1990, New Zealand, WM'92

Dreamseeds ignite the fire
for new revolutions.
Dreamseeds are the heart stone
for empowered choices
and conscious change.
excerpt ¤ JoAnne Dodgson 2009. WM'11

Integration © *Autumn Skye Morrison 2009, WM'11*

. . . and to PISCES she said:

To you my twelfth and last daughter, I give the energy of the _mutable flowing water_. Your task is to find that all is nothing and nothing is all, which can be a painful and depressing lesson. But your compassion will help you on this way. You will be the one who dissolves everything in a total flow of feelings. You feel at home in the oceans of the subconsciousness and you like to swim along on mystical waves. But you can also get very lost in the mud. You have the ability to take shape after your surroundings, so can adapt easily, feel into others and flow with every change. But take care: this passivity can also be your weak point.

_WM'85_

_WM'85_

♓ **Pisces**:
The Mutable Pisces Sun asks us to feel the ambient pools of unabashed emotion and be moved to compassionate action. As the bear stirs in its den, Pisces calls us to use the waning winter nights to explore our dreams.

excerpt, Heather Roan Robbins
© Mother Tongue Ink 2006, WM'08

The Trio
© A. Kimberlin Blackburn 1989, WM'92

Whale Song

I have a whale in my belly. Memories, vibrations, emotions swirl, their echoes, tangle me up, threaten to overwhelm. I remember to surface, swallow great gulps of air before I surrender again to the sea that is the world around me.

excerpt © Mari Selby 1991, WM'92

Waking Up From a Dormant Cycle
◻ Robyn Waters 2001, WM'11

MINA - FISH

art by Minerva © Creative Cronies,
Moon CalendarProductions 1990, New Zealand, WM'92

. . . and to ARIES she said:

You are my first daughter—nothing yet exists, all has still to be done—so to you I give the energy of the <u>starting fire</u>. Often you will not have the time to see things growing which you have started, because there will be always something new for you to begin. Therefore you will be quick, burning and spontaneous like a volcano, and you will have a strong will to get what you want. You will also always have your own and independent way. But beware not to get impatient, irritated or intolerant with the ones that are not like you.

WM'85

art by Minerva © Creative Cronies,
Moon CalendarProductions 1990, New Zealand, WM'92

Indelible
I speak in bold
permanent lines
that will
not fade in the wash.
excerpt © Karyn Milos 1999, WM'09

Aries
WM'85

♈ Aries:
As the Sun enters Cardinal Aries, it asks us to remember our fire, our personal reasons for being alive. It pumps up the volume on will and life force: raw, exhilarated, direct, rude and passionate. Use wisdom to focus this power; give it a goal.
excerpt, Heather Roan Robbins
© Mother Tongue Ink 2006, WM'08

Ahhh. . .

the celebration of
one's life. . .

the sweet joy in knowing
the truth,

that you are enough,
more than enough

a blossom
of magnificence
▢ e.g. wise 2006, WM'11

SoulFire
© Deborah Koff-Chapin 2008, WM'11

. . . and to TAURUS she said:

To you, my second daughter, I give the energy of the <u>fixed earth</u>, and the ability to be sensual. Because you are the one who will give life, love and substance to everything which Aries has started. You will be constructive, practical and concrete, and you will have the patience to hold out and finish things, so others can count on you. But don't get upset when others don't love the things like you do, and take care: your love feelings for everything you gave life to, can make you possessive, stubborn and closed for changes. And don't keep your feelings in you—learn how to show them.

WM'85

WM'85

*art by Minerva © Creative Cronies,
Moon CalendarProductions 1990, New Zealand, WM'92*

♉ Taurus:
Fixed Taurus brings Aries fire down to earth, enlivening the growing green world. Taurus brings life into matter: through growing crops and wildflowers, muscular strength and the sensuality of our bodies, the solidity of our material resources.

excerpt, Heather Roan Robbins © Mother Tongue Ink 2006, WM'08

Weeping for Joy

Come, lay your skin on mine. Bring your skin—somewhere out there listening—back to your self, then lay it on mine. They'll discover us, our skins, vulnerabilities thinly whispering, and when they're done making sure, kissing us hungrily. Come to me then with all your ties, with your skin flowing behind you like a bridal train. Come to me with all your daughters, and we'll arrange the beds border to border, like a rolling landscape, endlessly unfolding, like a woman's body unfolding, waist, then bony hip, then her down-soft inner thigh, weeping for joy.

© Janine Canan, WM'93

Prarie Lilith
© Carol Wylie 2002 , WM'04

. . . and to GEMINI she said:

To you, my third daughter, I give the energy of the <u>mutable air</u>. You will have the ability to ask questions from all sides. You are the one who brings a mental consciousness to what is there and your curiosity will show others, what they can see around them. You are open to meet anybody and you are very social. The duality within you will make you always open to see and hear the other side of everything. On your way you will meet also indecision, restlessness and confusion in yourself, which might confuse others and make you seem to go into all and nothing. So you will have to learn clarity.

WM'85

Elder Moon, Blue Moon *© Colleen 2002, WM'09*

♊ **Gemini**:

When the Sun enters Mutable Gemini, it asks us to weave networks with humor and communication. Gemini's purpose is to disperse ideas like milk thistle on the spring winds: time to travel, talk, explore and listen.

excerpt, Heather Roan Robbins
© Mother Tongue Ink
2006, WM'08

gemini WM'85

MITHUNA – LOVERS

art by Minerva © Creative Cronies,
Moon CalendarProductions 1990, New Zealand, WM'92

WM'85

© Eleanor Williams 2009, WM'11

. . . and to CANCER she said:

You are my fourth daughter to whom I give the energy of <u>soft cardinal water</u>, with which you will be able to bring feelings to the others. You like to spread around cosy, warm, joyful and caring energies, and you will be able to create a home for you and others wherever you are. Because you are very sensitive and therefore vulnerable, you will often protect yourself by hiding in your shell. It's important for you to learn how much you can give at one time, so you don't have to make walls around so hard and keep everybody far from your soft centerself.

WM'85

© Anna Oneglia 2001, WM'04

art by Minerva © Creative Cronies,
Moon CalendarProductions 1990, New Zealand, WM'92

Holy Water

I taste the saltiness
As tiny droplets wet my lips
And I am reminded
Of how much of me is fluid.
That my skeleton walks on water.

excerpt © Karen Haffey 2004, WM'08

♋ Cancer:

As the Sun swims through Cardinal Cancer, we dive into the sea of emotion and come Home again. We nourish connections with family, tribe, our body, garden and our temple's hearth, stretching our hearts until all Gaia is our home.

excerpt, Heather Roan Robbins
© Mother Tongue Ink 2006, WM'08

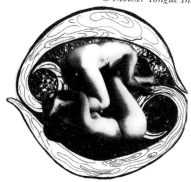

WM'85

© Sudie Rakusin, WM'92

203

. . . and to LEO she said:

You are my fifth daughter and to you I give the energy of the <u>fixed fire</u>, the sun. And like the sun you will bring warmth, happiness and fun. You can make everything shine with delight, and you will open all hearts. You will always need others around you and you will often feel in the center—because your pride can kill your innocence. Like a child you will like to play, but you should also learn that you have to lose sometimes. You love drama not only on stage, but also in your life.

WM'85

Gaia
© Gael Nagle 2000, WM08

WM'85

♌ Leo:

The Fixed Leo Sun asks us to shine our light on the crops of life and ripen its fruit: peaches of creative expression, plums of romance, wheat of familial warmth. Bask in the sun, cultivate with love, share the bounty of our culture and live fully.

excerpt, Heather Roan Robbins
© *Mother Tongue Ink 2006, WM'08*

Priestess, with your electric body
    be the wand   the lightning
that charges heaven and earth together
Spin out the miles of your nerves
    now the passion of trees holding the planet
    now the veins of gold that pierce her heart
    now the fibers of meaning
which are our great constellations

excerpt © Miriam Dyak 2008, WM'11

To Pele
Goddess of the Living Fire
© *Lilian de Mello 1997, WM'02*

SIMHA – LION

art by Minerva © Creative Cronies,
Moon CalendarProductions 1990, New Zealand, WM'92

204

. . . and to VIRGO she said:

To you, my sixth daughter, I give the energy of the <u>mutable earth</u>. You are the last one of this first half circle which is forming the "I". So it's up to you to review and analyze all that happened until now. You will have tendency to check things and criticize, but even though you will sometimes have to care for what others didn't see, don't forget to leave them their space, too.

You will sometimes need a leader to guide you and will be able to serve well without questioning. Your deep connection to the earth will often make you choose nature as your teacher and this will open you for magic, healing and a healthy way of life. Your ability to see details and give an order to things, will always help you on your way, but take care not to get stuck in them.

WM'85

WM'85

♍ Virgo:

The Virgo Sun asks us to weed, harvest, sort the wheat from the chaff and explain the summer to the winter. We grow introspective: we diagnose the world's ills and fertilize its strengths, make blueprints, prepare our health for autumn.

excerpt, Heather Roan Robbins
© Mother Tongue Ink 2006, WM'08

art by Minerva © Creative Cronies,
Moon CalendarProductions 1990, New Zealand, WM'92

Net
a most delicate
and invisible thread
carefully spun to encircle,
when woven in the proper way,
becomes a net
to cradle
and sustain.
© Joyce Ketterman 2004, WM'10

Awakening Heart
© Christina Smith 2004, WM'06

. . . and to LIBRA she said:

You are my seventh daughter and to you I give the energy of the <u>cardinal air</u>. You are starting the second half of this circle, so you are the first one to come out of her own world to meet the other. You can be very charming and you have a strong sense for beauty. You have love for everybody, and with your need for justice you will always try to harmonize, to balance. But therefore you will always need to find balance in yourself, to find your centerpoint. Mostly you will find it hard to choose, to make your own choice, because you can see the good side in everything.

WM'85

© Hawk Madrone, WM'89

Trust *© Lisa Seed 2003, WM'11*

♎ **Libra:**

The Cardinal Libra Sun asks us to strengthen all relationships with an infusion of justice, equality, communication, fairness and romance. We harvest what we sow, in our hearts and in our cultures. Honor our beloveds, two- and four-legged, winged and finned relations.

excerpt, Heather Roan Robbins
© Mother Tongue Ink 2006, WM'08

THULA – SCALE

art by Minerva © Creative Cronies,
Moon CalendarProductions 1990, New Zealand, WM'92

Jai Ma

The power of turning inside out,
and simply tuning in

deeper to the luminous crimson
shadow core that is

at once Shakti/Kali
breathing through my flesh.
excerpt ¤ Suzette Winona Summers 2009, WM'11

WM'85

206

. . . and to SCORPIO she said:

To you my eighth daughter belongs the energy of the deep <u>fixed water</u>. I give you the difficult task to experience and learn about death and rebirth. So you will be the ones who can show others the impermanence of all, you show to let go and free the way for something new. A vital force and sexual power will be available to you, because you have to deal with regeneration of life, which will bring you often in dark, depressing and destructive spaces. Your deepness will make you able to come to the bottom of everything, and then rise again like a colorful bird to the heights of the sky.

WM'85

Moonspell
© *Krista Lynn Brown 1998, WM'04*

♏ **Scorpio:**
The Sun in Fixed Scorpio asks us to reach into the wellsprings of our soul, our knowledge and our passion. Its purpose is to compost the old, peer into the lengthening nights and face our fears. Mysteries fascinate and instruct us; we bring our formidable attention to bear and seek new answers.

excerpt, Heather Roan Robbins
© *Mother Tongue Ink*
2006, WM'08

art by Minerva © Creative Cronies,
Moon Calendar Productions 1990, New Zealand, WM'92

Transcendence
I am That which I avoid.
I am That which I seek.

excerpt © Myra Dutton 2009, WM'11

WM'85

Coastal Water Dance
❑ *Jeanette M. French 2001, WM'08*

. . . and to SAGITTARIUS she said:

To you my ninth daughter I'll give the energy of the <u>mutable fire</u>. You will have the lightness, the optimism and the hope to look for truth of life, the 'why' of our existence, and to find it. With your love for adventures nothing can ever stop you to go after your goals. But this energy can also make you restless, because once you have reached your goal you won't be satisfied until you have found the next. Your search will never be just for yourself-you have a strong need to make it known, what philosophical answers you have found. You will be mostly very convinced of your own ideas but take care not to get dogmatic or fanatic.

WM'85

Firedance © *Jana Lamprecht 2004, WM'09*

✒ Sagittarius:

The Mutable Sagittarius Sun asks us to think big and use our restlessness and curiosity creatively. It's time to take a philosophical perspective and see ourselves as global citizens of a many-species existence. Expand horizons, explore our world and be grateful for all we have.

excerpt, Heather Roan Robbins
© *Mother Tongue Ink 2006, WM'08*

art by Minerva © Creative Cronies,
Moon CalendarProductions 1990, New Zealand, WM'92

i know how to be an arrow now

i know how to be the seizing power
    the searing core
i know how to pierce through, eyes open

and i know my body as a huge bright flame
my will directed is a deep wide beam

i know how to be an arrow now
i know how to be an arrow now

excerpt ¤ Marna 1995, WM'07

Release

afraid to move forward
hesitating in indecisiveness
back and forth
        back and forth
back and forth

until one morning
she wrapped herself
in purple silk
put roses in her hair
and shouted, "YES!"
to the sky

¤ *Tara Maher 2007, WM'09*

Diana
© *Alexandra Olenka Gadzik*
2003, WM'07

. . . and to CAPRICORN she said:

You are my tenth daughter, and to you I give the energy of the starting earth. While Sagittarius had still all the wildness in front of her to explore, you have reached the borders. You have a strong responsibility feeling and you will be able to bring structures, rules and discipline in life with others, where ever it's needed. You have a lot of endurance to go hard and lonely ways, but take care not to get lost in your ambition. Being so strongly grounded, you are able to make high jumps and come down again safely.

WM'85

art by Minerva © Creative Cronies,
Moon CalendarProductions 1990, New Zealand, WM'92

♑ Capricorn:

The Cardinal Capricorn Sun asks us to dive deep into the collective consciousness to find a worthy dream, and then do the work necessary to walk it to the mountaintops. It's time to ground ourselves in the traditions and rituals that connect us to our past, and refocus our resolutions.

excerpt, Heather Roan Robbins
© Mother Tongue Ink 2006, WM'08

WM'85

Request to Pluto

Oh, Precious Pluto,
Planet of Prescribed Burn—
while you are destroying
my old structures,
kicking my butt,
singeing outdated ideas
and illusions to ash,
could you spark a
fire in my heart,
reseed my dreams
like fireweed after
the forest burns, which
returns stronger, fuller,
more resilient, richer,
with greater color, longevity,
fortitude and strength?
With humble caution and
great respect,
     Capricorn

© Diane Bergstrom 2008, WM'10

Butterfly Woman
© Patricia Mary Brown 2000, WM'04

We'Moon's Saturn Return

In 2010-2012, We'Moon encounters its first Saturn Return—a crucial developmental stage for individuals and institutions in their 29th or 30th year. Born as the *We'Moon Almanac* on the Full Moon of Winter Solstice in 1980, We'Moon took off with its own astrological blueprint. We'Moon 2011, the 30th edition, also begins at the Full Moon of Winter Solstice. As Saturn returns to Libra, (We'Moon's 1980 location), it's time to re-ground and lay new foundations.

I entered We'Moon's story over 20 years ago, offering astrological perspectives for each sign in the "Year at a Glance." I am especially interested in the long view of Saturn's influences, as Saturn Returns occur after significant turning points every seven years. I have seen that We'Moon's herstory contains just such pivotal moments (there is more about these events in the Herstory section):

We'Moon begins at Kvindelandt, 1980; first US edition, 1987; Mother Tongue Ink incorporates, 1994; fire burns the office, 2001; the business restructures, 2008.

Structural transformations during this Saturn Return are critical to a sustainable future. Saturn rewards We'Moon's resilience and repeated ability to reconfigure. Saturn's stern eye demands intentionality, care with contracts and expectations, and encourages wise outside counsel.

Uranus, Neptune and Pluto also exert powerful influences upon We'Moon now. Pluto's paring knife peels away layers, revealing and reactivating We'Moon's 30 year-old passionate vision of offering inspired guidance for uncertain times. Uranus brings unexpected changes (2010-2011), requiring open-minded experimentation in this contracting economy. And Neptune follows, moving into its home sign Pisces in 2012, amplifying We'Moon's visionary work.

excerpt, Gretchen Lawlor © Mother Tongue Ink 2010, WM'11

Astro-Overview 2011: Groundswell

Change is rumbling underneath us, swelling from every crack in the culture and through every choice we make. We can resist and feel torn by its tremors or choose to roll with the waves, set our sails toward personal and cultural evolution, and see where the current takes us.

We are breaking down and rebuilding during an era-birthing T-square between Saturn, Uranus and Pluto, all in active Cardinal signs for most of 2011. These three have been dancing in and out of challenging aspects since 2009. Saturn then moves on and lets us lay new foundations, but Uranus and Pluto continue to square though 2015 to make sure we keep evolving.

A real disaster this year would be to try to prevent change; the tectonic plates of the earth and of the culture continue to move, and we have to adapt. Each day we need to hold on to our vision for ourselves and our world, and make decisions to move us in that direction.

Momentum builds toward a new creative era as expansive Jupiter conjuncts change-maker Uranus, and both trine warm-hearted Venus as 2011 begins—an aspect that flavors the whole year with hopeful and creative innovation. The planet Uranus speaks of innovation and technology, our nervous system, and our capacity to create and withstand change. Uranus can help us find the ingenious alternative fuels and technologies, as well as the new social constructs we need in order to progress.

We'll need balance as old rules fall by the wayside. We're compelled to take risks, to drop old modus operandi and do it differently. If our culture is willing to be honest, the Pluto/ Jupiter/Uranus T-square can help us make the radical adjustments needed to ameliorate climate change. But it may be hard to get anyone to work together. We can inspire, but have to let others find their way under this freedom-loving and rebellious aspect.

As the groundswell gains momentum, change can begin to feel like freedom, not breakdown.

*excerpt, Heather Roan Robbins, **www.roanrobbins.com***
© Mother Tongue Ink 2010, WM'11

The Yoga of Kinship
Cyclical and Evolutionary Shifts: 2012

Astrology provides us a profound symbolic language for understanding our participation in the flow of the cosmos. Over eons human beings have engaged in a co-creative relationship with the heavenly bodies circling in our skies. Wisdom is awakened when we use our own inner observatories, and through our own angle of perception, bring the phenomena of the world into focus.

During the cluster of years around 2011, Uranus energizes Aries, Pluto plunders Capricorn, and Saturn focuses Libra and Scorpio. These transforming planets form a "T-square" aspect (three planets 90° apart). This is a significant configuration that represents the crucible of tensions and dilemmas that we are facing in our personal and collective evolution. It calls on us to confront the selfish adherence to superficial rewards that rob the quality of life from future generations. It is like a square table with three legs that keeps tipping towards its missing point. Engaging the fourth cardinal sign of Cancer can allow us to restore balance, and reset our priorities. What resources we bring to this table, and how we serve and share among us, will be critical in defining the ascent or the decline of our humanity. We can choose to practice a "yoga of kinship" that values the integrity of the Earth and her people. As we come to recognize in each other our innate oneness, we will open in a heart-centered resonance with the life-giving divine Feminine.

There is a confluence of prophecy and mythic meaning from the Hopi, Maya, and Hindu traditions that considers this period as pivotal to our human destiny. The Mayan Long Count calendar ends a 5,125-year era on December 21st, 2012 (dates do vary). The calendar points to a harvesting of our history, or the "end of time" as we know it. According to some interpretations this is when the evolution of our human consciousness reaches an omega point, and we wake up to celebrate the Day of Creation in another cycle. While apocalyptic visions may abound, how we use this full dimensional identity crisis that is underway could be what saves us. With realities in flux, relinquishing our perceptions of separateness will allow us to engage fully in our conscious evolution

excerpt, Sandra Pastorius © Mother Tongue Ink 2010, WM'11

Arianrhod *© Hrana Janto 2000, WM'07*

From the perspective of the whole cosmos, where our universe revolves around a sun that is but one star in one galaxy whose closest stars we can barely see in the spiraling Milky Way, the entire span of earth life is hardly a blip. And yet this particular time span, encompassing the turn of this century, appears to hold great significance for the future of life on earth. Who knew? . . . that We'Moon would be exploring natural cycles and the creative consciousness of politically aware feminist women steeped in earth-based spirituality at this very time?

A time that is seen astrologically as the approaching alignment of our solar system with the center of our galaxy, kicking off a new 25,000 year era that ancient prophecy has foreseen as a critical turning point in even larger cycles of earth time! Whatever this might mean, the book you hold in your hands gives one look at how women (we'moon, womyn) view ourselves and our world in this period: a rarified time capsule. Look for the next chapter in We'Moon 2012 and beyond.

Musawa 2010

IV. Creative Spin

She Changes Everything She Touches © *Jakki Moore 2008, WM'10*

Freeplay combinations of art and writing celebrating thematic strands in the weave of We'Moon

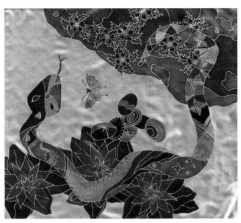

Snake, Eggs & Butterfly
◻ *Juliette Lagenour 2001, WM'07*

I Will

Listen, I've decided:
Life is too precious to ponder
the petty details any longer
and to put it bluntly
I will not participate.
I will not be coming to the party.
I will not be returning the call.
I will not be anything to anyone.
I will stare at the gray sky till it is blue.
I will walk in the green fields and
smell the wildflowers.
I will imbibe this life the way
it was meant to be imbibed.
I will listen only to my body
and the black crows.
I will live by the true laws of the Land.
I will pick wild blackberries and pet cats.
I will write poems I share
only with the wind.
I will raise a child
on the edge of nowhere.
I will nourish her on magic and honey.
I will teach her
the languages of fairies.
We will play in
the forest at twilight.
We will hurl all hardship
downhill to the sea.
© *Marni Norwich 2005, WM'07*

...to become a transformed Phoenix requires development of serenity, patience and peace of mind, which are not natural Phoenix traits. Phoenix sometimes pursues goals beyond her grasp and becomes disappointed when the task proves beyond her abilities. She benefits by learning to hold back criticisms and restraining the desire to dominate others and always be in the right. Instead, actively seek opportunities for growth, change and transformation. Keep your beak to the wind and fly Phoenix wemoon, fly!

excerpt, Susan Levitt © Mother Tongue Ink 2003, WM'05

Escape
© *Mickey Spencer 1991, WM'05*

The Fool and the Fire

My heart pumps hot blood faster as
we drum and rattle under August stars.
The guide has readied us well.
I watch the others one by one
walk the fire without harm.
Red coals wink and beckon,
This heated bed makes eyes at me!

Onto a new plane I move resolutely.
The crunch under my bare feet,
licks and steams, how on earth
can it feel cold as old popcorn?
Seven steps I walk as ten companions chant.
I part the curtain of fear. The world
changes. At the end of the bed.

I step laughing to my lover's arms.
She and I take hands to make the return.
I want to slow those moments down, sear
them into my heart. No challenge can
undo me now. What belief cannot be changed?
The curtain melts away. Expecting safety
I need no longer pursue it.
◻ *Susa Silvermarie 1998, WM'00*

The Woman Whose Body Became the Earth: Mythology for Re-Creation

Once there was a woman whose body became the Earth.
Her cells changed, turning from human form
          to animal, vegetable, mineral.
A cool stream pebbled down her throat and her center
became a pool with floating water lilies.
Her spine became an old Cedar,
her breasts grew into hillsides.
She took a breath and her lungs made grasses and grains.
The sun rose over the cave of her ribs and all the colors
of the desert mesa were etched along the horizon.
The woman squatted down
and her womb poured forth a fertility
that swam and crawled and galloped and flew;
that chirped and squeaked,
grunted and meowed and hissed.
And all this life made its way through the terrain of her flesh
until she was very full.

She Weaves Rainbows for Eternity
© Lupen Grainne 2006, WM'08

Once there was a woman
whose body became the Earth—
and became it, and became it and became it—
until the woman was no longer Woman.
All thought stopped.
The trees breathed. The mountains trembled.
The tides rose and fell under the eye of the Moon.
And the Earth rolled round and round
in the satin black sky.
No time passed. What was, Was.
The striving, dreaming, scheming,
willful, wonderful, conflicted,
clear consciousness of human mind slept deep
within her and the Earth rested.
Breathing. The Earth rested.
Stretching. The Earth rested.
And more no time passed.
And the Woman whose body had become the Earth,
who held all creatures inside herself,
and all the wild places
from pole to pole, rested, too.

excerpt © Christina Baldwin 2001, WM'03

Sheela na Gig ¤ *Monica Sjöö 1978, WM'96*

Woman as Potter

From the very first time she threw that hunk of clay on the wheel, she said, I'm going to throw a hell of a world. And from the rich recesses of the cool, dark earth, she hollowed out a bowl, a hand-held crater, into which she collected the rain. And as the rain shimmered down outside, she held the image of her world, and the redwoods and cedars drank deep from their roots, silhouetted against the silvery cusp of the moon. And as the arc of the moon tipped up on her pointed toes, the woman as potter settled her weight down on her hips, and gravity danced between them like lightning in the hills and rocked them in the deep rhythmic pull of the tides.

And as the carpet of leaves below hugged tightly around the chest of earth mother, the stars whirled around the elliptic on the potter's wheel, and as autumn spun through winter to spring, the little bulbs pushed their prayered hands up through the carpet of leaves, and the vision of woman as life-giver grew strong. No torn and tattered maiden, no servant, no rib; this woman was warrior, minstrel of fire, storm lover and mother of birth. You could see her splinter flint from her anvil, fire stones into stars in her kiln, wrack forth life like thunder, while her prayers ushered forth oracular and her children claimed life with both hands.

Paoro—Goddess who Gave the First Woman Voice
© *Lynn Dewart 2001, WM'05*

© *Julie Weber 2000, WM'03*

Young Goddess Creates New Toys
© *Robyn Waters 2002, WM'10*

© *Oriol Dancer 1991, WM'92*

"...To my Knowledge this turtle was one of the first animals, or is the first animal, and that was its duty, was to turn into the island, the earth. So to my knowledge that's the oldest animal and I give thanks for that spirit."
excerpt from an interview with Kayendres, Mohawk
© *Sandra Pastorious 1990, WM'92*

Prayer & Invocation
© Marcia Snedecor 2004, WM'07

when i am clear
with myself
clear
to the solid cavern
at my center
the world turns
luminous truly.
in the truth telling
orbs and edifice
of sense
i become a bell
my body becomes
a bell the wind rings
excerpt ¤ marna 2005, WM'09

Angel with Ladder
© Marianna Crawford 1994, WM'09

Betwixt and Between

Find a quiet place to sit outdoors. Settle in however you like—breathing, chanting, stretching or any kind of mind-body deepening. Make yourself comfortable enough to stay alert and relaxed for an indefinite period of time.

Lotus ¤ Melissa VanTil 2000, WM'03

Send your awareness to a place around you that is betwixt and between. In other words, find a point of energetic exchange where what exists is neither this nor that but rather in dynamic transaction.

For example, seek out the boundary between rock and river. Where does the river stop flowing into the rock? How porous is stone? How subject to erosion, to temperature change, to the insistent pressure of rushing water? What does the stone yield to the river? Or find the place where leaf becomes sunlight, where root penetrates soil, where your breath meets the air. Explore an edge of contact, experiencing the permeable and mutable qualities of so-called solid matter.

Let this perception lead you deeper into relationship with the numinous, vibrating energy of nature. If you still think the environment is outside you, try holding your breath. Perhaps you will discover that you are not separate from the world nor from the divine. Perhaps you will find yourself betwixt and between, neither here nor there, which is to say in the land of faerie. May you dwell in timeless time and know that you are blessed.

Return to normal perception slowly and gently. Or don't return at all. It's up to you.

¤ *Jessica Montgomery 1999, WM'01*

Swellspell
◻ *Padme Rain Crowe 2009, WM11*

We spill salt in circles
Shout in minor keys
We summon Diana Isis Hecate
We write wishes on rice paper—certain
We know what will make us happy.
We play witchery
We want change in conformity to our whims.
We want the universe at our feet.

We breathe deep, suckling Earthblood.
Her Power fills our wombs, our breasts
Our hands, our circle.
We drink, overflow, shine like stars.
We concentrate, conjure magic symbols,
Howl like wolvewomen, chant Her Names.
We imprint wishes on Astral Planes, those
Liquid Worlds where futures rest
Ripe for manipulation, artistry.
We know a secret: Imagination is magic.
We burn and banish.
So mote it be.
We play at witchery—certain
We know what will make us happy.
We hope we know what we're doing.

◻ *Diana Rose Hartmann, WM'93*

Altaring

My altar is a microcosm of myself, of my living, and not a static assemblage of things. Altar is not only a noun but also a verb. "To altar." I altar, which is to say that I focus, that I concentrate on whatever is up (illness, someone I want to sing heartfullness to, something I am grateful for); I give myself healing touch, speak my list of affirmations. A polished rock, a slice of petrified wood, an old wooden candlestick conjure the company of women who care about me.

The altaring I do daily in the inner circle of the house is similar to what I do with plants and soil: it feels the same to focus on the candle flame as to contemplate the earth's moisture rising to the sun, the same to hold a crystal and call healing to a friend as to splint a rose branch.

One day I stood a long while on the deck and considered the gardens, the snow lingering on the distant ridges, the huge white clouds, and understood the immensity, the mystery, and power of the altar that is the Earth herself.

On this altar I am an active sacred object. In the myriad details of my daily living, I manifest the goddess speaking her affirmations.

◻ *Hawk Madrone 1995,*
excerpted from Maize *(Summer 1995), WM'98*

Good Intentions

In magickal work, Intention is a priority to consider before beginning action. It is a way of focusing the mind and having a sense of purpose that leads to action. Intention is a determination to act in a certain way, a resolve to achieve something. It helps to be deliberate about our plans in order to organize the energy and actions that will bring about our desired results.

Much of creating Sacred Space is in Intention. Since we are performing a symbolic cleansing of an area, our Intention is very important to the process. If we are to reverentially set aside a location, a time or an action, we must be clear about what we want to accomplish, and how we plan to do that. In this kind of work, it matters how we do things, but it matters just as much why we are doing them and what attitude we bring to the situation.

Approaching a magickal working with full attention and an open heart is making use of Intention to guide our actions and focus our energies. When we come to stand in a Circle with "Perfect Love and Perfect Trust," we have begun an Intention of working together cooperatively. This magnifies the energy even more than the increased number of participants raises the vibration.

Live your life with Intention and you will see that every act becomes a sacred ritual, every thought a blessing.

◻ *Spiral Crone 2005, WM'07*

They Are
(The Ancestors)

They are like glass
     or water
the shimmer.
They are like heat
     or wind
the current.
They are like animals
     or dust
the river.
They are like moons
     or walking
the promise.
They are like wanting
     or fear
the insistence.
They are like ocean or
     mist
the deliverance.
They are like broom or
     flower
the exception.
They are like pattern
     or song
the artistry.
They are like babe
     or cane
inevitable.
They are like stones
     or mouths
our ancestors.

      ▫ *Patricia Worth 1998, WM'00*

Amazon Warriors of the Bronze Age ▫ *Monica Sjöö 2001, WM'02*

O Great Mother of Creation
A Prayer for (S)healing the Matrilineal Line

I take a deep bow to the foremothers.

I take flight with the foremothers
Who have been born aloft
by the spirit winds of vision
for liberation—
the foremothers, all the womyn
who ever paused,
wind in their hair, listening to bird
song, clarifying freedom.

I rise in conflagration's journey
in search to stars:
I crouch at fire's verge
with the foremothers
who have been burnt in
pyres of desolation,
And wind-whip-whinny,
air-alight, with all the womyn
who have ever gazed at bright
flame and changeling coals
of circle-fire,
and circled, and sang.

I stoop and drink the water
my foremothers drank
she-they who have floated
in the (s)healing waters,
with flower petals and sacred herbs,
and been restored,
Weeping and strengthened
with the moon's wild gyres.

I step onto this Earth
where my foremothers danced
Made
from my foremothers' dust
—the foremothers
who knew the cycle of return,
who grew garden
from seed to fruit and flower.

I inhabit the same womon's body
of wisdom and sinew and vim
My foremothers crafted.

I take a deep bow to myself
and smile the deepest smile
of delight and crafty knowing.

I hear the sacred blessing
from the foremothers forward
My deepest heart sparkles
with their radiant blessing.

     ▫ *marna 2006, WM'09*

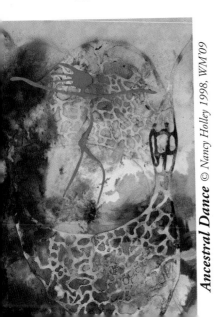

Ancestral Dance © *Nancy Holley 1998, WM'09*

Remembering ▫ *Gyps Curmi 2003, WM'09*

Horned Goddess Rememberance
© Oriol Dancer 1991, WM'92

Wakan

My wings were cut
By the scissors of the Diva,
Great angel whose body is the sun.

Her breath cast crystal stars
Of light across my shoulder blades
As she gently shaped my rainbow feathers.

The snowgoose, eagle, owl, and hawk
call to me repeating my name backwards.

With the voice of the serpent
I answer.

□ *Gentle Doe, WM'92*

Soul of Creation © Ann Beeching 2005, WM'08

Kindred Spirits

...I know animals as my guides, as my friends, and in my chakras. When I quiet myself I am able to listen to the information, pain, joy each animal has to share with me. Each one of my chakras has an emotional lesson, and my animals are there to assist me.

When I am asked to do healing in a "shamanic" way, through an altered state, animals are with me as a source of power and guidance. If I have to face other people's demons, or do a "soul retrieval," I am grateful for the animal's strength and wisdom. My animals help me to understand other people, whether they are clients who have come for healing, or my lover or friends.

excerpt © Mari Selby 1991, WM'92

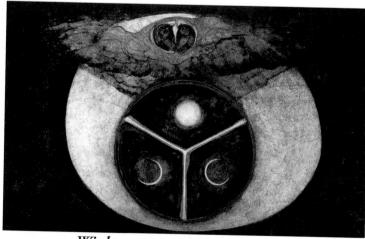

Wisdom □ *Meinrad Craighead 1983, WM'05*

The Dreaming Turtle © *Karen Russo 1997, WM'99*

After

Sister, when the flood is through
  and liquid evenings tell
of eternity's drunken power,
  take the avenue to still waters
where the dark sea incubates our love.

The rose red goddess will consume
  our secrets in one heaving moment.
Her chanting will rain
  these days to sleep.

And in her next dream
we blossom together—
  you are honey sweet tendrils,
  I am diamond pink petals—
in a misty morning bed,
  whispering under a summer sky.

¤ *Christine McQuiston 1998, WM'05*

Moon Guide

Pitch black dotted with sequins
View for sleepy eyes propped by anticipation
Wearily awaiting the rising moon
That brilliant jewel to illuminate nocturnal images
Providing light for clarity
Till fading into dawn
When waking vultures pick dreams clean

¤ *Kathryn A TePoel 1997, WM'99*

Magic of the Night

Each night I lower myself down
Into the magic depths of sleep
Oblivious to that embracing
Moment when it takes me deep
Into the silent world of nowhere
There, with others, animals and insects,
Even flowers
I live the other side of life that sleeps by day.

© *Marguerite Bartley 1999, WM'01*

***Dreams are filled with omens.
Listen, learn, fear not.***
© *Sudie Rakusin 1984, WM'93*

This is a YES! place
Love is a YES!
    Not a maybe
    Or a will see
    Or a if you do this & this & this
It's a brisk, clear water, earth, air
    And fire paradise!
We are whole and alive
    And brilliant and beautiful
And YES!!!

¤ *Joanie Levine 2000, WM'02*

Tongues of Fire ¤ *Dorothy Rossi 1998, WM'08*

© *Annie Ocean, WM'88*

True Friends are ones
who know the tune
of your heart
and hum it back to you,
when you have forgotten
the words.

excerpt ¤ *Galloway Quena Crain 2006, WM'08*

Mother & Daughter Storm

We walked gingerly
tonight
around the edges
of our storm.
The water rippled
and raged
almost tidal
at times
but we stayed
steady on the rocks
of our rendezvous
with old pain.

And then at last
we breached
as if we were killer whales
high above the sea
and then we crashed through
the glistening surfaces
deeper deeper
into the ocean's core
deeper deeper
into our heartspace
where the storm
finally ends

© *Pesha Joyce Gertler 2005, WM'08*

© *Sandra Lory 2008, WM'10*

Unfolding This Season

As the kindness of verbena
expresses in excess
of that expected
As the clemency
of pansy utters far beyond
demands of fairness
May my mouth make the round
sound of mercy
Enough of pursed lips, the straight
line of judgement.

May dianthus and alyssum
be the syllables I chant
Let my mouth now sing
compassion in the shape
of a perfect peony
Like lilacs awaited
for years of spring,
unfolding finally this season,
may mercy from my mouth
ring into the world.

¤ *Susa Silvermarie 2001, WM'02*

Our Relatives with Roots

We have a covenant with creation to carry on our responsibility, as those who have two legs, in relationship to our relatives that have fins, wings, hooves and roots. And so we have this food, Manoomin, which means "the most wondrous seed." This food is a central part of our culture as Anishinaabeg people. We have cared for those rice beds, for our lakes and rivers for as long as we have been Anishinaabeg.

When the University of Minnesota cracked the DNA sequence for Wild Rice, that set us up for genetic engineering and genetic contamination. One of our chiefs said, "Who gave them permission?" And that is the ethical question, isn't it? Who gave anybody rights to change the DNA sequence of life forms?

I didn't understand what seed slavery was until I met up with Monsanto. And then I understood why we had to ensure that they did not patent our rice and they didn't own it. And so, we as indigenous people have formed this indigenous seed sovereignty coalition; with us are the taro farmers of Hawaii, who are saying taro is our relative and you can not patent it. Our relatives in New Mexico look at protecting the indigenous corn varieties as their relatives. These are essential parts of who we are.

Our traditional foods, those really old indigenous varieties, are much higher in antioxidants, fiber, amino acids than anything you can buy at the store. Those foods are medicine. Those old biologically diverse seed stocks have the ability to adapt and will make it through climate destabilization. If we want to feed our people, we have to go back to our original heritage varieties, those original relatives that have roots.

excerpt © Winona LaDuke, Bioneers 2007 Conference, October 19-21, WM'09

White Earth Reservation, Winona and Ajuawak, Wild Rice Harvest ¤ *Betty LaDuke 2007, WM'09*

I used to have a button that said, "Violence begins with the fork"! Perhaps we ARE what we eat, and as we continue to torture our dinner, we become a more violent culture. Maybe little bits of frustration and anger creep into our world because of what we eat!

If everyone (or at least half of us!) switched to a vegetarian diet, or ate only free-range meat, factory farms would become unprofitable and go out of business. Mass production of livestock uses up many of our natural resources. Think of all the trees cut down in the rainforest to make way for cattle ranches. Over 50% of our water is used in some form of livestock production. It takes 2500 gallons of water to produce one pound of meat compared to 25 gallons for one pound of wheat. A vegetarian diet can conserve about one and a half Olympic pools of water a year per person. We have lost about 56% of our topsoil because of livestock production. 15 vegetarians can be fed on the same amount of land that it takes to feed one person on a meat-based diet.

My dream is to see the factory farm become extinct before I do.

¤ *Ann Southcombe 2006, WM'08*

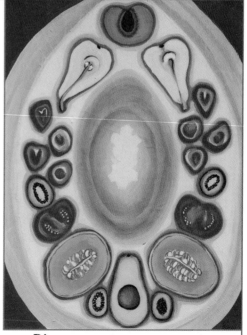

Ripe ¤ *Rebecca D'Elena 2001, WM'04*

Angel of Mercy © Marla Faith 2006, WM'09

Legacy'd

for Beverly Brown, 1951-2005

Will you really, finally die
after I use all the Sweetmeat squash seeds
you gave us years ago?
Your fat, happy seed children.
I still plant lettuce seeds, Buttercrunch,
that came from your serious saving.
Will you fade when the envelope is empty
of life rattling around in seed form?

There is nothing quite like
putting your seeds in the ground
legacy of trust in tomorrow
despite the end of your today.

How you loved the science of the cycles—
the dormant, the swelling,
the opening push of tender
miracle sprout hungry and thirsty

the crowded carrots
the giant mustard leaves
the hot rank summer of lusty success
    the triumph of Food
Food to share, food to dry, to can
before the shrivel and pucker of pods
where the next generation of seed babies
snuggles down in the cold nursery of winter
to await the next incarnation
while decay enjoys its own feast
and compost works its slow resurrection.

excerpt © Bethroot Gwynn 2008, WM'10

My Down Home Religion

"Composting is my religion," I like to say with a mischievous smile. Composting! Such a dull term to refer to the miracle that changes the dirty, the rotting, the slimy, the smelly, the broken, the unwanted, the leftovers, the sticky, the too many, the not enough, and the repulsive—into the very stuff of life. Into that beautiful dark crumbly soft moist fertile soil that will eventually become air to breathe, food for energy, the pleasures of color and scent, and indeed the very ground on which we stand.

To consciously participate daily, hourly, in this process, is my religion. I believe it is Hers, too. The Tao of the Universe: to support life, enhance it, expand it, transform it, continue it.

In my Spring garden, the ground is moist and crumbling. The sun is warm on my back and robins keep watch with song as I prepare for planting. Dreams of thick green bushy plants full of blossoms, then heavy with fruit, and visions of rows of jars of vegetables and sauces fill my head as the wetness seeps through the knees of my jeans.

Kali. I am Kali now, and soon Aphrodite, Demeter, Hestia. Now I kill. I kill everything that grows in my path. Not in anger or vengeance or indifference. I kill within the circle of this garden. In the service of my need for food and beauty. I am partner in the life-death-life cycle which I see surrounding me as I walk these woods. So much green-growing. . .so much broken-rotting: each becoming the other in the Great Mysteriousness.

□ Jean Mountaingrove 1996, reprinted and excerpted from
The Sage Within *(Summer Solstice 1996), WM'98*

Share the Seeds © Sandra Lory 2008, WM'10

Coo Coo Coo Chew

Turkey vultures flap overhead,
swooshing kites of black and red, something's dead.
Stink invades my brain, wings seduce my eyes.
The promise of flight
uplifts an ancient segment
of the flesh and spirit sandwich I inhabit
tickling capillaries deeper than the mind,
flicking the veil aside.
The Universe revealed as a spinning donut
in an onanistic reverie,
a closed system like the symbol for recycling,
infinity a Möbius strip
that does have a meaning after all. What's rot and filth to me
is lunch-time at the Ritz for my distinguished visitors.
This refreshes my tolerance
for "the seeming inequities," "the perceived injustices"
the limbless children searching through rubble for their parents
the smarmy fat cats profiting from this week's pillage.
Thank you, turkey vultures for a job well done.
You gobble up the putrid mess,
turn it into gliding feathers
slicing arcs of rapture through the sky.
It's all one dance one dancer
one applauding audience one ensemble cast
The golden rule has been mistaken for injunction.
The truth is simpler:
Whatever we do, we do to ourselves.
We are the deer. We are the vulture.
We are the eggplant.
Coo coo coo chew.

© *La Tigresa (Dona Nieto) 2006, WM'08*

Emergence
© *Ann Beeching 2007, WM'09*

I am the world and the world is in me.
I am a tree, a rock, a puddle of water
Moon pulls me.
The tears in my eyes have tides
that rise higher some nights than others,
beholding the world in the sleeper's gaze.
They lied to us.
Said we are separate from creation.
We are not.
The molecules of this planet are all the same.
Break me down, break me down—
the skin, the bones,
the muscles, the soft organs—
to the level of absolute matter
you cannot tell me apart
from anything else.
I am every body—
the magpie's tail, the pinion bush,
the pebble, the dog's hair—
the same body as your body.

excerpt □ Christina Baldwin 1996, WM'98

The Self and Other Dreams
© *Emerald Goldman, WM'93*

Biosexual

I think I'm biosexual.
Flowers turn me on. I have eco-erotic thoughts.
The liquid trickle of the stream-flow lapping over the rocks
makes my juices flow. My loins are moist soil.
My nipples respond to the tiny cupped lips of flower petals.
And a flower is really nothing but spread-open botanical labia—
love-lips smiling at the world.
A flower is a sexual invitation luring insect pollination.
Trans-species sexuality is what makes your garden grow.
Soft green moss on the velvet loveseat of a fallen tree trunk
seduces my skin with the promise of sweet sensation.
Delicate blue and purple wild flowers entice me
like little faerie poems printed on flower-vellum,
and in the center of each one, five tiny secret hearts
like a cluster of elfin candy valentines
within the flower vulva, protected by luscious flower lips.
Some blossoms closed, some shamelessly spread open.
My own juices begin to trickle,
my own labia swelling with desire as I write this.
And when I timidly stroke the deep green velveteen
of the outer flower cover
it feels like I'm rubbing skin on teensy-tiny bad-girl buns
encased in eensy-weensie velvet panties
and I feel the tingle of desire squirt through all my inner folds
like I haven't felt from an erotic encounter with nature
since those apple blossoms seduced me down in Santa Cruz
with their ripening adolescent bud-breasts
and flouncy petal skirts of pink and white chiffon;
Am I a botano-phile? A pan-sexual?
Or just a moist pink mammal
sniffing all the painted perfumed floral floozies
flirting well outside my species,
lusting after my long-forbidden sisters
hungry to embrace this whole green planet
unable not to taste the nectar of love
where ever it finds me.

excerpt © LaTigresa (Dona Nieto) 2004, WM'06

Fertility and Choice
© Jennifer Lynn Shifflet 1998, WM'01

The Lesbian Mind: Metaphors II & III *© Judy Springer 1991, WM'93*

44 Salmon

The scientists snare numbers with charts of statistics
while you squint from the river boat into folds of water
arching and mottled with wind spittle
and deeper into where the numbers school,
upcurrent over the teeth of dams,
unharmed by turbines and the suck of pumps, so they say.
The scientists multiply numbers like fish eggs hatching
spawned by reasons and equations.
What happens when numbers die?
The scientists arrange them in pi and square roots
and declare there is still plenty to go around.
Meanwhile, the salmon disappear.

When the scientists suspend their numbers like hooks
do you bite into the belief of longevity,
the river's ability to look out for herself and the salmon?
Or do you cast your line without hesitation,
the river thick with equations, so they say.
What difference will 44 salmon make this year
if next we have 45?
They offer fractions as bait, calculations as hope.
Meanwhile, the salmon disappear.

What good will the rivers be if they are empty and sour?
And which scientist will make a salmon
from electricity or a pristine prime number?

excerpt © Amy Schutzer 1994, WM'02

Listen They Know © *Diana Tatiana Leaf 1993, WM'08*

Prayer to Live with Paradox

I want to be young in wonder again,
to hold a single seed to the sky and marvel
that it owns the energy of a star. I want to
be grown big enough for my vast protective arms
to encompass whole rainforest miracles
of tree-dazzle, life-power. I want to be light
as a leaf on the earth. I want to be the weight
that carries promise-flowers to fruit, greens
Darfur to peace and nurtures Lebanon's vineyards
through all four seasons gift to eye and tongue.

I want to learn the use of grief that honours those
creature-spirits who leave us, that long, on-going
shadow-procession: Nightjar and Loggerhead,
Gold-ringed Tanager, Arabian Gazelle,
Yellow-shouldered Blackbird, howler monkey,
Hyacinth Macaw and salamander, sea mink
forever swimming to horizons beyond the blue —

I want to learn the use of joy in those who stay,
somehow still keeping faith
in the family of humankind:
cranes and sweet horses,
rainfrogs and mountain lizards,
Bald Eagles, elk and caracal,
Mexican Spotted Owls
thriving on the rooftops of Los Alamos, chaffinch
in the lilacs, coyote, otter, Golden Jackal,
huge herds
of shining white-eared kob runing on the sands
of South Sudan,
parakeets thriving wild in London—

So much I want, a whole world I want.

© *Rose Flint 2007, WM'09*

Goddess of the Ark © *Lindy Kehoe 2004, WM'07*

© Jacqueline Young 2001, WM'09

© Kanoa 1991, WM'92

I want to dream of wolves and bears again
I want to get in touch with my family...
excerpt © Berta R. Freistadt 1990, WM'92

CreatureSpeak

Who shall speak for the voiceless ones?
In a language we all can understand
The ones in chains, in costumes, labs
The ones whose habitat fell to concrete
What queen of nature, of spirit, of grace
Shall speak for these creatures
Honor the animals, the earth, ourselves
excerpt ¤ Casey Sayre Boukus 2000, WM'08

Calistos © S. J. Hugdahl 1989, WM '00

Three Ravens © Lisa de St. Croix 1999, WM'01

Golden Eagle
© Elizabeth Diamond Gabriel 2000, WM'08

Cry Freedom   © Mira Michelle 2000, WM'06

Saraswati
© Meganne Forbes 2009 WM'11

Why I Sing

I sing because it feels good. As one sound starts bubbling up from my belly and resonating in the cathedral of my chest, it feels as if the whole earth is breaking open and that a river is running up my serpent spine until the gate of my heart is sprung and I wiggle free from this tight suit of skin. When I sing, something bigger than just me emerges, chanting the life force in an ancient language of tone, breath and rhythm. My heartbeat is the percussion, my breath the space between notes; I am a bellows breathing fire into the heartland to ignite and blaze, not only for me, but for everyone. To sing is to invoke, to chant, to yell, to moan, to sigh, to sob, to coo, to laugh, to reach for and to empty all in one.

I sing because it keeps my muscles lithe, my mind loose, my flesh warm, my bones supple, my blood rich and my heart ripe. I sing because it makes me cry when I need to, makes me express what is tangled and pent up and makes me celebrate what is joyful. When I sing, I am able to let go of my smaller self to communicate with the divine in a language beyond language—*before* language, when tone, melody and emotion were the only language.

I sing because it is my way of placing a prayer in the open palm of the goddess, and my song is an armful of wildflowers gathered at sunrise and placed on her altar like a million tiny tongues chanting their harmonies to the universe, calling out the names of every being, everywhere, to come home.

© Meredith Heller 2005, WM'07

The Muse Listening

The Muse is listening for
a silence she can erupt through.
An emptied mirror
she can reflect in.
excerpt © Lorraine Schein 2002, WM'04

Potter's Hands and Pot:
pottery ¤ Greta Boann Perry 1993;
photo © Tangren Alexander 1996, WM'98

© Rebecca Guberman-Bloom 2005, WM'10

Night of One Thousand Birds

Thought Woman

Thought Woman is one of many names pervasive in tribal origin stories from all over the world for the essence of powerful feminine creative intelligence.

My intelligence is complete and unique. I am a wise descendant of Thought Woman, brilliant in my own creative ways, valuable to the Whole.

excerpt © Jane (Saya) Wolf 1999, WM'03

Dear Sappho *© Lorraine Inzalaco 2001, WM'04*

A Writer on Beltane

Curves swelling,
flowing lines
oozing out of my hands
through my pen,
in honor of Goddess.
I know her;
She is in me now.
I am acutely aware of energy
and emanations on this day.
I don't want to write words;
don't want to make well-formed,
structured letters or meanings.
I want to let my pen lead me all over the page,
taking me into unknown spaces,
forming who knows what.
Then maybe I'll be led off the page,
out of the chair, down the stairs,
picking up paints and dyes,
dripping color on my walls,
making thick, juicy lines
and swirls of color
I'll want to lick and taste
because they seem alive.
Then maybe I'll be led outside,
to my gardens,
small and ready for attention,
dripping my own thick colors into them.
And maybe I'll have to lie
in some sweet folds of soft earth,
all juicy and aroused.
The stories in my body telling themselves
to the listening Mother.
Secrets she already knows.

▢ Katryn Lavanture 2003, WM'06

© Heike Montreal 1996, WM'98

Home Is Where You Are

Basketeer

Black hands split white pine
sass blonde fibers into composed laths
folding one, pulling tight
each a splice for a banjo seat
tucking there, weaving fast
while the fat baby sleeps
Cakewalk over lattice unfettered
and full of hickory smoke,
fragrant slats burned to bend
giving breath to vessels
for eggs and glass beads
spools of blue thread
dandelion greens
and pinto bean jars
with thoughts in slience
of ginger-root fingers
casting the spellwork down.

© *Terri Jewell, WM'91*

Bharti's Kalash © *Susan Kullmann &*
Marvelle Thompson 2004, WM'08

healing hands

   hands slick with warm oil, she glides her fingers
between mine. thumbs rub the belly of my palm. she
is scented orange and almond. sparks rise like fountains
in my thighs. she slides up my wrist, circles the pulse,
slicks the tiny hairs with oil. loosens the bicep, tricep,
rocks the shoulder in its socket. the blade slips into her
hands. she polishes the bone until it shines like a song.
vessels sigh open. muscles swing. her fingers like water
swirl between tendons, lift and carry bones. thought-
petals drift. she cradles, envelops, encloses me. rocks
me in a hammock of hands. she caresses my ears until
I hear sparrows. an outbreath of wind. the whispery
dances of leaves. she pours my body full with lullabies,
with sacred chant, with grace.

© *Natascha Bruckner 2003, WM'05*

Creation © *Rebecca Hickman 2004, WM'08*

Cave Walls © *Sierra Lonepine Briano 2008, WM'00*

Moon Lodge

I want to build a moon lodge
where old womyn braid my hair
brushing slowly, gently
the tangles of my life free
where there are no walls
only painted warm cloth
flowing, circling
blanketing me from the world
hanging between strong trunks and branches
of old growth wisdom
where I can smell flowers
and soil, rotting wood
where I can bleed in the moss
moan down the river
shed hidden tears, inner skin
breathe, drink, and sing
fresh strength
all day, three days
five days every month
whenever I need to, want to
hide, heal, hold hands
with wise womyn
who want to build a moon lodge

□ Jessica Todd 1997, WM'99

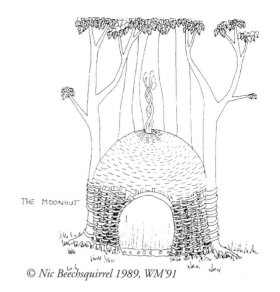

THE MOONHUT

© Nic Beechsquirrel 1989, WM'91

Dragon Salve

my brew is red
it comes form the dark
it boiled inside my cauldron
and for three days and
three nights it overflows
I reach my fingers into it

I paint it on my brow
I smear it on the
bottoms of my feet
I smell the hotness of it
I smell the soil inside it
and I mend myself

© Karen Van Fossan 1992, WM'94

Luteal Phase—Ovulation to Bleeding
Days 16–28 of the menstrual cycle

Slowly we pull back from the fullness, regathering what we have sent out. We start to turn our energy away from others, rearranging the pieces of our selves that were jostled by our full moon dash through the wild. We may need to be firm with those who demand our attention. The crone once again beckons, softly at first, but louder until we heed her call to lose ourselves in the ending that is a new beginning. As we move inward we may find ourselves experiencing mood swings. Teas or tincture of fresh Borage or Lemon Balm supports the nervous system, counteracts mind depression, and helps us feel less vulnerable.

After ovulation, progesterone levels rise to a peak and then taper off. Our liver works hard to break down hormones. Metabolism slows, calcium is absorbed less efficiently; changes in carbohydrate metabolism can cause sugar cravings, If the follicular (waxing) phase is a time of building, then the luteal (waning) phase is a time of breakdown and cleanup. The most helpful category of herbs we can use at this time are the liver tonics—Dandelion root or Burdock which can be taken as tea or tincture.

© Colette Gardiner 1998, WM'99

Resacarlize the Feminine
© Katheryn M. Trenshaw 1999, WM'03

Touching Southern Ocean

Your body
      folded in the arms of ocean
      weaving your legs around the
         legs of ocean

brushed by rhythmic
      lips of ocean—the lips
      calling home all your metaphors
         of tears

and crooning instead
      their silky tones along
      every surface of your skin—
         that membrane

thin and salty,
      the purse where you carry
      the tide pool that is
         the whole

of your life.
      And at that life's jostled
      and liquid center
         the ancient caress

of every wave
      in the round and panting
      instant
      before

         it breaks
         across the long thigh of a continent.

         ¤ *Mary Clare 1996, WM'99*

Brush with Beauty ¤ *Jill Dalton 1995, WM'99*

Eve
© *Sandra Stanton 1996, WM'03*

Persephone
© *Selina Maria di Girolamo 1998, WM'00*

232

Dancing as Liberation

There are countries where it is
a punishable crime
to dance.

Women must cover their heads,
never raise their voice in song and
never ever display such immoral conduct
as dancing.

Those who forbid the dance forbid life.

If they tied me in ropes
Held a gun to my head
And forbid me to dance
I would dance in my head.

If I woke up tomorrow
Without limbs that would move
I would dance in my soul.

If dance was taken from me
I would snatch it back.
I would dance with my eyes.
I would dance in my breathing.
I would dance completely still.
I would dance with the atoms
moving inside me.

I would dance in the mingling
of voices around me
Layering transcending
swooping into each other.
I would dance in the red-blushed sky
that caresses the tree line.
I would dance on the call of the geese
that cut through the sky above me,
my winged partners in the dance.

If dance was taken from me
I would snatch it back.

I would dance passion.
I would dance pain.
I would dance magick.
I would dance at my labor
and dance at my rest.
I would dance my power.
I would dance my palpable joy of existence.

In some countries it is illegal to dance.
It is illegal to display such immoral conduct.

Dancing is an act of liberation.
It is for those who must dance in stillness
that I open myself up and dance.

□ *Victoria Day 2007, WM'09*

*Hard Times
Require Furious
Dancing*
© *Alice Walker 2007,
WM'09*

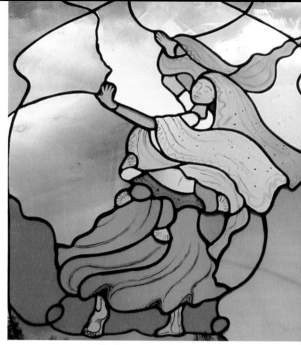

Bismillah © *Lupen Grainne 2003, WM'07*

Kali Epiphany

I am in dance class, gazing at an image of the Goddess: the fierce eyes of Kali-Durga, weapons in Her several hands framing Her serene face, Her lips curved in the hint of a smile. I ache inside, grieving over the world—poverty, hunger and suffering, the many wars, the violence. How can She be in bliss in the midst of all this?

Grace
© *Victoria Christian 2004, WM'06*

How can I dance now, when even *You* hold weapons of war in Your hands? I cling to my anguish, refuse reconciliation of the paradox—between Her serene face and her weapon-filled hands, between a suffering world aching for a Mother's love and its armed Mother.

But I am the teacher and I must dance   "it doesn't make sense" *surrender* "to believe the Mother's love and bliss is everywhere while this suffering happens" *surrender* "this is escapism!"   "self indulgence!" *surrender* "How dare I be in pleasure when there is so much suffering?!" *let go*

The pleasure of the Dance soaks me like exquisite perfume. I feel the charred bodies and battlefields around my feet—the ultimate horror of nuclear devastation. I inhale the inner fragrance of my pleasure, a million jasmine blossoms intoxicating me with bliss, curving my lips into the hint of a smile. Words float up on the fragrance—*If you want suffering, I give it. If you want pleasure, I give you that. I am your Mother. I give you your desire. Why not choose pleasure?*

© *Vajra Ma 2003, WM'09*

Back at the farm,
the starlings warble in the cottonwoods,
overlooking the pond.
Fresh mint scents the air,
and sheep bleat in the field
Ten years have passed since I left school,
with a fancy, advanced degree.
Over time the polish wore off
the diploma,
and smiles from would-be employers
grew dim.
New jobs, like springtime sprouts,
never reached the time of harvest.
Every time I got hired, I thought,
"this is it."
Relieved to have an income,
and grateful to have my gifts in use.
But now at middle-age,
I'm facing an uncertain future.
With no job, and no savings,
I may as well stand on a street corner
and hold up a sign,
"Overeducated woman of color,
please help."
Back at the farm,
plums and blackberries
hang on branches,
gracing my nose
with purple fragrance.
I turn my attention
to grooming the land,
as our ancestors have done
at one time or another.
Like a beloved's skin under my hand,
the earth heaves to my touch
with a strong pulse.
The farmland spreads
Her life-death cycle before me.
I offer to Her tenacity,
devotion, my life-long gifts.

excerpt ¤ Jean-Marie Zubia 2005, WM'07

*Coffee
Shop
Blues*
© *Cosima
Hewes 2005,
WM'07*

This Work of Women

Yes. It is time for a revolution in women and path, women and money, women and business, women and art, women and marketplace. We do not choose to give our works of any kind away for nothing. We are not starving or frivolous artists. We are creators whose creations save lives, heal the world, heal wounds. This work of women, priestesses and practitioners of every kind is VISIONARY WORK.

Your work is vital. Essential. Needed. This work of women must include creating livelihood. This is not easy, quick, fun nor likely. This is not accepted or encouraged. But this is what we must do:

Cause an abundance revolution. We must create our own path. We must create our own money. We must create art. We must create our own marketplace. We must be compensated.

We are creating our own mystical cosmic luminous overflowing BANK. A bank that does not cause, contribute or condone the suffering of others for profit. A women's bank. Believe it. Create it. Deposit into it. Draw from it. Invite other women to it. Enter the income stream in your little golden boat and dream and work and pray and play and do not stop. Keep going. It will almost always seem impossible. But we will make miracles. Miracles are organizing themselves around our dreams, our work, right now.

Believe it.

© *Shiloh Sophia McCloud 2005, WM'07*

Sheetrockin' Sister
¤ *Deborah Jones 2002, WM'04*

Hazelnuts ¤ *S.J. Hugdahl 1994, WM'96*

Women's Laughter

talking the night away
kitchen sink humour
laughing like drains
cackling like crones

hooting like owls
howling like wolves
gut wrenching
belly laughs

filthy jokes
foulmouthed
spitting it out
old bags and bad girls

table thumping
trivial, tribal,
tremendous
the power

of women's laughter

□ Cora Greenhill 2005, WM'10

Ester © Sequoia 2007, WM'10

Nicole's Wild Side © Angie Coffin Heiney 1998, WM'98

laugh

laugh
when there is nothing left
grief has eaten you
laugh.

fill the belly and the lung
with air the healer and the cleanser.
sing throat songs bird songs
smile: tooth grin and air roaring.
laugh to remember
what moves all moves you.

if you close your gateway of mouth
bitterness will linger, will
coat your mouth and organs with
long decaying staying.
movement reprieves us, relates us,
reminds us:

belly dances nose singing
mouth chortle   laugh.

□ marna 1995, WM '00

Greenham Women's Peace Encampment
¤ *Tracy Litterick 1985, WM'97*

Like a Mountain

SING DOWN ONE OCTAVE

words and music by Naomi Littlebear

Nobody can push back an ocean.

It's gonna rise up, in waves. And

nobody can stop the wind from blowin',

Stop a mind from growin."

Somebody may stop my voice from singing,

But the song will live on and on. You can't

kill the spirit, It's like a mountain,

Old and strong It lives on and on.

Nobody can stop a woman from feeling She

has to rise up like the sun.

Somebody may change the things we're saying,

But the truth will live on and on. You can't

kill the spirit, It's like a mountain,

Old and strong, It lives on and on...

© *Naomi Littlebear Morena 1977, WM'90*

Women's Magic Overcomes!

The fence around the US military occupation of Greenham Commons (UK) finally came down!—twenty years after the first women, mothers and children, marched from Wales across England to set up camp around the ten miles of fence surrounding the base. Since 1981, thousands of women from around the world came to protest, bear witness to and take action against the military maneuvers of the Cruise Missile housed there. Greenham was home for many women who lived there days, months, even years at a time, in impossible conditions: outside in the rain, facing eviction daily, cooking meals over wood fires, sleeping in makeshift "benders." They monitored the activities inside the gates and notified a network of concerned citizens when the Cruise missile was about to come out. They were continually arrested and "zapped" with radioactive currents, all the while keeping their spirits up with creative acts of magical power, cutting holes in the fence and pulling off incredible stunts inside the base and outside the gates, keeping the pressure up and the spotlight on the illegal US military nuclear presence in Greenham Commons. Thank you, Greenham women, for your courageous ongoing magic; we celebrate your success.

WM'97

Love For Missing Women Project

I heard about the missing women of Ciudad Juarez from a Mexican artist who was visiting the Gulf Islands. I was so moved, I painted these images. There are over 400 paintings of women's bodies on pages of the Bible. They are strung together and hung like Buddhist Prayer Flags. They are my prayers for these women and all women missing everywhere.

© *Amarah Gabriel 2002, WM'06*

Women's Work

Send the camouflaged men home
Ship the guns back
  Let the metal rust
  Defuse the bombs
  Detonate the mines
Sands shifting with a new wind.
    Gone! Gone! Gone are the ghosts.

Array the women in silver
  daughters of the world's
Great Goddesses
  bearing medicines and gruel
  seeing their hidden sisters in the shadows
Hear them shout across the line
  "Do your children have enough to eat?"

        ¤ *Lyrion Ap Tower 2008, WM'10*

The Line, Up ¤ *Katya (Nina Sabaroff) Taylor 1973, WM'08*

Wanted: Earth Healers
To Start: Immediately
Job Description: Care for the Earth.

Anyone need some work, or a life purpose? If so, look no further than your own backyard. There are billions of openings for hardworking folks in the field of permaculture, with demand for people to grow their own food, produce renewable energy, build sustainable communities and heal damaged ecosystems! Thanks to corporate plunder, our once abundant natural resources are in rapid decline. As fossil fuels diminish and global oil prices rise, much of the job market will become unstable. What's the unemployed truck driver, factory worker, industrial farmer, Enron executive and the rest of us to do?

Work for the earth! This big blue ball we have been living on needs every hand She can get. There are permaculture jobs to suit everyone. You can design food systems, heal the soil, purify water, provide habitat for wildlife and produce tons of organic food on as little as a quarter of an acre. Jobs building energy-saving homes (with local materials like recycled lumber, cob and straw bale) are in high demand. These homes use passive solar energy, living roofs, grey water recycling and composting toilets. The ancient jobs of sustainable woodcutting, fishing, wild crafting, animal husbandry, weaving, baking and natural healing are returning with vigor! Educators, bicycle mechanics, bio-fuel brewers, recyclers, community mediators, craftspeople, artists, herbalists, midwives, and creative people everywhere are needed now!

To apply: Please look over your current lifestyle and answer the following questions. Where does your food come from? How are your energy needs met? Where does your water come from, and where does it go after it leaves your home? Does your lifestyle/job enhance air, water and soil quality? In an emergency situation, how would you meet your basic needs for transportation and resources? Share your answers about this new career path with your sister earth healers!

Salary: The Earth is willing to pay top wages for integrating with and enhancing Her life systems. Organic food, abundant energy, clean water, shelter, community-based childcare, education and comprehensive natural healthcare are available to all successful applicants. The benefits increase the longer you work and will be passed on to future generations. So start now and build a better future for yourself and the planet—learn permaculture today!

        ¤ *Ginger Salkowski 2006, WM'08*

Poland: Brezezowka Village Hen Project
¤ *Betty LaDuke 2005, WM'10*

Timber Sales: Lost & Saved

An amazing set of coincidences saved the forest in the Cobble Creek timber sale area.

A group of forest activists I was a part of discovered BLM (Bureau of Land Management) cutting a few old trees illegally. We stopped them and reported them to other agencies. Soon afterward, I went for a hike in the area with my friend Abbey, a lichenologist. She found a very, very rare lichen on the downed old trees—a lichen which usually grows *only* in the very tops of trees over 400 years old and only at relatively low elevations. No one would ever have known about it, if those few old trees hadn't been cut and if Abbey and I hadn't happened to go for a hike to the right place. Abbey informed BLM of her discovery, and BLM has not been able to find a way around the law forbidding them to destroy this lichen site.

650 Year-old tree, Paw Timber Sale, Umpqua National Forest

photo and writing □ Francis Eatherington 2000, WM'02

Bless you, silent menders of a planet
torn by strip mining, clear-cutting, toxic waste dumping,
soil stripped of nutrients,
your web, of strongest single-celled strand mycelium,
unseen but for the fruiting of your mushroom flowers,
you hold us, mend us, heal us.

□ Barbara Dickinson 2007, WM'09

□ Marjorie Corbin 2007, WM'09

Elders

Nobody told her to lock herself with a bike chain to the logging truck but when the forest service workers stopped arguing with "them darn tree-huggers," there she was—five foot tall, tanned and tough as a nut, smiling serenely, locked to their immense vehicle.

"Hell," one of the officials said, "it's late." Besides, this white-haired lady looked like any of their grandmas or Mother Theresa, so the driver kicked a rotting log inhabited by nematodes, bark beetles, spaghnum moss, bracken fern, and the tottering seedlings of mountain hemlock, offering to leave if she would please unlock herself from his truck. "But first tell me," he pleaded, "you look like a nice lady, why did you do that?" She looked up at him, rain following the paths of wrinkles down her face. "Because," she said, nodding towards the trees, "they were here first."

© Amy Minato 2003, WM'07

Photo Credit © J. Fisher-Smith 2003, WM'07

Current Events

A small splash of news from the air waves.
I flood with the Absurd. Let me tell you:
In Bolivia, these days, it is illegal for people to catch rainwater.
Centuries of rainwater falling from roofs into barrels and tubs,
buckets of life from the sky for crops and herds, baths and drink.
It is illegal to catch raindrops. Corporations bought the water.
In South Asia, corporations copyright pollen.
Seeds that make plants that make seed become contraband.
Generations of botanical care wiped out by company patent.
Perhaps soon they will sell bottles of sunshine.
Clouds will wear brand names, and if you do not have
the price of air, you will not breathe.
Greed clutches the planet, sucks her juices,
gorges on the fat of the land,
will bloat/will choke/will strangle
on the ferment of stolen harvest,
on the rising tide of earthwise peoples
catchers of rain, savers of seed, planters of hope.
Let me hope. Let me hope.

Epilogue: In Bolivia, these more recent days,
raincatchers rose up like a boiling flood
and swept the absurd corporations
our of their watershed, out of their country.
Like I told you.

© Bethroot Gwynn 2002, WM'04

Global Cooling Incantation
© D.J. Webb 2007, WM'10

Statistics of Hope

Every seven minutes,
somewhere in the world, someone is falling in love.
Every six minutes,
two women pour tea and sit down for a good talk.
Every five minutes,
someone, somewhere is doing a good deed.
Every four minutes,
someone stops and says, "Thanks, I needed that."
Every three minutes,
someone hugs someone else in need.
Every two minutes,
someone comforts a crying child.
And every minute of the day and night,
someone, somewhere in the world,
someone is at prayer, saying
"Thank you. . ." to the sacred Mystery which sustains us all.

□ *Christina Baldwin 1996, WM'98*

Walking on Thin Ice *© JoAnn George 1991, WM'93*

V. Appendix

Acknowledgments

I am forever indebted to the talented, experienced and committed We'Moon team who, after I spent at least a year in the "broody hen" stage (brooding over thousands of pages of past We'Moons, with the help of my partner, Eagle) took "the egg" out from under me and skillfully produced an Anthology out of it "in no time at all." Actually, it was in "expando-time"—an intense time-warp we go into as the Creatrix—which was particularly intense after just producing We'Moon 2011. We turned around and created the Anthology immediately afterward, in time to go out with the 30th edition of We'Moon. Normally considered our "down time," this early Spring/Summer turned into a veritable vortex of activity that took everything else in our lives with it into an energy swirl capable of condensing coal into diamonds. Out of this a book was born: *In the Spirit of We'Moon*. We went through our ups and downs, like the Moon through all phases of light and shadow—the whole mandala—and survived it with humor and love. Blessed be this team that will continue to carry We'Moon with aplomb in the years to come.

In particular, I want to express my deepest appreciation for:

• Sequoia, our graphic artist who doubled as a race horse and a work horse to get the job done; she did a beautiful job of designing every page and rendering the art anew, whether or not she had the originals to work from.

• Barb, the production coordinator who claimed the inch worm as her totem and ended up going over every inch of it, while also excelling as Spider Woman, mistress of the mistress list, weaving in all the strands.

• Bethroot, the night owl with an eye on every detail whose special editing skills worked magic with visual and verbal art together, never missing a part, while priestessing the whole process with heart.

• Myshkin, who, like a hummingbird, darted here and there as needed, extracting the nectar from every flower, applying her art as a musician to composing the pages with intricate harmonies.

• Eagle Hawk, who searched far and wide for We'Moon artists and writers—and connected with and remembered so many—while giving me her unconditional Whale Heart support all along in helping coordinate this project.

Thanks also to: Renée, who compiled the initial lists of We'Moon artists and writers; Amanda, who helped with web searches; the land residents and the wwoof volunteers who cooked meals and worked around us in good spirits during the Creatrix. Special thanks to all the womyn who participated in the Anthology Weaving Circles and shared their love of these glorious out-pourings. And deep appreciation to Sue and Lou in the Portland office, who kept the Matrix of Mother Tongue Ink work going while we were busy Creatrixing for the Anthology.

Anthology Creatrix Team
(left to right) Myshkin, Musawa, Barb, Sequoia, Bethroot, Eagle, Whiskey Pickles and Zia the doggies.

We honor wemoon who shared their art and writing in the pages of We'Moon over these past 30 years, and who have crossed over between the worlds of life and death. The list grows longer every year. This listing is of contributors whose work graces the pages of this Anthology, and who are now with us only in spirit. They bless us always.

Berta Freistadt (1942-2009) British lesbian writer, actor, beloved teacher of drama and creative writing. Her poems and stories were widely anthologized in feminist publications on both sides of the Atlantic. Irony, depth, and humor marked her work.

Charlotte Tall Mountain (1941–2006), artist and poet, was a We'Moon contributor whose work focused beautifully on Spirit and nature. Of Iroquois ancestry, she was a strong and passionate defender of the natural world. Her poem "For the Love of the World" was widely circulated in the media.

Christine Pierce (1954-1998) was the soul of gentleness: adoring of creatures, plants and song. She was an Oregon artist, incest survivor, a magical and playful six-foot tall sprite who sought vocation and family.

Deb Meadows-West (1954-2005) was a devoted single mom, a loyal friend and fan of We'Moon, a gifted special needs educator and care giver. Deb loved camping, hiking, rafting, rock collecting and cats.

Dwayne Campbell (1960-2002) Feminist, anarchist, activist, photographer.

Judith Anderson (1934 - 2008) Judith's prints have been published in many periodicals and books, including Elinor W. Gadon's *The Once and Future Goddess: A Symbol for our Time.* Her work explored themes of Jungian thought, nature, women, and political injustice.

Marcia Patrick (1943-1989 and buried at We'Moon Land) An artist, cabinet-maker, early goddess researcher, and member of WITCH (Women's International Terrorist Conspiracy from Hell, guerrilla theater action on Wall St., 1968).

Marsha Gomez (1951-1998) was a clay sculptor, art educator, community organizer for environmental and community rights. She was co-founding mother of the Indigenous Women's Network in 1988, and directed the Alma de Mujer Retreat Center for Social Change.

Martha Courtot (1941-2000) was a poet whose work was an inspiration to lesbian feminists, especially with her poetry books *Tribe* and *Journey,* published in 1977. She was a member of Fat Chance, a fat women's dance/performance group in California's Bay Area.

Mau Blossom (1935–2007) was a lesbian artist, healer, and musician. Golden Light, the land she homesteaded in the Ozarks for 36 years, and Golden Light Center, the alternative health care clinic she established there in 1974, still continue on today, lesbian owned and operated.

Monica Sjoo (1938-2005) was at home in Sweden, Wales and U.K. She was a prolific artist, writer and activist, devotee of the Great Mother and Her sacred sites, and long time beloved We'Moon contributor. www.monicasjoo.com

Moon de la Mar (1938-1997) was a pioneer of womyn's land, lover of Earth, radical community activist, craftswoman extraordinaire. Her loving presence and principled ethics inspired all who knew her.

Pat Ray (1932-1994) A brilliant artist skilled in any medium, beloved by many. Her work is not forgotten.

Rose Johnson (1954-2010) Occasional artist and poet, Rose was good at anything she chose to do. Her iconic poem (p. 171) companions women far and wide at memorial circles for our ansisters.

Shekinah Mountainwater (1939-2007) described herself as "a muse-ical mystical magical woman who loves the Goddess and women, a foremother of the Womanspirit movement, a teacher of Women's Mysteries, and a priestess of Aphrodite."

Tee A. Corinne (1944-2006) was an innovative and influential lesbian artist: accomplished painter, writer of fiction and poetry, avid historian of lesbian culture, teacher of art and memoir. She was an extraordinary muse, urging everyone she touched toward creative work.

Terri Jewel (1954–1995) Black feminist lesbian poet and writer. A best friend and sister sorely missed. Terri would be pleased to know that after 30 years, We'Moon is still inspiring women in the struggle.

Bamboo Bridge © Diana Gardener 2007, WM'09

© COPYRIGHTS AND CONTACTING CONTRIBUTORS ▢

Copyrights of most individual works belong to each contributor. Please honor the copyrights: © means: <u>do not reproduce without the express permission of the artist, author, publisher or Mother Tongue Ink</u>, depending on whose name follows the copyright sign. Some wemoon prefer to free the copyright on their work: ▢ means: <u>this work may be passed on among women who wish to reprint it "in the spirit of We'Moon."</u> In all cases, give credit to the author/artist and to We'Moon, and send each a copy. If the artist has given permission, We'Moon may release contact information. Please email inquiries to mothertongue@wemoon.ws or directly to contributors whose email addresses are in bylines.

Many pieces of art and writing reprinted in this Anthology were not originally credited or copyrighted, and many others were printed with an open copyright permitting use "in the spirit of We'Moon." Since 2005, We'Moon Contributor Licenses have included permission for reprinting. Every effort has been made to contact all contributors and copyright holders. Please contact the publisher if you are among those whom we were unable to reach.

A. Kimberlin Blackburn (Kapaa, HI) happily lives on Kauai farming and making art. Please see her work at www.akimberlinblackburn.com. **p. 12, 81, 199**

Abby Mariah Wentworth (Seward, AK) I grew up in N. Berwick, ME, and have lived in Alaska for ten years. I cherish both families and both coasts in the ebb and flow of my life. **p. 174**

Alexandra "Olenka" Gadzik (Davenport, IA) is a music and inter-media artist whose global fusion songs address themes of women, spirituality and belonging. Her visual arts, inter-media performances and writing draw upon research in mythology and economic anthropology. Olenka's work can be accessed through www.olenka. com **p. 208**

Alice Walker (Berkeley, CA) I am experiencing the bliss of living with animals. Together we are a family pack, loving our friends who come to visit us and our solitude when they don't! Living in this time of so much threat and trouble is a grand adventure we are happy to witness. **p. 233**

Alix Greenwood (Oakland, CA) **p. 130**

Amarah Gabriel ((Salt Spring Island, Canada) loves nature, art, family, friends, gardens and swimming. Currently she writes, paints and studies art history and film at University of Victoria, BC. Her recent work, *Rabbit Ears,* addresses the power and privilege of institution versus nature, and hopes to stop the cull of rabbits at UVIC. **p. 124, 182, 236**

Amber Amanita Darkwood (Olympia, WA) I dream of living sustainably on land and creating a tribal community with my dearest friends and family. I wish to re-connect with the earth and rhythms of nature. I sing in a project called Elysium+Obscura. PNW Cascadia forests and mountains is home. **p. 135**

Amy R. Hanford (St. Paul, MN) **p. 80**

Amy Minato (Portland, OR) **p. 238**

Amy Schutzer (Portland, OR) is heartily busy writing poems and her fourth novel. Read her first book, *Undertow.* She is a dedicated gardener and recently bacame manager of the community gardens across the street from her home. **p. 88, 131, 132, 181, 226**

Anah Holland-Moore **p. 79**

Angela Von Lintel Lobitz (Carlos, MN) The process of drawing mandalas, being the soul's expression, is very therapeutic as I recover from a year of ill health and multiple surgeries. I hope to pass this beautiful expression of personal and universal insights to others for their healing and return to wholeness as we all journey, spirit connected, in the matrix of life. **p. 72**

Angela Werneke (Santa Fe, NM) is a gardener, dreamer, flower essence practitioner, and astrologer. Angela finds that there are many tools on the path to healing and wholeness, not the least of which derive from the rich dimensions of myth and nature. **p. 79**

Angie Coffin Heiney (Portland, OR) owns an artsy boutique called Frock, practices photography, and has an accessories line called Gung Ho. www.frockboutique. com **p. 168, 235**

Angie Lazaro (Capetown, South Africa) is a South African photographer specializing in fashion, food, décor and portraiture. As a student her documentary work became part of a river rehabilitation and management project in the Kat River Valley. www.angielazaro.com **p. 151**

Ann Beeching (Fort Wayne, IN) For 25 years, Ann has studied and painted our co-partnership with the physical and spirit world of nature and animals. To see more of her work, order prints or commission a portrait, visit her website. www.annbeeching.com **p. 219, 224**

Ann Filemyr (Santa Fe, NM) leads workshops and seminars recently for the Conference on Consciousness and the Association for the study of Women and Mythology. She is dean of the College of Contemporary Native Arts at the Institute of American Indian Arts in Santa Fe. **p. 108, 117**

Ann Southcombe (Hugo, OR) has dedicated her life to working with captive animals to make their lives as happy as possible. "My hope is to help bridge the gap between humans and animals, so all creatures are treated with compassion and respect." sulango@ terragon.com, www.kinshipwithanimals.com **p. 222**

Ann-Rosemary Conway (Victoria, Canada) Creating a better world for my daughter, Jennifer, inspired me to create a better world for myself and for all women. In my painting, teaching and community life I evoke reverence for our Heritage of Honor, the Sacred Feminine, Woman and Mother earth. www.gobc. ca/goddessworks **p. 151**

Anna Oneglia (Santa Cruz, CA) is a compulsive maker of things who is always trying to figure out how to get spirit into image. **p. 109, 116, 150, 160, 203**

Annalisa Cunningham yoga teacher, author, travel guide offers yoga vacations & retreats in Mexico, Hawaii, Peru, New Zealand and Northern California. Please visit her website: www. openingheartjourneys.com **p. 21**

Anne Benvenuti (University Park, IL) is currently at work on projects related to *The New Archaic,* including a book on neuroscience and spiritual practices, *Soul and Synapse* (April 2011). web.me.com/anne.benvenuti/ site **p. 140**

Anne Berg **p. 65**

Annie Ocean (Roseburg, OR) Country Dyke, Oregon-born witch, 12 stepper, Sufi, water baby, goddess worshiper, pie Queen, Naturalist, VW cultist, photographer, moon swooner, house painter extraordinaire, singer, songwriter, loving being 60! beloved@jeffnet. org **p. 15, 22, 66, 87, 155, 157, 162, 221**

Antiga **p. 75**

Antonia Matthew (Bloomington, IN) born in England, a member of the women's writing group Five Women Poets. She is a member of the Reformed Congregation of the Goddess International and a graduate of their Women's Theology Institute. **p. 120**

Arisika Razak **p. 57**

Autumn Sky Morrison (Canada) In creating art I find my stillness, rhythm, my teacher and passion. Each painting offers a reflection of the light and shadow of our humanity, our sublime geometry, and our timeless divinity. May we celebrate this fantastic adventure, inspire, and be inspired. **p. 198**

Barbara Dickinson (Sunny Valley, OR), artist, gardener, lover of the wild places and open spaces. **p. 153, 238**

Barbara J. Raisbeck (Eugene, OR) writes, photographs and speaks out on human, animal and environmental rights issues. She is currently working on a book project re. the genocide of women in Asia. **p. 101**

Bedo (Cottage Grove, OR) World journeyer, Euro-Asian and survivor of a Japanese P.O.W. concentration camp, cherishing independence and needing freedom, still a creating Crone-Grandmother. **p. 168**

Berta R. Freistadt (see Ansisters, p. 241) **p. 227**

Beth Beurkens (Mt. Shasta, CA), M.A. has been a teacher of shamanism, a shamanic practitioner, and a vision quest guide for 20 years, leading dynamic seminars in the U.S. and Europe. She is an instructor at Rouge Community College, a faculty member at the Foundation for Shamanic Studies, and a creative writing teacher. Her first collection of poetry, *Shaman's Eye,* was released in 2009, and the *2011 Shaman: Spirit Walker Calendar* is out this year. **p. 155, 173**

Beth Ferguson **p. 185, 195**

Beth Freewomon (Santa Cruz, CA) gratefully living her life near the sea and applying spiritual principles to life's circumstances. Blessing and being blessed through sharing sacred music, food as medicine (www. iamtheopenhearth.com), and prayer as a movement in consciousness. Inner Light is my spiritual home now www.innerlightministries.com. **p. 60**

Beth Lenco (Chester, Nova Scotia) Thank you ancestors and all we'moon for helping and encouraging me to shine from my truth. I am blessed daily with your support. May we walk in beauty together on this Earth for life now, and for our descendants after us. www.starflower.ca **p. 148**

Bethroot Gwynn (Myrtle Creek, OR) is blessed to be Special Editor for We'Moon. She lives at Fly Away Home women's land (34 years now): writing, growing food, making theater and ritual. FFI about spiritual gatherings, work visits, and possible residency, send SASE to POB 593, Myrtle Creek, OR 97457 **p. 52, 119, 138, 143, 147, 151, 153, 170, 223, 239**

Betty LaDuke (Ashland, OR) Through my publications, art, and work in the academic world, I honor and give visibility to international women artists who have inspired my work. *Dreaming Cows* is a new book depicting a 100-foot mural created in collaboration with Heifer International, an organization I have been dedicated to since 2003. www.bettyladuke.com **p.64,78,90,138,144,222,237**

Billie Miracle (Murphy, OR) **p. 51, 56, 62, 88**

Billie Potts **p. 41**

Boudyke **p. 77**

Calley O'Neill (Kamuela, HI) www.calleyoneill.com **p. 20**

Camp Sister Spirit (MS) **p. 93**

Carmen Rodriguez Sonnes (Talent, OR) Artist, mother, grandmother, sister. Carmen paints to express the feminine experience in the form of grace, strength, wisdom, and beauty. **p. 96, 101**

Carol Bridges (Nashville, IN) is author of *The Medicine Woman Tarot* and other books on living in harmony. She leads women's retreats at her Nine Harmonies School. Her schedule can be viewed at www.sacredarts.info and her art quilts can be seen at www.carolbridgesartquilts.com. **p. 151**

Carol Schaefer (New York, NY) author of *Grandmothers Counsel the World,* is a writer, photographer and speaker. She has appeared on Good Morning America, CNN and MSNBC for her memoir *The Other Mother: A Woman's Love for the Child She Gave up for Adoption.* **p. 20, 22, 91**

The Elders ◻ *Jeanette M. French 2008, WM'11*

WITH THESE WORDS WE
OPEN THE CIRCLE:

WE WANT TO ACKNOWLEDGE AND GIVE THANKS TO THE SPIRITS OF THE NORTH, AND THE EARTH ELEMENT WHICH EMBODIES & GIVES FORM TO SPIRIT IN THIS LIFE.

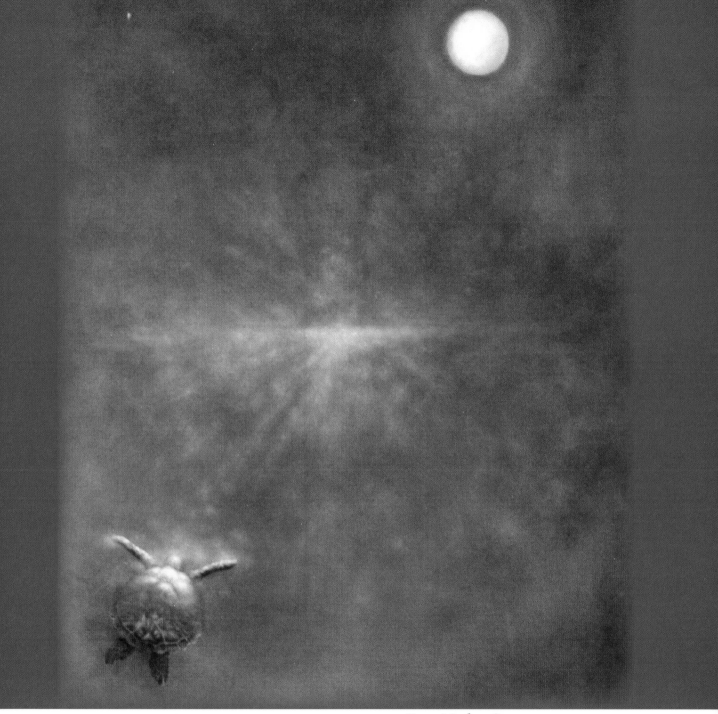

Deep Mother Ocean ¤ *Dorrie Joy 2006, WM'08*

We acknowledge and give thanks to the Spirits of the West, and the element of Water that flows through us all.

Agua est vida!

Steamy Rendez-vous © *Lilian de Mello 2002, WM'04*

WE ACKNOWLEDGE AND GIVE THANKS TO THE SPIRITS OF THE SOUTH AND THE ELEMENT OF FIRE THAT LIGHTENS, BRIGHTENS, AND WARMS US IN ITS DANCE OF TRANSFORMATION.

Wind □ *Heather Jarry 2003, WM'05*

WE ACKNOWLEDGE AND GIVE THANKS TO THE SPIRITS OF THE EAST AND THE ELEMENT OF AIR FOR THE POWER OF INSPIRATION! . . . AND TO ALL THE WOMYN WHO HAVE CONTRIBUTED TO WE'MOON OVER THE YEARS, WHETHER OR NOT YOUR ART OR WRITING MADE IT INTO PRINT. YOU ARE THE MUSES WHOSE CREATIVE ENERGY IS THE LIFE FORCE OF WE'MOON!

A Thousand Years of Healing

With this turning we put a broken age to rest.
We who are alive at such a cusp
now usher in
a thousand years of healing.
From whence my hope, I cannot say,
But it grows in the cells of my skin,
my envelope of mysteries.
In this sheath so akin to the surface of earth
I sense the faint song.
Beneath the wail and dissonance
this singing rises. Winged ones
and four-leggeds,
grasses and mountains and each tree,
all swimming creatures.
Even we, wary two-leggeds,
hum, and call, and create
the changes. We remake our relations, mend
our minds, convert our minds to the earth.
We practice blending our voices,
living with the vision
of the Great Magic we move within.
We begin
the new habit, getting up glad
for a thousand years of healing.

© Susa Silvermarie 1998, WM'00

Yemaya Offering the Healing Waters © *Mira Michelle 2005, WM'07*

We acknowledge and give thanks to the living Spirit in all the elements, all the directions, all beings: in You we are All ONE! Thank you for coming through all these years In the Spirit of We'Moon.

Great Blessings! Amamma